Bonpo Dzogchen Teachings

Bonpo Dzogchen Teachings

according to
LOPON TENZIN NAMDAK

*Dzogchen Teachings from the Retreats in
Austria, England, Holland and America*

Vajra Publications
Kathmandu, Nepal

Vajra Publications
Kathmandu, Nepal

Distribution:
Vajra Book Shop
PO Box 21779
Kathmandu
Nepal
http://www.vajrabooks.com.np
Tel/fax: 977-1-4220562

Transcribed and edited, together with Introduction and Notes,
by John Myrdhin Reynolds

© 2006 by John Myrdhin Reynolds. All rights reserved. No part of this book may be reproduced in any form or by any means, electronic or mechanical, including photography, recording, or by any information storage or retrieval system or technologies now known or later developed without permission in writing from the publisher.

Photos © 2006 by Elisabeth Egonviebre

ISBN 99946-720-5-3

Printed in Nepal

Contents

Preface to the First Edition   ix

Preface to the New Edition   xiii

Introduction to Bon   1
    Bon and Buddhism in Tibet   1
    Tonpa Shenrab and Olmo Lung-ring   3
    The Causal Ways of Bon   9
    The Four Portals and the Treasury   11
    Yungdrung Bon   12
    Hidden Treasure Texts   14
    The Nine Ways of Bon   15
    Shenchen Luga and the Revival of Bon   20
    The Traditions of Bonpo Dzogchen   22

1. **Introduction to the Practice of Dzogchen**   25

2. **The Attaining of Buddhahood according to Sutra, Tantra and Dzogchen**   37
    The Hinayana View   37
    The Mahayana View   38
    The Tantra View   40
    The Dzogchen View   41

3. **Four Essential Points for Understanding Dzogchen**   49

4. **The View of Shunyata found in Madhyamaka, Chittamatra and Dzogchen**   57
   - The View of the Sutra System   57
   - The View of Madhyamaka   58
   - Madhyamaka and Dzogchen on the Two Truths   66
   - The View of Chittamatra   73
   - Chittamatra and Dzogchen   82

5. **The Views of Tantra, Mahamudra and Dzogchen**   89
   - The View of Tantra   89
   - Mahamudra and Dzogchen   99

6. **The View of Dzogchen**   107
   - Dzogchen as the Highest Teaching   107
   - The Base   109
   - Commitment to the Dzogchen View   111
   - The Dzogchen View   112
   - First Contradiction – Chittamatra   114
   - Second Contradiction – Madhyamaka   115
   - Third Contradiction – the Lower Tantra   117
   - Fourth Contradiction – the Higher Tantra   119
   - Inseparability   120

7. **The Practice of Dzogchen**   123
   - View   123
   - Meditation   135
   - Action   149
   - Fruit   153
   - Conclusion   155

8. **Rushans: The Preliminary Practices of Dzogchen**   157
   - Rushan Exercises   157
   - Impermanence of Life   157
   - Karmic Causes and Consciousness   158

Methods of Purification	165
The Outer Rushans	166
The Inner Rushans	170
The Secret Rushans	172
Recognizing the Nature of Mind	173
Meditation	177
Continuing in the View	182
How to Practice Meditation	183
Disturbances to Meditation	185
Signs of Right Meditation	187
9. Introduction to Thekchod and Thodgal	**189**
The Natural State	189
The Three Series of Dzogchen Teachings	190
Thekchod and Thodgal	193
Thodgal Visions	194
Development of Visions	199
The Four Lamps	201
The Rainbow Body	203
Appendix	**209**
The Biography of Lopon Tenzin Namdak	209
The Curriculum of Studies at Triten Norbutse Monastery	224
Notes	**231**
Selected Bibliography	**265**

Preface to the First Edition

During 1991, the Bonpo Dzogchen master, Lopon Tenzin Namdak, visited the West twice, coming first to Europe and later to America, where he taught a number of meditation retreats and gave a series of public talks on Bon and Dzogchen. In March and April, Lopon Rinpoche taught a meditation retreat focusing on the practice of Dzogchen at Bischofshofen, south of Salzburg in the Austrian Alps, and several weeks later he gave a series of talks on Dzogchen at the Drigung Kagyu Centre in Vienna. After that he went to Italy where he taught two retreats in Rome, and also briefly visited Merigar in Tuscany, the retreat center of Namkhai Norbu Rinpoche. Coming to England next, the Lopon taught a ten-day Dzogchen retreat in Devon in the west of England, at a locale near Totnes, and after that he gave several talks in London. Proceeding later to Amsterdam, he taught a five-day retreat on Dzogchen in the city at the beginning of June. With the exception of the Italian visit, I was present on all of these occasions and served as a facilitator and sometime translator for the teachings.

Then in October, Lopon Rinpoche visited New York city at the invitation of H.H. the Dalai Lama and Tibet House, to participate in the Kalachakra Initiation and in other activities connected with the Year of Tibet. In particular, the Lopon was the first speaker in the afternoon series called "Nature of the Mind Teachings." During the Devon retreat, the Lopon had prepared a brief paper on the Bonpo teachings for presentation in this series in New York. I translated this into English as "The Condensed Meaning of an Explanation of the Teachings of Yungdrung Bon" and this has been published elsewhere. [1] During his time in

New York city, the Lopon gave three further talks, at which I was again the facilitator as I had been in Europe. Towards the end of the month, at the invitation of the Dzogchen Community of Conway, known as Tsegyalar, the Lopon gave a weekend seminar at Amherst College in western Massachusetts. In November, I met up with the Lopon in San Francisco where, again at the invitation of the Dzogchen Community, he gave a two-day seminar on Guru Yoga practice. After that he went to Coos Bay, Oregon, where for eight days he held a retreat on the Dzogchen teachings.

On these occasions also I served as facilitator and translator and made detailed notes on the teachings. These notes again served as the basis of the transcripts found herein of the Lopon's teachings in America. Although the Lopon spoke in English, on many occasions he asked me to translate technical terms and help clarify various other technical points. All of this I recorded in my notes. In order to further clarify matters, he requested that after each portion of the teaching I repeat from my notes what he had said. So the transcripts found here result from our collaboration together. Nevertheless, I alone must take responsibility for any errors that might be found. I have done some editing of the transcripts, adding any additional clarifications required as well as any sentences needed to link the various paragraphs or topics. But generally, I have left the language in the style of the Lopon's oral presentation and have not rendered the text into a literary presentation since the present collection of teachings is not envisioned as a commercial publication, but as an aid for practitioners of Dzogchen.

I have included only transcripts directly related to the Lopon's teachings on Dzogchen, and to where the views of Sutra and Tantra are contrasted with that of Dzogchen. The Lopon's teachings on Guru Yoga, the Rite of the Guardians, specific Tantric teachings such as the practice of Zhang-zhung Meri, and so on, as well as the Dzogchen teachings from specific texts of the

Zhang-zhung Nyan-gyud, are found elsewhere in the publications of the Bonpo Translation Project. [2]

I began working on the translation of Bonpo Dzogchen texts first with Geshe Tenzin Wangyal in Italy some years ago, and continued doing this with Lopon Tenzin Namdak on his three visits to the West. As a consequence of this work, I organized the Bonpo Translation Project in order to make translations of Bonpo texts and prepare transcripts and monographs on the Bonpo tradition available for interested students and practitioners in the West.

Before the arrival of these two learned Bonpo Lamas in the West, my interest in the Bon tradition was stimulated by Namkhai Norbu Rinpoche, head of the Dzogchen Community. Rinpoche, although not a Bonpo Lama himself, was for many years interested in the Bonpo tradition because he was researching the historical roots of the pre-Buddhist Tibetan culture known as Bon. [3] He was also very interested in discovering the historical sources of Dzogchen teachings, for which there exist two authentic lineages from at least the eighth century CE, one found among the Nyingmapas and the other found among the Bonpos. [4] More than any other Tibetan teacher, Namkhai Norbu Rinpoche has played a key role in transmitting Dzogchen teachings to the West, and for this he has the profound gratitude of all of us.

For their help and assistance in various ways during the retreats with Lopon Rinpoche and also later while compiling and editing these transcripts, I wish to thank Gerrit Huber, Waltraud Benzing, Dagmar Kratochwill, Dr. Andrea Loseries-Leick, Armin Akermann, Ken Rivad, Tim Walker, Lee Bray, Florens van Canstein, Michael Katz, Des Berry, Dennis Waterman, Bob Kragen, Michael Taylor, Anthony Curtis, and last, but not least, Khenpo Nyima Wangyal and Geshe Tenzin Wangyal. It is also my hope here as translator and editor that this small collection of Lopon Tenzin Namdak's teachings on Dzogchen according to the Bonpo tradition, its view and its practice, will prove of use and benefit to Western students and practitioners of Dzogchen.

MU-TSUG SMAR-RO

John Myrdhin Reynolds (Vajranatha),
Amsterdam
March 1992

Preface to the New Edition

Even though these teachings on Dzogchen were given by Lopon Tenzin Namdak Rinpoche some years ago in 1991, and have circulated privately as transcripts, they remained in need of some further editing regarding repetitions and annotations. This has been provided here, as well as a new introduction to Bon in general, and some further material on the education given to young monks and nuns at Lopon Rinpoche's monastery in Kathmandu, Triten Norbutse (Khri-brten nor-bu'i rtse). This further material is found in the appendix. The monastery is primarily an educational institution for monks and nuns, aimed at preserving and perpetuating the ancient culture of Bon, rather than a residential monastery. After finishing their education here, the former students will go elsewhere and serve as teachers or enter lay life. Students are drawn from the Bonpo areas of Nepal, such as Dolpo and Mustang, as well as from Tibet itself, where a traditional Bonpo education is becoming progressively more difficult to obtain.

The educational program at Triten Norbutse includes the thirteen-year course in Geshe studies at the Dialectics School or Lama College (bshad-grwa), at present under the direction of the chief teacher of the Dialectics School (mtshan-nyid bshad-grwa dpon-slob), Lopon Tsangpa Tenzin. The focus is on the philosophical studies (mtshan-nyid) found in the Bonpo tradition, and on cultivating skills in correct thinking and the art of debate (rtsod-pa). In addition, a number of traditional secular sciences (rig-gnas) are studied and mastered. Upon completion of the course and passing several examinations, the student is awarded a Geshe degree (dge-bshes), the equivalent of a Western doctorate. Independent of this program in Geshe studies, there is also a Meditation School (sgrub-grwa) at the monastery which has a four-year program for the study and practice of the four major systems of Dzogchen found in the Bonpo tradition. Whereas in the Dialectics School, the emphasis is on academic study and learning the skills of debate, here the emphasis is on the actual meditation practices of Dzogchen in a semi-retreat situation. This school is at present under the direction of its Abbot (sgrub-grwa mkhan-po), Kenpo Tsultim Tenzin. During these courses of study and practice, the students are housed and fully supported by the monastery. Frequently young monks and nuns come as refugees from Tibet seeking a Bonpo education and possess no funds of their own at all.

With Lopon Rinpoche now in retirement at the age of 80, the monastery is under the able direction of its present Abbot, Khenpo Tenpa Yungdrung. However, Lopon Rinpoche continues to teach on occasion at the monastery, in sessions open to both monks and lay people, and also to Westerners at his new meditation center in France, Shenten Dargye Ling, near Saumur in the Loire region, south-west of Paris. Moreover, Lopon Rinpoche's collected works (gsung 'bum) in thirteen volumes were published last year by the monastery. A number of Geshes at the monastery, with the help of modern computer technology provided by Japanese friends, have been digitalizing the basic Bonpo texts which are studied at the monastery, including those of Dzogchen. The texts are then published in India and Nepal for the use of students.

Now that Bon is becoming increasingly recognized in the West as an important spiritual tradition in its own right, and as an original component of the Tibetan culture and civilization which continues and even thrives today both in Tibet and in exile, it was felt that these teachings of Lopon Rinpoche on Dzogchen should be republished for a wider reading audience. My thanks, as the editor of these teachings, go to Vajra Publishing of Kathmandu for undertaking this project, to Elisabeth Egonviebre for providing the photographs included here, and to Dr. Christine Daniels for her editorial and other help while completing this project. I would especially like to thank Khenpo Tenpa Yungdrung for supplying additional information on the expanded educational program at Triten Norbutse. It is my prayer that these rare explanations of Lopon Tenzin Namdak Yongdzin Rinpoche, being exceptionally lucid and clear, will help to clarify the relationship between Dzogchen and Madhyamaka, Chittamatra, Tantra and Mahamudra, for interested Western students.

MU-TSUG SMAR-RO!

John Myrdhin Reynolds (Vajranatha),
Kathmandu, Nepal,
Losar, February 2006

Introduction to Bon

Bon and Buddhism in Tibet

Bon is the name of the pre-Buddhist religious culture of Tibet and often in Western books in the past it has been equated with a kind of primitive North Asian shamanism. Indeed, shamanism as a traditional practice still exists among Tibetans, both in Tibet itself and in adjacent regions such as Ladakh, Nepal, Bhutan, and Yunnan. Such practitioners were known as Pawo (dpa'-bo) or Lhapa (lha-pa) in Tibetan. But this is not Bon. In terms of religious affiliation, these shaman practitioners are usually Buddhist, belonging to the old tradition of the Nyingmapa.

Nowadays Tibetan Bonpo Lamas are not shamans but monks and scholars with a monastic system fully comparable to the four contemporary schools of Tibetan Buddhism, that is, the Nyingmapa, the Sakyapa, the Kagyudpa, and the Gelugpa. Bonpos have a learned literary and scholastic tradition extending back to the early period of the eighth century of our era, and even before. Moreover, since 1988, when H.H. the Dalai Lama visited the Dialectics School at the Bonpo monastery in Dolanji, northern India, Bon has been officially recognized by His Holiness and by the Tibetan Government in Exile as the fifth Tibetan school. The Bonpos have now been given representation on the Council of Religious Affairs at Dharamsala.

If Bonpo practitioners possess institutions, practices, and teachings similar to the four Buddhist schools, what then is the difference between them? Tibetans themselves clearly distinguish *Bon* from *Chos*, which is their name for the Buddhism of Indian origin. Both sides agree that the difference is principally a matter of lineage. Whereas all the Buddhist schools of Tibet look back to the historical Buddha Shakyamuni, who flourished in southern Nepal and northern India about two thousand five hundred years ago, as the source of their tradition and teaching known as the Buddha Dharma, Bonpos look back to an earlier prehistoric Buddha in Central Asia, named Tonpa Shenrab Miwoche (sTon-pa gShen-rab mi-bo-che) as the ultimate source of their spiritual tradition known as Yungdrung Bon (g.yung-drung bon), the Eternal Dharma.

The Tibetan term "Yungdrung" means "eternal, everlasting, indestructible," and corresponds to the Buddhist term "vajra" or "dorje" (rdo-rje), meaning "diamond," and hence indestructible. The term "Bon" means "dharma," the teachings of the Buddhas about the nature of reality, the practice of which will bring release from the cycle of rebirth and thus the ultimate enlightenment of a Buddha. It has usages similar to the Tibetan Buddhist term *chos*.

Like Buddhists, Bonpo practitioners take refuge in the Triratna, or the Three Jewels of the Buddha, the Dharma, and the Sangha, that is to say, the teacher, his teachings, and the community of practitioners of the teachings, the Great Bodhisattvas. This Dharma is believed to have been taught by all the enlightened Buddhas who have appeared throughout history and before, not only on this planet earth, but in all world systems inhabited by intelligent life forms. Therefore, this Dharma is said to be eternal and indestructible but, of course, the actual presentation of the Dharma depends on the capacities of disciples, and so there exists a plurality of ways or vehicles to enlightenment. All of these ways are complete and valid within their contexts and circumstances. Thereby all of the teachings and practices derived from Indian Buddhism, although imported from outside by non-Tibetans, are regarded by Bonpo Lamas as authentic Dharma, the teachings of the Buddhas. Since the Dharma is like the light of the sun, it is omnipresent; its revelation is not dependent upon a single historical figure or restricted to a single period in history.

Nevertheless, the Dharma and the Sangha, the teachings and the community, do not represent the ultimate refuge. Both of them are dependent on the Buddha for their existence. Thus, the Buddha is the ultimate and supreme refuge. However, there have been many Buddhas in the past history of this planet, the historical Buddha Shakyamuni merely being the last in their number. According to ancient Indian Buddhist belief, there have been six prehistoric Buddhas who preceded Shakyamuni, namely, Vipashyin, Shikhin, Vishvabhu, Krakucchanda, Kanakamuni and Kashyapa. It was said that even in his own day when Shakyamuni was still a young prince, a few followers of the earlier Buddha Kashyapa still existed. The great Stupa of Baudhnath in Nepal is said to contain the relics of this earlier Buddha. An inscription of the Buddhist emperor Ashoka, from pre-Christian times, records the repairing of a stupa in Nepal said to contain the relics of the Buddha Kanakamuni. Another list in early Buddhist scriptures records twenty-four Buddhas from Shakyamuni back to the Buddha Dipankara in the distant past.

These Nirmanakaya Buddhas, who manifested in time and history, appeared not only in India, but in Central Asia as well, for in ancient times India and Central Asia formed a single cultural region. Moreover, both Buddhists and Bonpos agree that Maitreya will be the next Buddha, whose advent will be some time in the indefinite future. [1]

Tonpa Shenrab and Olmo Lung-ring

Thus Bonpo Lamas look to a prehistoric Buddha from Tazik (stag-gzig), in Central Asia, as the source of their tradition. The title Tonpa (ston-pa) means "teacher" in the sense of the original founder of a spiritual tradition, who is the source of this revelation. According to Bonpo belief, Tonpa Shenrab was not merely a priest or a shaman, but a fully enlightened Buddha (sangs-rgyas). Shenrab was a Nirmanakaya manifestation of Buddhahood, appearing in time and history, whereas his Sambhogakaya aspect known as Shenlha Odkar (gShen-lha 'od-dkar), corresponds to the Buddhist Vajrasattva (rDo-rje sems-dpa'). The Dharmakaya aspect is known as Kuntu Zangpo (Kun tu bzang-po, Skt. Samantabhadra), as is also the case in the Nyingmapa system. [2] The title Shenrab Miwoche means "the great human being who is the supreme Shen practitioner." The ancient word *gshen* is untranslatable and is sometimes used as a synonym for Bon and Bonpo. Shen was also the name of the clan to which Tonpa Shenrab belonged, that is, *dMu-gshen*, the celestial Shen. The Shen clan (gshen gdung-rus) continues as one of the principal Bonpo lineages even today. In the early days, transmission of the teachings was often through family lineages.

Tonpa Shenrab was said to have already been enlightened in his celestial pre-existence as Chimed Tsugphud ('Chi-med gtsugphud). In this guise, on a higher plane of existence, he transmitted the teachings of Dzogchen and Tantra to a prince from Tazik named Sangwa Dupa (gSang-ba 'dus-pa, Skt. Guhyasamaja), who returned with them to earth. Thereafter he propagated the teachings and subdued many gods and demons for the benefit of humanity. It is said that in a future incarnation this prince became the Buddha Shakyamuni. According to Bonpo Lamas, this would account for the similarities in teaching and practice between Indian Buddhism and Bon. They both have the same ultimate source. [3]

According to Bonpo accounts, namely the hagiographies of Tonpa Shenrab, the *mDo- 'dus,* the *gZer-myig* and the *gZi-brjid* [4], he is said to have manifested himself as a human being, as a royal prince, in the country of Olmo Lung-ring ('ol-mo lungring), located somewhere in the Iranian-speaking region of ancient Central Asia known as Tazik. This would correspond to the present-day republics of Tajikistan and Uzbekistan and parts of northern Afghanistan. In this region, Iranian-speaking people are still known as Tajiks. However, Olmo Lung-ring is not considered by the Bonpos to be an ordinary geographical location that a tourist might visit. It is a hidden land, or Beyul (sbas-yul), the Bonpos nowadays identify with Shambhala which, in turn, is well known in the West as the mysterious land that is the source of the Kalachakra Tantra. As in the Buddhist understanding of Shambhala, Olmo Lung-ring exists in a higher spiritual dimension and only those who have evolved to a higher level spiritually are able to travel there and find entrance. For ordinary, deluded human beings, Olmo Lung-ring and Shambhala lie in concealment, although they remain a source of great spiritual inspiration for unawakened humanity. Symbolically, Olmo Lung-ring represents the center of the world and in the middle of that sacred land is the cosmic mountain, the nine-tiered indestructible Swastika Mountain (g.yung-drung dgu brtseg). [5]

It was in Olmo Lung-ring that Tonpa Shenrab demonstrated the process of becoming enlightened for the benefit of humanity in terms of twelve great deeds:

1. Accomplishing the Deed of Rebirth in a human body (sku bltams-pa'i mdzad-pa). The Lord was born into the royal clan of dMu at the palace of Barpo Sogyed (bar-po so-brgyad) in the country of Olmo Lung-ring in Tazik. The Brahman who examined the child found that he possessed all the thirty-two marks and eighty characteristics of a great being. This is said to have occurred approximately 18,000 years ago.
2. Accomplishing the Deed of Disseminating the Teachings (rnam-par spel-pa'i mdzad-pa). During the course of twelve years in his youth he taught the Four Causal Ways of Bon, as well as the remaining ways among the Nine Successive Ways of Bon, and in addition he taught the Four Portals of Bon and the Treasury to his followers.

3. Accomplishing the Deed of Subduing Beings (rnam-par 'dul-ba'i mdzad-pa). He emanated aspects of himself as the Six Dulshen ('dul-gshen drug) into the six realms or destinies of rebirth.
4. Accomplishing the Deed of Guiding Beings (rnam-par 'dren-pa'i mdzad-pa). He subdued, and led into virtue, great beings such as Trishi Wanggyal, Halaratsa, Guwer Gyalpo, and Guling Mati who were dominated by aversion, jealousy, pride and lust respectively,
5. Accomplishing the Deed of Definitive Marriage (rnal-par nges-pa'i mdzad-pa). Beseeched by the gods, he married the princess Horza Gyalmedma (Hor-za rgal-med-ma), the incarnation of the great wisdom goddess Jyamma (Byams-ma).
6. Accomplishing the Deed of Emanating his Progeny (rnam-par sprul-pa'i mdzad-pa). He fathered eight sons and two daughters, and conferred the teachings of Bon upon them.
7. Accomplishing the Deed of Conquering the Mara Demons (rnam-par 'joms-pa'i mdzad-pa). Fearing that the teachings of Bon would empty Samsara of sentient beings, the Mara demons attacked the Lord. Then the demon prince Khyabpa Lag-ring seduced Shenrab's youngest daughter and afterwards stole his horses, only to be subdued and converted in the end.
8. Accomplishing the Deed of Vanquishing the Rakshasa Demons (rnam-par rgyal-ba'i mdzad-pa). He came to the aid of the king Kongtse Trulgyi Gyalpo (Kong-tse 'phrug gyi rgyal-po) who, when he attempted to build a temple on an island in the sea, was attacked by the Rakshasa demons. He then imparted the Four Portals and the Treasury to the king.
9. Accomplishing the Deed of Knowledge (rnam-par rig-pa'i mdzad-pa). Then in order to teach beings the path of renunciation and defeat the afflictions caused by the Mara demons, he demonstrated the method of renouncing worldly life to become a monk and practice the ascetic path.

10. Accomplishing the Deed of Retirement (rnam-par dben-pa'i mdzad-pa). He retired to the forest on the nine-tiered Swastika Mountain to practice meditation and he taught his followers according to their capacities as superior, intermediate, or inferior.
11. Accomplishing the Deed of Liberation (rnam-par grol-ba'i mdzad-pa). He taught his disciples the progressive path to enlightenment in terms of compassion and the Ten Perfections, and entrusted his teachings to his respective followers.
12. Accomplishing the Deed of Final Realization (rnam-par grub-pa'i mdzad-pa). Finally, he demonstrated the impermanence of life and the inevitability of death by passing beyond this present life.

At the end of his earthly career, it is said that his various teachings were collected together and put into writing. These were translated into many different languages, including the language of Zhang-zhung from which, in turn, they were translated into Tibetan. Among his many disciples, it was Mucho Demdruk (Mu-cho ldem-drug) who was principally entrusted with organizing the master's teachings in written form and he turned the wheel of Bon for three years. He was followed by the six great translators, namely,

1. Mutsa Trahe (dMu-tsha tra-he) of Tazik
2. Trithok Partsa (Khri-thog spar-tsa) of Zhang-zhung,
3. Huli Parya (Hu-li spar-ya) of Sum-pa,
4. Lhadak Ngagdrol (Lha-bdag ngags-grol) of India,
5. Legtang Mangpo (Legs-tang rmang-po) of China, and
6. Serthok Chejyam (gSer-thog lce-byams) of Phrom (the West).

These were the six scholars known as ornaments of the world. Each of them was said to have translated the teachings of Tonpa Shenrab into their own languages. [6]

During his career in Olmo Lung-ring, Tonpa Shenrab is said to have visited Tibet only once and then briefly. He went there in pursuit of his seven horses that had been stolen by the magician and demon prince Dudje Khyabpa Lag-ring (bDud-rje khyab-pa lag-ring). The demon hid them in Kongpo in southeastern Tibet. Tonpa Shenrab came there and fought ferocious magical battles with the demon prince, whereby, it is said, they literally hurled mountains at each other. Shenrab set down a crystal mountain of light on the north bank of the Tsangpo river, which then settled matters. Since then this holy mountain of Kongpo Bonri has been a place of pilgrimage for Bonpos and remains so even today.

After further contests, Tonpa Shenrab utterly defeated the demon prince in magical combat and as a result he became the Buddha's disciple. At that time, human beings in Tibet were in an exceedingly primitive state, living in caves, and were greatly oppressed and afflicted through the activities of evil spirits. Humans had no grasp of the higher spiritual teachings and so Tonpa Shenrab only taught them the art of practicing shamanism, and this in order to free themselves from the baleful effects of these evil spirits. He taught ritual magical actions including *lha gsol-ba* (invoking the positive energies of the gods), *sel-ba* (exorcising the negative energies of demons and evil spirits), and *g.yang 'gug* (summoning prosperity). Such rituals are now found among the Causal Ways of Bon. However, before departing again for Olmo Lung-ring with his recovered horses, he prophesized that the higher spiritual teachings of Bon, in the form of Sutra, Tantra and Dzogchen, would be brought to Tibet from Tazik and Zhang-zhung when the Tibetans were ready for them. This process began in the time of the second king of Tibet, Mutri Tsanpo (Mu-khri btsan-po).

The Causal Ways of Bon

It is true that the Bonpo tradition does preserve many texts of archaic rituals, totally un-Indian in character, which maintain traditions and myths from the times before Indian Buddhism came to Tibet. These old rituals invoke and placate the gods of the mountains (yul-lha) and the spirits of wild nature (gzhi-bdag) in a manner that we might term shamanic.

In the older classification of Bonpo texts, such shamanic practices were known as *Chab-nag*, which in contemporary Tibetan would mean "black waters." However, in ancient times, the word *chab* may have had a different meaning, perhaps that of "ritual practice." *Nag* or "black" refers not to an evil intent, as in the West, but to the exorcising, expelling, and dissolving of negative energies, whereas *dkar*, "white" refers to the invoking of positive energies. Thus these shamanic practices of evoking and exorcising spirits comprise one of the four doorways or Portals of Bon (bon sgo bzhi) in the system of classification known as the Four Portals and the Treasury which is the Fifth (sgo bzhi mdzod lnga).

Like the Nyingmapa school of Tibetan Buddhism, the Bonpo tradition also divides the teachings of the Buddha into nine successive vehicles to enlightenment (theg-pa rim dgu). According to the classification system of the Southern Treasures, the shamanic practices in question constitute the Causal Vehicles (rgyu'i theg-pa) or the Bon of Causes (rgyu'i bon). These represent the first four ways among the nine ways or vehicles of the teachings of Bon, namely,

1. the way of the practice of prediction (phywa gshen theg-pa),
2. the way of the practice of visible manifestations (snang gshen theg-pa),

3. the way of the practice of magical power ('phrul gshen theg-pa), and
4. the way of the practice of existence (srid gshen theg-pa).

Many of the practices found here have been adopted and assimilated into the various Buddhist schools for the purpose of harmonizing the relationship between our human world and the other world of the spirits. Indeed, one possible origin of the word "bon" is an ancient verb meaning "to invoke the spirits", and this certainly is one principal activity of the shaman, as well as the priest. [7] Again, in ancient times, there seems to have been a variety of religious practitioners designated by the term Bonpo. Nowadays, among Tibetans at least, Bonpo refers exclusively to a practitioner of Yungdrung Bon. Like their Buddhist colleagues, Bonpo Lamas are adamantly opposed to the practice of blood sacrifice (dmar mchod), which is still carried out by practitioners of shamanism in Nepal and some other regions. In both Buddhism and Yungdrung Bon, the use of torma (gtor-ma), or offering cakes, often elaborately sculptured, has come to replace blood sacrifice as a suitable offering for the gods and spirits.

We find here not only archaic shamanic rituals and magical practices, the aim of which is to secure worldly benefits for the practitioner and his patrons in this present life, but also the higher spiritual teachings of Sutra, Tantra and Dzogchen (mdo sngags sems gsum). The aim of these latter teachings is not just worldly benefits here and now, but the transcendent goal of liberation from the suffering of Samsara, the beginningless cycle of death and rebirth, and attainment of the enlightenment of a Buddha, the ultimate potential of human development and evolution. In contrast to the above Causal Bon (rgyu'i bon), these higher spiritual teachings are known as the Fruitional Bon ('bras-bu'i bon).

The Four Portals and the Treasury

The Four Portals of Bon and the Treasury, which is the Fifth (bon sgo bzhi mdzod lnga), represent an ancient system for the classification of the Bonpo teachings into four groups known as the Four Portals (sgo bzhi). This system appears to be independent of the classification of the teachings into the Nine Ways and is probably earlier. These groups or classes of teachings are as follows:

1. The Bon of "the White Waters" containing the Fierce Mantras (chab dkar drag-po sngags kyi bon): this collection consists of esoteric Tantric practices focusing on the recitation of wrathful or fierce mantras (drag sngags) associated with various meditation deities. Within this class are included the Chyipung cycle or "General Collection" (spyi-spungs skor), that is to say, the practices associated with the Father Tantras (pha rgyud). [8]
2. The Bon of "the Black Waters" for the continuity of existence (chab nag srid-pa rgyud kyi bon): this collection consists of various magical rituals, funeral rites, ransom rites, divination practices, and so on, necessary for the process of purifying and counteracting negative energies. This collection would seem to correspond, by and large, to the Four Causal Ways described above. Here the term "black" refers not to the practitioner's intention, but to the expelling of negativities, which are symbolically black in color.
3. The Bon of the Extensive Prajnaparamita from the country of Phanyul ('phan-yul rgyas-pa 'bum gyi bon): this collection consists of the moral precepts, vows, rules, and ethical teachings for monks and also for lay people who have taken one to five vows and remained householders. In particular, the focus is on the philosophical and ethical system of the Prajnaparamita Sutras, which are preserved in the Bonpo version in

sixteen volumes known as the *Khams-chen*. This collection basically represents the Sutra system, whereas the *Chab dkar* above represents the Tantra system. [9]
4. The Bon of the Scriptures and the Secret Oral Instructions of the Masters (dpon-gsas man-ngag lung gi bon): this collection consists of the oral instructions (man-ngag) and written scriptures (lung) of the various masters (dpon-gsas) belonging to the lineages of transmission for Dzogchen.
5. The Bon of the Treasury, which is of the highest purity and is all-inclusive (gtsang mtho-thog spyi-rgyug mdzod kyi bon): this collection contains essential material from all Four Portals of Bon. The Treasury, which is the fifth (mdzod lnga), is described in the *gZer-myig*: "As for the highest purity (gtsang mtho-thog), it extends everywhere. As insight, it belongs to the Bon that is universal (spyi-gcod). It purifies the stream of consciousness in terms of all four Portals." [10]

Yungdrung Bon

Yungdrung Bon (g.yung-drung bon) as such consists of the teachings and the practices attributed to Shenrab Miwoche himself in his role as the Teacher, or the source of revelation (ston-pa), and, in particular, this means the higher teachings of Sutra, Tantra and Dzogchen. He is said to have revealed these teachings to his disciples in Olmo Lung-ring on earth, as well as elsewhere in a celestial realm in his previous incarnation as Chimed Tsug-phud ('Chi-med gtsug-phud). [11] These teachings of Tonpa Shenrab, already set down in writing in his own time or in the subsequent period, are said to have been brought at a later time from Olmo Lung-ring in Tazik to the country of Zhang-zhung in western and northern Tibet where they were translated into the Zhang-zhung language. Zhang-zhung appears to have been an actual language, distinct from Tibetan, and apparently related to the west Himalayan Tibeto-Burman dialect of Kinnauri. Thus, it was not some artificial creation fabricated by the Bonpos in order to have an ancient source language corresponding to the Indian Sanskrit of the Buddhist scriptures. [12]

Beginning with the reign of the second king of Tibet, Mutri Tsanpo, it is said that certain Bonpo texts, in particular the Father Tantras (pha rgyud), were brought from Zhang-zhung to central Tibet and translated into the Tibetan language. [13] Thus the Bonpos assert that Tibetan acquired a system of writing at this time, based on the *sMar-yig* script used in Zhang-zhung which, therefore, would have been ancestral to the *dbu-med* script now often used for composing Tibetan manuscripts, especially among Bonpos. [14]

The Bonpos subsequently experienced two persecutions in central Tibet, the first under the eighth king of Tibet, Drigum Tsanpo (Dri-gum btsan-po), and the second under the great Buddhist king of Tibet, Trisong Detsan (Khri-srong lde'u-btsan) in the eighth century of our era. According to tradition, on both occasions the persecuted Bonpo sages concealed their books in various places in Tibet and adjacent regions such as Bhutan. These caches of texts were rediscovered from the tenth century onwards. Thus they are known as rediscovered texts or "hidden treasures" (gter-ma). [15]

Certain other texts were never concealed, but remained in circulation and were passed down from the eighth century onwards in a continuous lineage. These are known as *snyan-rgyud*, literally "oral transmission," even though they are usually said to have existed as written texts even from the early period. One example of such an "oral tradition" is the *Zhang-zhung snyan-rgyud* which, in the eighth century, the master Tapihritsa allowed his disciple Gyerpungpa to write down in the form of his pithy secret oral instructions (man-ngag, Skt. upadesha). Alternatively, the texts were dictated during the course of ecstatic visions or altered states of consciousness by certain ancient sages or certain deities to Lamas who lived in later centuries. One such example of this was the famous lengthy hagiography of Tonpa Shenrab known as the *gZi-brjid*, dictated to Lodan Nyingpo (bLo-ldan snying-po, b.1360) by the ancient sage Tangchen Mutsa Gyermed (sTang-chen dMu-tsha gyer-med) of Zhang-zhung. [16] This classification is quite similar to the Nyingmapa classification of its canon of scriptures into *bka'-ma* and *gter-ma*. [17] This form of Old Bon has flourished in western and central Tibet down to our own day.

The teachings of Bon revealed by Tonpa Shenrab are classified differently in the three traditional hagiographical accounts of his life. In general, Tonpa Shenrab was said to have expounded Bon in three cycles of teachings:

1. The Nine Successive Vehicles to Enlightenment (theg-pa rim dgu);
2. The Four Portals of Bon and the fifth which is the Treasury (sgo bzhi mdzod lnga);
3. The Three Cycles of Precepts that are Outer, Inner and Secret (bka' phyi nang gsang skor gsum). [18]

Hidden Treasure Texts

These Nine Ways or Nine Successive Vehicles to Enlightenment are delineated according to three different systems of hidden treasure texts (gter-ma) that were said to have been concealed during the earlier persecutions of Bon and rediscovered in later centuries. These hidden treasure systems are designated according to the locations where the concealed texts were rediscovered:

1. The System of the Southern Treasures (lho gter lugs): these were the treasure texts rediscovered at Drigtsam Thakar ('brig-mtsham mtha' dkar) in southern Tibet and at Paro (spa-gro) in Bhutan. Here the Nine Ways are first divided into the Four Causal Ways which contain many myths and magical

shamanic rituals, and which principally concern working with energies for worldly benefits. Then there are the five higher spiritual ways known as the Fruitional Ways. Here the purpose is not to gain power or to ensure health and prosperity in the present world, but realization of the ultimate spiritual goal of liberation from the suffering experienced in the cycles of rebirth within Samsara. The final and ultimate vehicle found here in this nine-fold classification is that of Dzogchen.

2. The System of the Central Treasures (dbus gter lugs): these treasure texts were rediscovered at various sites in central Tibet, including the great Buddhist monastery of Samye (bsam-yas). In general, this classification of the Bonpo teachings is quite similar to the system of the Nine Vehicles found in the traditions of the Nyingmapa school of Tibetan Buddhism. Some of these Bonpo texts are said to have been introduced from India into Tibet by the great native-born Tibetan translator Vairochana of Pagor, who translated works from both the Buddhist and the Bonpo traditions. [19]

3. The System of the Northern Treasures (byang gter lugs): these treasure texts were rediscovered at various locations north of central Tibet. However, according to Lopon Tenzin Namdak, not much is currently known regarding this system. [20]

The Nine Ways of Bon

The Nine Ways of Bon or, rather, the nine successive vehicles of Bon (bon theg-pa rim dgu) as classified in the System of the Southern Treasures (lho gter lugs), is expounded in as many chapters in the *gZi-brjid*, the most extensive hagiography of Tonpa Shenrab. Here the Nine Ways are listed as follows:

1. The Way of the Practice of Prediction (phywa gshen theg-pa): literally *theg-pa* means a vehicle or conveyance, rather than a

road or a way. *gShen*, a word of obscure origin and meaning, can here be translated as "practice" or "practitioner" according to the Lopon. And the term *phywa* means prediction or prognostication. This way or vehicle is principally concerned with divination (mo), astrological and geomantic calculations (rtsis), medical diagnosis (dpyad), and the performing of healing rituals (gto).

2. The Way of the Practice of Visible Manifestations (snang gshen theg-pa): this way is principally concerned with visible manifestations (snang-ba), perceived as positive manifestations of the activities of the gods (lha) who come to the aid of humanity. Therefore, the emphasis is placed on invoking the gods (lha gsol-ba) for their aid. This includes such classes of deities as the *Thugs-dkar*, the *sGra-bla*, the *Wer-ma*, and so on.

3. The Way of the Practice of Magical Power ('phrul gshen theg-pa): this way is principally concerned with magical rituals to ensure prosperity and control over the spirits evoked, especially the rites of exorcism (sel-ba) to eliminate negative energy and the negative provocations of evil spirits (gdon) who come to disturb human existence. The practitioner works with these energies in terms of evocation, conjuration and application (bsnyen sgrub las gsum).

4. The Way of the Practice of Existence (srid gshen theg-pa): here the term "existence" or "becoming" (srid-pa) properly refers to the processes of death and rebirth. This way is also known as *'Dur gshen*, the practice of ceremonies for exorcising ('dur) the spirits of the dead who are disturbing the living. It is, therefore, principally concerned with the three hundred and sixty kinds of rites for accomplishing this, as well as methods for ensuring the good fortune and long life of the living. These four represent the Four Causal Ways of Bon (bon rgyu'i theg-pa bzhi). They are followed by the higher ways of a more spiritual nature, whose goal is liberation and

enlightenment, collectively known as the Fruitional Ways ('bras-bu'i theg-pa).

5. The Way of the Virtuous Lay Practitioners (dge-bsnyen theg-pa): this way is principally concerned with morality and ethics, such as the ten virtuous deeds (dge-ba bcu), the Ten Perfections or Paramitas, and so on, as well as pious activities such as erecting stupas, especially on the part of lay practitioners (dge-bsnyen, Skt. upasika).
6. The Way of the Ascetic Sages (drang-srong theg-pa): the term *drang-srong* (Skt. rishi), meaning a sage, has here the technical significance of a fully ordained monk who has taken the full complement of vows, corresponding to the Buddhist bhikshu (dge-slong). The principal concern is with the vows of the monk and the rules of monastic discipline ('dul-ba).
7. The Way of the White A (A-dkar theg-pa): this way is mainly concerned with the Tantric practice of transformation by way of visualizing oneself as the meditation deity, and the practices associated with the mandala. Here are included both the Lower Tantras and the Higher Tantras.
8. The Way of the Primordial Shen (ye gshen theg-pa): this way is concerned with certain secret Tantric practices including the proper relationship with the Guru and with the Tantric consort, as well as with the methodologies of the Generation Process (bskyed-rim) and the Perfection Process (rdzogs-rim) and the conduct connected with them.
9. The Ultimate Way (bla-med theg-pa): this ultimate and unsurpassed (bla na med-pa) way is comprised of the teachings and practices of Dzogchen, the Great Perfection, which describes the process of enlightenment in terms of the Base, the Path and the Fruit, as well as the practice of contemplation in terms of view, meditation and conduct.

The Nine Ways according to the System of the Central Treasures (dbus gter lugs) are also divided into the Causal Vehicles (rgyu'i theg-pa) and the Fruitional Vehicles ('bras-bu'i theg-pa). These are as follows:

1. The Vehicle of Gods and Men where one relies upon another (lha mi gzhan rten gyi theg-pa), that is to say, this is the vehicle of those disciples who must first hear the teachings from another. This vehicle corresponds to the Shravakayana in the Buddhist system and the philosophical view is that of the Vaibhashikas.
2. The Vehicle of the Shenrabpas who understand by themselves alone (rang-rtogs gshen-rab kyi theg-pa). These practitioners do not need to hear the teachings first from another, rather, they discover the meaning of the teachings for themselves in their meditation practice. This vehicle corresponds to the Pratyekabuddhayana of the Buddhists and the philosophical view is that of the Sautrantikas.
3. The Vehicle of the Compassionate Bodhisattvas (thugs-rje sems-pa'i theg-pa). This vehicle corresponds to the Mahayana Sutra system or Bodhisattvayana vehicle in the Buddhist system. In particular, the reference is to the Bodhisattvas who practice the Ten Paramitas of generosity, morality, patience, vigor, meditation, strength, compassion, commitment, skillful means and wisdom. The philosophical view is that of the Yogacharins or Chittamatrins (sems-tsam-pa) who discern the absence of any inherent existence in terms of the internal self, as well as external phenomena.
4. The Vehicle of the Bodhisattvas that are without conceptual elaborations (g.yung-drung sems-pa'i spros med-pa'i theg-pa). This vehicle also corresponds to the Bodhisattvayana in the Buddhist system. The Bonpo term *g.yung-drung sems-dpa'*, literally Svastikasattva or "Swastika being," has the same significance as the Buddhist term Bodhisattva (byang-chub sems-dpa'). Here one finds the same practice of the Ten Paramitas. However, the philosophical view of emptiness and the ab-

sence of any inherent existence in the internal self and external phenomena is understood by way of Madhyamaka (dbu-ma-pa), rather than Chittamatra (sems-tsam-pa). These four lower ways represent the Causal Vehicles (rgyu'i theg-pa), while those which follow are known as the Fruitional Vehicles.

5. The Vehicle of the Primordial Bon of pure conduct and ritual activity (bya-ba gtsang-spyod ye bon gyi theg-pa). Focusing on ritual activity (bya-ba, Skt. kriya) and purity of conduct, this vehicle corresponds to the Kriyatantrayana in the Nyingmapa system. In terms of method, the Wisdom Being (ye-shes-pa) is invoked into one's range of vision and treated as a great lord being petitioned by a humble servant. Thereby the practitioner receives the knowledge (ye-shes) and the blessings (byin-rlabs) of the deity.

6. The Vehicle of the Clairvoyant Knowledge that possesses all of the aspects (rnam-par kun-ldan mngon-shes kyi theg-pa). The focus is equally on external ritual action and internal yoga practice. This vehicle corresponds to the Charyatantrayana in the Nyingmapa system. Together with the practice of the Ten Paramitas and the Four Recollections, the presence of the Wisdom Being is invoked, but this time the deity is regarded as an intimate friend rather than as a superior lord. These two vehicles represent the Outer or Lower Tantras (phyi rgyud), while the vehicles that follow represent the Inner or Higher Tantras (nang rgyud).

7. The Vehicle of Visibly Manifesting Compassion in terms of the Actual Generation Process (dngos bskyed thugs-rje rol-pa'i theg-pa). This vehicle corresponds to the Yoga Tantra and to a certain extent to the Mahayoga Tantra and the Anuttara Tantra in the Buddhist system of classification for both the Nyingmapas and the Newer Schools. Establishing oneself in the higher view of the Ultimate Truth and remaining in the original condition of the Natural State, one engages

in the Generation Process (bskyed-rim) and transforms oneself into the meditation deity, thereby realizing the qualities attributed to that manifestation of enlightened awareness.

8. The Vehicle wherein Everything is Completely Perfect and Exceedingly Meaningful (shin tu don-ldan kun rdzogs kyi theg-pa). Becoming established in the Ultimate Truth and the original condition of the Natural State, as was the case above, here one places the emphasis on the Perfection Process (rdzogs-rim) rather than on the Generation Process (bskyed-rim), so that Space and Awareness are realized as inseparable (dbyings rig dbyer-med). And particularly in terms of the meditation deity, the practitioner comes to realize the gnosis or pristine awareness of the inseparability of bliss and emptiness (bde stong ye-shes). This vehicle corresponds to the Mahayoga Tantra and especially the Anuyoga Tantra classifications of the Nyingmapas.

9. The Unsurpassed Vehicle of the highest peak of the primordial Great Perfection (ye nas rdzogs-chen yang-rtse bla-med kyi theg-pa). This vehicle comprises the Dzogchen teachings in terms of the Mind Series (sems-sde), which emphasize the awareness side of the Natural State and the Space Series (klong-sde), which emphasize the emptiness side, as well as the Secret Instruction Series (man-ngag sde), which emphasize their inseparability.

Shenchen Luga and the Revival of Bon

In the year 1017, Shenchen Luga (gShen-chen klu-dga') came from eastern Tibet and discovered two large wooden boxes containing many Bonpo texts in the Tibetan language, which had been buried at Drigtsam Thakar ('brig-mtsham mtha' dkar) in Tsang Province, near the ancestral seat of the Shen clan. [21] It was principally this discovery that led to the revival of Bon in central Tibet in the eleventh century, a revival similar in character to the revival of Buddhism among the Nyingmapas at the same time. In part, this renaissance was a reaction to the development of the Sarmapa of the New Tantra movement of that century, a movement inspired by the translations of Indian Buddhist texts, many of them previously unknown in Tibet.

Among his disciples, Shenchen Luga commissioned Druchen Namkha Yungdrung (Bru-chen nam-mkha' g.yung-drung), together with his son, Khyunggi Gyaltsan (Khyung gi rgyal-mtshan), to copy and record the philosophical texts (mtshan-nyid) which he had recovered from this treasure hoard of the Shen clan. The cache was reportedly concealed during the persecution of Bon in the eighth century by Dranpa Namkha, Lishu Tagring and other Bonpo Lamas. This persecution occurred in central Tibet in the time of King Trisong Detsan. This large collection of Termas, or hidden treasure texts, became widely known as the Southern Treasures (lho gter), and they came to be classified into the Nine Successive Vehicles of Bon (bon theg-pa rim-dgu). As outlined above, also contained in this collection of rediscovered texts were the *Gab-pa dgu skor* and the *Sems phran sde bdun*, representing an important cycle of Dzogchen texts closely related to the *Zhang-zhung snyan-rgyud*.

According to the Bonpo histories, the Dru lineage became pre-eminent in the transmission of the Bonpo philosophical tradition. Druchen Namkha Yungdrung himself wrote a commentary on the *Srid-pa'i mdzod-phug*, the main Bonpo cosmological text, and his son Khyunggi Gyaltsan wrote a commentary that established the philosophical and exegetical tradition of this lineage (mtshan-nyid kyi bshad srol). Both father and son had listened to the master Shenchen expound the philosophy and cosmology of this text. Then in 1072, Druje Yungdrung Lama (Bru-rje g.yung-drung bla-ma, b. 1040) established the Bonpo monastery of Yeru Wensakha (g.yas ru dben-sa-kha) in Tsang Province that became the fountainhead of this tradition and the foremost Bonpo monastery of its time. When it was destroyed in a disastrous flood, it was re-established on higher ground by Nyammed Sherab Gyaltsan (mNyam-med shes-rab rgyal-mtshan) in 1405 as the monastery of Tashi Menri (bkra-shis sman-ri), where later Lopon Tenzin Namdak served as principal teacher for a time.

The Traditions of Bonpo Dzogchen

In general, within the Bon tradition, a number of different lines of transmission for the Dzogchen teachings exist, three of which are collectively known as *A rdzogs snyan gsum*. The first two of them represent Terma traditions based on rediscovered treasure texts, whereas the third is an oral tradition (snyan brgyud) based on a continuous transmission through an uninterrupted line of realized masters. These transmissions of Dzogchen are as follows:

1. A-khrid

The first cycle here of Dzogchen teachings is called *A-khrid* (pronounced A-tri), that is, the teachings that guide one (khrid) to the Primordial State (A). The white Tibetan letter A is the symbol of Shunyata and of primordial wisdom. The founder of this tradition was Meuton Gongdzad Ritrod Chenpo, who was frequently known simply as Dampa, "the holy man." [22] He extracted these Dzogchen precepts from the *Khro rgyud* cycle of texts. Together with the *Zhi-ba don gyi skor*, these texts formed part of the *sPyi-spungs yan-lag gi skor* cycle of teachings that belong to the Father Tantras (pha rgyud), originally attributed to Tonpa Shenrab in his celestial pre-existence as Chimed Tsugphud ('Chi-med gtsug-phud). To this collected material, Meuton added his own mind treasure (dgongs gter) and organized the practice of the cycle into eighty meditation sessions extending over several weeks. This was known as the *A-khrid thun mtsham brgyad-cu-pa*. The instructions were divided into three sections dealing with the view (lta-ba), the meditation (sgom-pa), and the conduct (spyod-pa). Upon a successful completion of the eighty-session course, one received the title of Togdan (rtogs-ldan), that is, "one who possesses understanding." The *A-khrid* tradition, where the practice is very systematically laid out in a specific number of sessions, in many ways corresponds to the *rDzogs-chen sems-sde* of the Nyingmapa tradition. [23]

2. rDzogs-chen

Here the term *rDzogs-chen* does not indicate Dzogchen in general; the reference is to a specific transmission of Dzogchen whose root text is the *rDzogs-chen yang-rtse'i klong-chen*, "the Great Vast Expanse of the Highest Peak which is the Great Perfection," rediscovered by the great Terton Zhodton Ngodrub Dragpa (bZhod-ston dngos-grub grags-pa) in the year A.D.1080. This discovery was part of a famous cycle of treasure texts hidden behind a statue of Vairochana at the Khumthing temple at Lhodrak. This root text is said to have been composed in the eighth century by the Bonpo master known as Lishu Tagring. [24]

3. sNyan-rgyud

The third cycle of transmission of the Dzogchen teachings within the Bon tradition is the uninterrupted lineage of the oral transmission from the country of Zhang-zhung (Zhang-zhung snyan-rgyud), which was revealed to Gyerpung Nangzher Lodpo (Gyer-spungs snang-bzher lod-po) at the Darok lake in northern Tibet in the eighth century. Gyerpungpa was thus a contemporary of the great Tibetan king Trisong Detsan who invited Padmasambhava and Shantirakshita to Tibet, built the first Buddhist monastery in Tibet at Samye, and established Indian Buddhism as the official religion of his kingdom. Before that, in the seventh century, it is said that Tapihritsa, a native of the country of Zhang-zhung, had received the Dzogchen precepts from his own master Tsepung Dawa Gyaltsan (Tshe-spungs zla-ba rgyal-mtshan). After practicing Dzogchen in a cave for nine years, he attained realization and liberation as the Rainbow Body of the Great Transfer. [25] Later he reappeared to Gyerpungpa on several occasions and transmitted to him the precepts for Dzogchen (bka' brgyud). After that he allowed him to set down these precepts in the Zhang-zhung language for the first time. They were translated into Tibetan in the next century. Because this tradition has a continuous lineage extending back to at least the eighth century of our era, and so does not represent Terma texts rediscovered at a later time, it is of particular importance for research into the question of the historical origins of Dzogchen. [26]

4. *Ye-khri mtha'-sel*

This fourth major cycle of Dzogchen, together with the above three, is included within the four-year training program of study and practice in the Meditation School (sgrub-grwa) at Triten Norbutse Monastery in Kathmandu. It is said that in the eleventh century, the Bonpo master Lungton Lhanyen (Lung-ston lha-gnyan) actually met Tsewang Rigdzin (Tse-dbang rig-'dzin) in person in the guise of an Indian sadhu. The latter revealed to him the Dzogchen teachings he had received from his father Dranpa Namkha (Dran-pa nam-mkha', eighth century). Having acquired the power of long life (tshe dbang) by virtue of his yoga practice, Tsewang Rigdzin is said to have lived for centuries. Some of these texts, such as the *Nam-mkha' 'phrul-mdzod* present Dzogchen in a much more systematic and intellectual manner comparable to the Dzogchen Semde (sems-sde) class of the Nyingmapas.

Having previously taught the *A-khrid* and *Zhang-zhung snyan-rgyud* extensively to Western students both in Nepal and in the West in recent years, Lopon Tenzin Namdak Yongdzin Rinpoche has been focusing on the teaching of the *Ye-khri mtha'-sel*, convinced that Western students are especially suited to the practice of Dzogchen.

CHAPTER 1
Introduction to the Practice of Dzogchen

Talk by Lopon Tenzin Namdak,
Vienna, Austria, April 1991.
Compiled and edited by John Myrdhin Reynolds.

It is necessary for us to know what Dzogchen is, how to practice it, and the result of this practice. Even in Tibet it was not easy to get these teachings. They have been kept very secret since the eighth century. Even before that there were twenty-four masters of Dzogchen in the Zhang-zhung Nyan-gyud lineage, all of whom realized Jalu ('ja'-lus), or the Rainbow Body. However, each of them only gave the transmission to a single disciple. [1] Furthermore, from the eighth century until today this Dzogchen lineage has remained unbroken. It was kept very secret, but now in the second half of the twentieth century because circumstances have changed, both the Dakinis and the Guardians have given permission to teach Dzogchen much more openly. [2]

These days, we Tibetans have lost our native country. My own master prayed to the Guardians and positive signs appeared, so now we can teach Dzogchen much more openly to those disciples who are ready. We give a two-year course in the Dzogchen teachings at Dolanji where we have our monastery. This course is part of the nine-year program for the Geshe degree (Ph.D.) and in it we give a very logical and systematic presentation of Dzogchen. This tradition has remained unbroken from earliest times until today.

The Dzogchen teachings are the same in both Bonpo and Nyingmapa, but the lineages are different. This is the principal difference. Historically speaking, the Zhang-zhung Nyan-gyud (Zhang-zhung snyan-brgyud) is the most important lineage for Dzogchen. It came not from Tibet, but from the ancient kingdom of Zhang-zhung to the west, centered in the Mt. Kailas region. Dzogchen was the highest teaching in the religious culture of Zhang-zhung and from there the Dzogchen tradition was transmitted to Tibet. [3]

Some years ago, Namkhai Norbu Rinpoche came to our monastery at Dolanji with fourteen of his Italian students in order to receive the transmission for the Zhang-zhung Nyan-gyud and the empowerment for its patron deity, or Yidam, Zhang-zhung Meri. However, Namkhai Norbu is not a Bonpo Lama; he is a Drugpa Kagyudpa Tulku, who received a Sakyapa education at Derge Gomchen Monastery, and whose principal Dzogchen master was a famous Nyingmapa Lama in Derge named Changchub Dorje. Rinpoche was very interested in the Bonpo tradition because he was researching the historical roots of Tibetan culture and Dzogchen. These roots are Bonpo; in general, Bon was the name for the pre-Buddhist religious culture of Tibet. In Zhang-zhung it was called Gyer. [4] Both the Bonpos and the Nyingmapas have a system of Thegpa Rimgu (theg-pa rim dgu), or nine successive vehicles to enlightenment, and in both cases the ninth and highest vehicle is Dzogchen.

According to the Paramita system, or Sutra system, it takes three incalculable kalpas to attain the realization of Buddhahood. But according to the Tantra system, it only takes seven lifetimes. The goal is the same in both the Sutra system and the Tantra system, namely, Buddhahood, but the methods or paths are different. There are four classes of Tantra in the Bonpo system:

1. Jyawe Gyud (bya-ba'i rgyud), or Kriya Tantra,
2. Chyodpe Gyud (spyod-pa'i rgyud), or Charya Tantra,

3. Yeshen Gyud (ye-gshen gyi rgyud), and
4. Yeshen Chenpo Gyud (ye-gshen chen-po'i rgyud).

Each of these classifications of Tantra has its own views which are the foundations of practice. Therefore, we find that a difference necessarily exists in terms of the time it takes to realize the fruit or result of the practice. The methods are not all the same; some are far more potent and bring quicker results.

In Dzogchen there are three divisions in the teachings:

1. Semde (sems-sde), or the Mind series,
2. Longde (klong-sde), or the Space series, and
3. Manngagide (man-ngag sde), or the Upadesha (secret instruction) series.

Dzogchen as a teaching has three inherent qualities: awareness (rig-pa), emptiness (stong-pa nyid), and their unification or inseparability (dbyer-med). But in the Natural State (gnas-lugs), which is the Nature of Mind (sems-nyid), these distinctions are not found because therein everything is primordially unified and inseparable from the very beginning, and never otherwise. But in talking about and describing the teachings, we make these distinctions. Semde, the Mind series, emphasizes much more the Awareness side or aspect (rig-cha); Longde, the Space series, emphasizes much more the Emptiness side or space aspect (stong-cha). And Manngagide, the Upadesha series, emphasizes the inseparability of awareness and emptiness (rig stong dbyer-med). Each of the three series of Dzogchen teachings, however, recognizes Yermed (dbyer-med), or inseparability, as fundamental; the distinctions are only a matter of emphasis.[5] In terms of this classification into three series, the Zhang-zhung Nyan-gyud is Upadesha or Manngagide because it principally teaches the inseparability of awareness and emptiness.

The state of Dzogchen, the Great Perfection (rdzogs-pa chen-po), is described as being Kadak (ka-dag), that is, primordial purity or pure from the very beginning. It has never had any obscurations in it, as is the case with our ordinary functioning mind (yid) and consciousness (rnam-shes). This Natural State of Dzogchen is naturally and inherently pure, and never otherwise. Therefore, it represents primordial Buddhahood (ye sangs-rgyas). This is the Base (gzhi) for the Path (lam) and for the realization of the Fruit ('bras-bu), or result of the Path. Thus we speak of three Buddhas:

1. Zhi Sangye (gzhi'i sangs-rgyas), Buddhahood of the Base,
2. Lam Sangye (lam gyi sangs-rgyas), Buddhahood of the Path and
3. Drebu Sangye ('bras-bu'i sangs-rgyas), Buddhahood of the Fruit.

The Buddhahood of the Base means this state of Kadak, or primordial purity, and the term is synonymous with Shunyata or emptiness (stong-pa nyid). It has no obscurations whatsoever, either emotional or intellectual. It is like the nature of a mirror which has the capacity to reflect whatever is set before it. But, although this inherent Buddha nature exists in all sentient beings, it is necessary to practice the Path in order to realize its nature which, at the moment, goes unrecognized by the individual. It is like the face of the sun obscured by clouds so it cannot be seen and goes unrecognized, even though it is present in the sky all the time. As the source, this inherent Buddha-nature is already pure and clean and unmixed with defilements, whether emotional or intellectual. The process of coming to realize this fact is called the Buddhahood of the Path. By way of practicing the Path, we come to attain realization and this realization is called the Buddhahood of the Fruit.

Introduction to the Practice of Dzogchen ~ 29

Now, both the Buddhahood of the Base and the Buddhahood of the Path are called "Buddha", but they are not the real Buddha because this Buddhahood is latent and potential at this time and not actually manifest. We must still purify ourselves of adventitious obscurations, accumulated in countless lifetimes from time without beginning, in order to attain the realization of manifest Buddhahood. If we say that all beings are already Buddhas, then why is there any necessity to do practice? It is because this Buddhahood is not yet manifest and visible, but it is present in potential at the core of every single sentient being.

In the practice of Dzogchen, we do not find it necessary to do visualizations of deities or to do recitations like the Refuge and Bodhichitta. Some would say that these are not necessary to do at all, but this is speaking from the side of the Natural State only. They say in the Natural State, everything is present there already in potential, and so there is nothing lacking and nothing more to do to add or acquire anything. This is fine. But on the side of the practitioner, there is much to do and practices such as Refuge and Bodhichitta are very necessary. [6]

In its own terms, Dzogchen has no rules; it is open to everything. But does this mean we can do just what we feel like at the moment? On the side of the Natural State, this is true and there are no restrictions or limitations. All appearances are manifestations of mind (sems kyi snang-ba), like reflections seen in a mirror, and there is no inherent negativity or impurity in them. Everything is perfectly all right just as it is, as the energy (rtsal) of the Nature of Mind in manifestation. It is like white and black clouds passing overhead in the sky; they equally obscure the face of the sun. When they depart, there are no traces left behind.

However, that is speaking only on the side of the Natural State, which is like the clear, open sky, unaffected by the presence or absence of these clouds. For the sky, it is all the same. But on the side of the practitioner, it is quite different because we mistakenly believe these clouds are solid, opaque, and quite real and substantial. As practitioners we must first come to an understanding of the insubstantiality and unreality of all these clouds which obscure the sky of our own Nature of Mind (sems-nyid). It is our Tawa (lta-ba), or view, our way of looking at things, which is basic and fundamental, and we must begin here. Then we must practice and attain realization. So on the side of the practitioner, practice and commitment are most certainly required. The Natural State in itself is totally open and clear and spacious like the sky but we, as individuals, are not totally open and unobstructed.

The principal point in Dzogchen is the view, that is, recognizing the Natural State and continuing in the Natural State. This is the highest of all ways or vehicles. But arrayed below it are eight other yanas (vehicles), where the practitioner, no matter how subtly or unconsciously, still clings to grasping at reality ('dzin-pa) and to activity (bya-ba), where we try to accomplish something. Dzogchen, on the contrary, is absolutely without any grasping or apprehending of anything ('dzin med) and without any deliberate activity (bya bral).

When we begin as practitioners on the path of Dzogchen, we first need a direct introduction to the Natural State from someone who has directly experienced the Natural State personally. [7] But just meeting it for one time, like meeting a new acquaintance, is not enough. We must discover the Natural State within ourselves over and over again, so that we have no doubt about it. For this reason we do practice and look back at our thoughts, observing them arise, stay and then pass away again. We look to find from where they arise, where they stay, and where they go. In this way we discover that thoughts are insubstantial; they just arise and disappear again, leaving no trace behind. If we do not interfere with them or try to modify them, they will liberate and dissolve in themselves. And so we must learn how to keep ourselves in this Nature and how to remain without modifications. There is nothing to change or modify or correct (ma bcos-pa). Thoughts just arise and then they liberate. [8]

At first it is sufficient to remain like that. When we truly experience the Natural State, we do not need to keep checking and waiting for thoughts to disappear. Thoughts arise and dissolve of their own accord. At the moment when a thought dissolves, just leave everything as it is until the next thought arises. We find ourselves in a condition which is very clear and alert. The Tibetan term Rang-rig means self-seeing, being self-aware. If we allow ourselves to follow after a thought, it will carry us away on a trip, and it will obscure and cover over our sense of presence, and we will forget to be self-aware. The Natural State is inexpressible in words. We may be all clarity, and yet, in our practice, if we think or say "I am clear!" we lose it. There should be no checking or evaluating at all by the mind or intellect when we are in the Natural State. Such mental activity is not the Natural State. When a thought dissolves, we leave it alone just as it is. But we remain alert and clear.

The Natural State possesses the qualities of being empty (stong-pa) and clear (gsal-ba). And so we can speak about these qualities, but in the Natural State itself, we find no separate or distinct qualities; everything is whole and unified (dbyer-med). The Natural State is just itself and nothing else, yet it encompasses everything. If it did not encompass everything, then it would possess an unchanging individual inherent existence (rang-bzhin). And, therefore, there would be no possibility for any change to occur in ourselves or in the world. Change would be impossible because everything would be locked into a rigid inherent nature or essence (rang-bzhin). But everywhere in our experience we see change, and so everything is insubstantial and lacking inherent existence (rang-bzhin med-pa). Whether there are many clouds seen in the sky or not, the nature of the sky in itself remains unchanged and undisturbed. It is the same with the

Nature of Mind. It is only our vision that is disturbed and obscured.

So we should not allow ourselves to be distracted by the thoughts that arise in meditation; we should try to remain in the Natural State. Eventually our contemplation will become stable, but at first many distractions will arise. We may begin by focusing our attention on a single point so that we can come to recognize what disturbs our contemplation. We must recognize this right away, so that we do not fall into the wrong way of practicing contemplation.

There are various ways to be introduced to the Natural State. We can use Shamatha meditation (zhi-gnas) for this purpose, for example, by concentrating our attention one-pointedly on the white Tibetan letter A. Initially this fixation allows no space for thoughts to arise and distract us, but then when we relax our fixation a little, thoughts arise again. But the thoughts that arise are only like the clouds that appear in the sky, and when they dissolve, they leave no trace behind. So we do not need to examine them and think about them, asking ourselves: "Are they emptiness or are they clarity?" We eventually find ourselves in a calm state, where few or no thoughts arise.

This, however, is the result of fixation and it is not Rigpa, or the Natural State. It is only an experience (nyams). Rigpa, the Natural State, is neither the calm state nor the movement of thoughts, but a state of pure immediate awareness which transcends all thought and workings of the mind. It is like a mirror reflecting whatever is set before it, without judgment or thought. When we enter into the Natural State, we are not practicing the cultivation of positive thoughts nor are we trying to repress negative thoughts. That is the method of the Sutras, namely, the application of antidotes to negative thoughts and emotions. But that is not the method of Dzogchen. The practice of Dzogchen means just continuing in the Natural State of Rigpa and allowing whatever thoughts arise, whether positive or negative, to self-liberate.

Dzogchen has been kept very secret in India and Tibet because it can easily give rise to wrong views. Dzogchen speaks of a state beyond cause and effect, so its practice is not a matter of cultivating positive thoughts and repressing negative ones. Why has Dzogchen been kept so secret? Not because it is a heresy or because it has anything to hide. If some individual is not ready for this teaching and hears it and misunderstands it, then this can be of harm to himself and of harm to others when he speaks to them regarding his wrong understanding. Therefore it has been better to keep the teachings secret and private.

How do we practice Dzogzchen? First we must practice Guru Yoga. [9] But Guru Yoga visualization is something created by our minds. Mind creates this object. The same is the case with the white Tibetan letter A. So, although we begin with such practices, they do not represent the principal practice. That involves entering into a state beyond the mind and we call that state Rigpa. Fixating on some object like the white letter A is only an aid to discovering Rigpa.

After we have fixated the mind on the white A and find ourselves in a calm state, then we look back into our minds to see who has fixated on this object. We look for the source of mind. We look for the source of thoughts. From where do they arise? Where do they stay? Where do they go? Do we find that they have any color or shape? When thoughts go, do we find any trace left behind? That is all on the object side. But now we look back to the subject side. Who is this watcher? Who is it that has created this visualization. Do we find two things here, the watcher and the watched? We search and search and we find nothing. We look for a subject and we find no trace of it. We look back and at that moment, the watcher and the watched dissolve.

Then we just remain in that presence without changing anything. We just leave everything as it is. When there is no interference, thoughts dissolve naturally. So we allow the thoughts to be just as they are without judging them. It does not matter at all what comes into the mind. The Dzogchen texts tell us that the emptiness side of the Natural State is primordial purity (ka-dag) and that the clarity or awareness side of the Natural State is spontaneous perfection (lhun-grub). But when we find ourselves in the Natural State, we are not thinking this, nor are we making any analyses or judgments. This Natural State is beyond conception by the intellect and inexpressible in words. Once we have been introduced to the Natural State, we will know what it is and not forget it. Then our task is to enter into it again and again and to continue in it. Contemplation or continuing in Rigpa, the Natural State, is the principal practice of Dzogchen. [10]

Here there are three principal obstacles which can disturb contemplation: chyingwa ('bying-ba) or drowsiness, mugpa (rmug-pa) or dullness, and godpa (rgod-pa) or agitation. We may try to keep in the Natural State continuously but find that it has become mixed with drowsiness, and so a renewal of energy is necessary here. We need to observe our contemplation in order to discover if it has become mixed with any of these three faults. Dullness means our clarity thickens and loses its transparency; the object appears dull. We lack energy. The opposite of dullness is alertness and the clear appearance or visualization of the object. We must check and see what is needed as an antidote. If we add too much energy, we will find ourselves in a state of agitation. With not enough energy we can be dull and drowsy.

So here a relationship exists between contemplation and energy. We must discover this for ourselves because it varies with the capacity and constitution of each individual practitioner. Generally, agitation is easy to recognize. But there are two kinds of agitation: coarse and subtle, and subtle agitation is very difficult to recognize. Thoughts arise and if we allow ourselves, consciously or unconsciously, to identify ourselves with them, immediately they lead us away from the Natural State. Remaining in the Natural State is the great highway leading directly to our destination, but distraction by thoughts leads us into bye-ways where we become lost and only with difficulty do we find our way back.

So what can we do? With drowsiness there are two principal things to do. First, get some fresh air and, second, shake and move the body and do some deep breathing. If coarse agitation arises, then stop the meditation practice for a while. Take a rest and do something else. Subtle agitation is more difficult to handle because we do not even realize that we have it. But when we do, we also need to stop and take a break. Dullness is handled in much the same way as drowsiness. When practicing Dzogchen we should always remember never to force ourselves, and to give ourselves plenty of space. It is much better to practice in many short sessions with refreshing breaks in between, rather than trying to force ourselves prematurely into long sessions of practice. This will only give rise to obstacles. In any event, what is most important, both at the beginning and later on, is to relax. The Natural State is already fully present from the very beginning, and so there is no need to cajole or coerce it. Just relax and let it all be. It is all there. That is the way of Dzogchen.

CHAPTER 2

The Attaining of Buddhahood according to Sutra, Tantra and Dzogchen

Taught by Lopon Tenzin Namdak,
Devon retreat, May 1991.
Edited by John Myrdhin Reynolds.

The Hinayana View

Mahayana recognizes the Trikaya, the Three Bodies of the Buddha, but Hinayana does not do so. The followers of Hinayana only recognize the existence of a historical Buddha who lived in the past. That Buddha, Shakyamuni, was like an Arhat, one who had purified all of his kleshas (passions or negative emotions) and vasanas (karmic traces). After his enlightenment, the residual karma that remained with him was represented by his physical body. This impure body persisted for a time, but his mind was entirely purified of obscurations. Then after passing into Parinirvana, absolutely nothing remained behind, neither body nor mind.

So when we pray to the Buddha, this action is no more than a commemoration because there is no one there to hear us. We receive no blessings and no wisdom from him because the Buddha is no more. There is only the memory of his teachings and example found recorded in the scriptures. Nonetheless, he showed the path to liberation from the sufferings experienced in Samsara and we can follow and practice that same path. The goal, according to Hinayana, is to liberate oneself alone from Samsara, that is, to become an Arhat. However, by practicing the path of

Hinayana, we realize only the status of an Arhat, and not the full enlightenment of a Buddha.

The Mahayana View

According to the traditional cosmology found both in Bon and in Buddhism, there are three principal levels of existence in the universe:

(1) The Kamadhatu, or Desire World, where all sentient beings, including the gods or Devas, are dominated by their sense desires (kama),
(2) the Rupadhatu, or Form World, the abode of the gods who have exceedingly subtle bodies (rupa) and sense organs of light, and who are no longer dominated by gross sense desires (kama), and
(3) the Arupadhatu, or Formless World, where beings have no visible form (arupa) and exist in a dimension of cosmic consciousness.

The highest plane of existence found at the summit of the Rupadhatu is known as Akanistha, or Ogmin ('og-min) in Tibetan, and at that level of existence, the Akanistha Devas ('og-min lha) reside. As we ascend upward through the celestial planes of the Rupadhatu, we find that the bodies of light of the Devas residing on each plane become progressively more subtle, clear and pure. When we are ready to attain Buddhahood, after an existence as a human being here below on earth, we find ourselves reborn in the Akanistha heaven. This is because there on that plane the manifest form, which embodies the enlightenment experience of a Buddha, is the most suitable. That is to say, we acquire a subtle and highly refined body of light by virtue of our rebirth in the Akanistha realm. Here in this Akanistha heaven we continue to practice in order to purify our stream of consciousness of all obscurations, even the most subtle and unconscious of obscurations. Once purified of all shadows, we attain Buddhahood in Akanistha as the Sambhogakaya. That is to say, we realize the Sambhogakaya form. This is how one attains Buddhahood according to the Sutra system of Mahayana.

According to Bon, one must first be reborn in Akanistha as an Akanistha Deva in order to possess a suitable body or form for enlightenment. Here the individual attains the Sambhogakaya, and then descends into the lower worlds in order to manifest as the Nirmankaya on the physical earth plane. The Mind of the Buddha is the Dharmakaya, which possesses the two-fold purity, that is, an intrinsic purity, as well as a freedom from all adventitious impurities. This Dharmakaya is inconceivable and inexpressible; it is without limits. But the manifestation of the Buddha's Energy (thugs-rje) is the Sambhogakaya, in a purified form of light and energy. It is something visible. This is the Speech aspect of the Buddha. The great Bodhisattvas, when they have attained the higher Bhumis or stages, can perceive this glorified Body.

But there are also the countless suffering beings of the Kamadhatu, who with their obscurations cannot perceive the Sambhogakaya. For their sakes the Buddha manifests innumerable projections or emanations (nirmitas) of his forms into all inhabited world systems, and these are known as Nirmanakayas, or Emanation Bodies (sprul-sku). These bodies can be perceived by beings whose minds are obscured by the kleshas (passions) and by sense desires. The Sambhogakaya is like the sun in the sky and its light shines everywhere. There is only a single sun in the sky, but there are many reflected images of this single sun in the many vessels of water set upon the ground. These reflected images are the Nirmanakayas. But only when the practitioner has attained the path of vision (the Darshana-marga, the third among the five paths), have we sufficiently purified our obscurations so that we can see the Sambhogakaya and hear its teachings directly.

Ignorant sentient beings are only capable of perceiving the Nirmanakaya that appears in time and history.

The Tantra View

In the Tantra system, we find a different method described where it is not necessary to be reborn first in the Akanistha heaven in order to obtain a subtle body of light. This method is known as Mayadeha, the Illusion Body or, in Tibetan, Gyulu (sgyu-lus). In this case, during our lifetime here on earth, we do the practice of Dzogrim (rdzogs-rim), which is the second phase of Tantric transformation, and we create in our heart center a very refined Illusion Body by way of a union of subtle prana and mind. This Gyulu, or Illusion Body, provides a suitable base for the manifestation of the Sambhogakaya, and so it is not necessary to seek this base in any other dimension of existence. We create this Gyulu during our lifetime on earth by way of our practice, and then, at the time of our death, we transfer our Namshe, or consciousness, into it and it then becomes the vehicle for our Sambhogakaya manifestation.

There are, however, two kinds of Gyulu, one pure and the other impure. If at the time of our death, we have not attained perfect realization and purified all our subtle obscurations, both emotional and intellectual, then this subtle body born of the unification of prana and mind is known as an impure Illusion Body. In that case, we must do further purification practice in that body in order to realize perfect enlightenment. Only when we attain that state can we speak of a pure Illusion Body. The manifesting of this Gyulu has wrongly been called a Rainbow Body ('ja'-lus) or a Body of Light ('od-lus). It is neither because the manifestation of this Sambhogakaya form depends on our prior practice and realization of both Kyerim (bskyed-rim), the process of generation, and Dzogrim (rdzogs-rim), the process of perfection. [1] Where the view and the practice are different, then the fruit or result will be different. So these manifestations, the Illusion Body and the Rainbow Body, are not at all the same.

The Dzogchen View

From the standpoint of Dzogchen, this creating of a Gyulu through the unification of subtle prana and mind (the Tantric method) and the attaining of rebirth as a Deva in the Akanistha heaven (the Sutra method) do not represent real Buddhahood. Nor does an Arhat, the state realized through the Hinayana method, represent a real Buddha. Once the Arhat has attained this state of having cut off all his kleshas, or defilements, at their roots, he need no longer be reborn as a human being. Nevertheless, at a more exalted level of existence, he must continue the process of purifying his stream of consciousness because he is still afflicted with various intellectual obscurations. [2]

Finding himself now at a higher level existence after his last human rebirth, the Arhat must enter into the practice of the Mahayana path in order to realize Buddhahood. Similarly, the Tantric practitioner who has realized the Gyulu does not need to take another human rebirth. But since this Gyulu is something that arises from causes, and the same is true of rebirth in Akanistha, it is therefore not permanent. If knowledge of the Dharmakaya were brought about by such antecedent causes, it also would be something that is impermanent. We cannot proceed from our conditioned existence to an unconditioned state. There is no way for this to occur.

There are two aspects or perspectives with regard to the Dharmakaya, first when it is viewed from the standpoint of the Sutra system and the Lower Tantras, and second when viewed from the standpoint of Dzogchen and some of the Higher Tantras such as the Ma Gyud. According to the Mahayana Sutra system, the cause which brings about the realization of the Dharmakaya is the accumulation of wisdom, meaning the understanding of

Shunyata or emptiness. The cause which brings about the realization of the Rupakaya, which includes both the Sambhogakaya and the Nirmanakaya, is the accumulation of merit accomplished by way of the practice of the Ten Perfections for three immeasurable kalpas of time. According to the Tantra system, the cause for the realization of the Dharmakaya is also the understanding of Shunyata but, in addition to the practice of the Ten Perfections, the cause for the Rupakaya is the practice of Kyerim and Dzogrim (visualizing oneself as the Yidam, or meditation deity, during the course of sadhana practice), thereby producing the Gyulu, or Illusion Body.

However, Dzogchen asserts that if Buddhahood is brought about by antecedent causes, it is not an unconditioned state. It would not be permanent. It would come to an end eventually, just as any mystical experiences brought about by meditation practice come to an end and thereafter we resume an ordinary, deluded level of consciousness. The fundamental principle here is that all conditioned things are impermanent, and this truth has been taught by all the Buddhas. However, according to the Sutra system, the accumulation of wisdom is the cause of the Dharmakaya and the accumulation of merit is the cause of the Rupakaya. Therefore, in this perspective of Sutra and Tantra, the Dharmakaya would be something impermanent and conditioned, whereas according to Dzogchen, the Dharmakaya is unconditioned and non-temporal. So, there is a logical contradiction to be found here.

How then does the practitioner realize the Dharmakaya, if the Dharmakaya is present all of the time? Here there is an example. Just as there exists the boundless infinity of space that pervades everywhere and, at the same time, there is the space found inside an earthen jar, which takes thereby a specific and particular shape, so it is with the Dharmakaya and the individual sentient being. The one is permanent and the other is impermanent and conditioned, temporarily confined by the clay walls of the jar. When the jar is broken, they are only one space. However, would this mean that, if there is only a single Dharmakaya, like the space that pervades everything, then all Buddhas are one and the same? No. [3]

Again, according to the interpretation of the Sutra system, after attaining enlightenment, the Buddha reappears in the world to teach the Dharma to sentient beings as the Nirmanakaya because of his Bodhichitta and his individual Pranidhana vow made previously. Therefore, that vow is the cause for his manifesting as the Rupakaya, as well as his individual accumulation of merit. But this Rupakaya appears to us because of our needs as individual sentient beings, and not because the Buddha has any desires or aspirations. He teaches sentient beings through the vehicle of Speech, that is to say, the Sambhogakaya, the manifestation of his energy, even though it is only the Great Bodhisattvas who perceive that manifestation visibly and directly.

Nevertheless, his Mind remains unmoved as the Dharmakaya. According to the theory, this Dharmakaya is unconditioned; it is in no way afflicted or limited by thoughts and desires which exist in time. It is like the clear, open, unobstructed sky, whereas the Sambhogakaya is like the sun in the sky. It sheds its light everywhere, impartially and indiscriminately and these rays of the sun are like the individual Nirmanakayas perceived by sentient beings. But if we are sitting in a cave on the north side of a mountain, we must then come out of that cave in order to see the face of the sun, even though its light shines everywhere outside. It is the same with the Sambhogakaya. In its essence, the Dharmakaya is empty and formless like the sky; it is unconditioned and permanent. But from the perspective of the Sutra system, on the side of wisdom the Dharmakaya would be impermanent because this wisdom arises from causes, the meditations that bring about the accumulation of wisdom. So, how can the real Dharmakaya arise from an accumulation of wisdom as the cause? There is a contradiction here.

However, matters stand quite differently according to Dzogchen. In the Dzogchen Upadesha teachings, we have the practices of Thekchod and Thodgal. Thekchod means we enter into and continue in the state of contemplation (rig-pa), which is the Natural State (gnas-lugs). Thodgal means that, while in the state of contemplation, the potentiality of the Natural State (rig-pa'i rtsal) has the occasion to manifest spontaneously as vision. The medium for the manifesting of this potentiality is either sunlight, total darkness, or the open space of the sky. [4] The ultimate culminating result of this prolonged Thodgal practice is the attaining of the Rainbow Body, or Jalu ('ja'-lus).

According to Dzogchen, we have attained the Sambhogakaya already because it is contained in potential in the Natural State. It is not something that is brought about historically by antecedent causes. Rather, it has been primordially present because it represents the inherent potentiality or energy of the Natural State (rig-pa'i rtsal) itself. This method of Thodgal is only found in Dzogchen and not in the other vehicles. Here the Sambhogakaya is not caused by something else other than itself, such as a vow or even Dzogrim practice. It is a spontaneously self-perfected manifestation (lhun-grub). But in terms of our experience, it is a visible thing and like all visible things it is changeable and impermanent. Therefore, a Rupakaya manifestation is always impermanent, as well as being individual. For us, it does not just sit on a throne in the sky throughout eternity, unchanging century after century.

Indeed, Thodgal does possess a method for dissolving the impure physical body, at the time of death or even before, and then this allows the Rainbow Body of Light to come into manifestation. But this is not a process of transforming an impure physical body into a pure Sambhogakaya. The method proper to Dzogchen is not the path of transformation, as is the case with the Tantras, but the path of self-liberation. Therefore, the procedure in Tantra and in Thodgal is quite different. To effect a transformation in vision and in energy, Tantra employs visualization in terms of Kyerim and Dzogrim practice. [5] We visualize ourselves in a Sambhogakaya form, whether this Yidam be a peaceful or a wrathful manifestation.

But in Dzogchen there is nothing to be visualized and nothing to be transformed. The visions which arise during the course of Thodgal are not visualizations. Visualization represents the work of the mind; visualizations are created by the mind. But Dzogchen is a state beyond the mind. So these visions which arise in Thodgal are not created by the mind or by unconscious karma. They are a manifestation of what is already primordially present in the Natural State. The vision is not something created by causes, but it is Lhundrub (lhun-grub), or spontaneously perfected. Since the Sambhogakaya is already fully inherent in the Natural State, it simply manifests. Dzogchen alone discloses our real nature; Dzogchen has already discovered this inherent Buddhahood, our real nature, and so it can manifest the Sambhogakaya effortlessly.

At the culmination of the Thodgal process, at the stage of vision called the exhausting of everything into Reality (bon-nyid zad-pa), all of the visions that the practitioner experiences, whether pure or impure, come to dissolve into the Natural State. This includes our physical body, which itself is the result of past karmic causes and represents our impure karmic vision. For the practitioner, everything dissolves. This sets the stage for the spontaneous manifestation of the Sambhogakaya which has been present in potential in the Natural State from the very beginning. Since it is already there, no primary cause for its manifestation is needed. The secondary causes for its manifestation, however, are the purifications of obscurations along the path. This is like wind removing clouds from the sky, so that the face of the sun becomes visible, or like opening the doors to the temple, so that the image of the Buddha can clearly be seen. [6]

If we examine the notion of Buddhahood from the logical standpoint, we find that the Nirmanakaya and the Sambhogakaya are impermanent, whereas the Dharmakaya alone is permanent.

But when we further examine the Dharmakaya, we discover that there are two sides to it. On the side of Shunyata or emptiness, it is permanent, but on the side of wisdom, it is impermanent. The Kunzhi, the basis of everything, is permanent because it is emptiness itself, but Rigpa is impermanent because it is not always manifest. Nevertheless, these two, Kunzhi and Rigpa, are always inseparable (dbyer-med) in the Natural State. On the side of emptiness (stong-cha), there is permanence, but on the side of clarity (gsal-cha) or awareness (rig-cha), there is impermanence. So, the manifestation side is impermanent, even when it represents pure vision. It is changing all of the time, whereas the emptiness side is constant and permanent. We can logically distinguish these things when we speak about the Natural State, but the Natural State is a totality and a perfect unity. Within it, emptiness and clarity are inseparable and never otherwise. This inseparability, or Yermed (dbyer-med), is the essence of Dzogchen. To fall either on the side of emptiness or on the side of manifestation is to deviate from the Dzogchen view and to fall into partiality and extreme views.

To realize the Rainbow Body means that we have practiced Thodgal and not some other method. The visions that arise are not specifically created, but appear spontaneously (lhun-grub) in the presence of secondary causes such as sunlight, total darkness, and the clear, open sky. They arise spontaneously from the Natural State; no Kyerim or Dzogrim practices must be accomplished first as preparation. All that is required is the capacity to remain with stability in the Natural State. This is called stable Thekchod. Then the Thodgal visions come automatically, whether in sunlight or total darkness or in the empty sky. Gradually all the pure visions of the deities arise, and these visions develop by way of four stages (snang-ba bzhi) until completion. Then they all dissolve into the Natural State. Our personal reality of pure and impure vision (snang-ba) dissolves into Reality (bon-nyid) which is the Natural State.

At the same time that our visions dissolve, our physical body also dissolves because it is just one manifestation of our impure karmic vision, the product of our past karmic heritage. Our normal everyday impure vision has the same source as the Thodgal pure vision, and now both equally dissolve into their source, the Natural State. There is a single primordial Base, the Natural State, but there are two Paths, impure karmic vision and pure vision, and two Fruits or results, Samsara and Nirvana. Having returned to the ultimate source, then the potentiality of the Natural State manifests as a Rainbow Body, the real Rupakaya.

Thereafter, this Jalu, or Rainbow Body, can appear in a material sense to sentient beings in order to teach them. The Rainbow Body is not something material as such, but appears to be so since it can act on all of the senses of a sentient being simultaneously. The Sambhogakaya can be perceived only by the Aryas, the Bodhisattvas who have ascended the third, fourth, or fifth paths. [7] They can hear the actual teachings of the Sambhogakaya, whereas ordinary beings cannot see or hear this manifestation. Thus, it is the Nirmanakaya that ordinary beings can hear and perceive. To human beings this Nirmanakaya appears as human. In other worlds and with other species of beings, the situation will be different. But the Rainbow Body, as the potentiality of the Natural State, is not limited to any particular form. It can appear in a myriad different forms. Since the Natural State has been with us from the very beginning, we have done nothing more than rediscover it, continue in it, and allow its potentiality to manifest. That is Buddhahood.

CHAPTER 3

Four Essential Points for Understanding Dzogchen

Talk by Lopon Tenzin Namdak,
New York City, October 1991.
Transcribed and edited by John Myrdhin Reynolds.

The short text we have before us here is from the *Nam-mkha' 'phrul mdzod* collection. [1] Here there are four essential points for understanding the nature of Dzogchen. First, Dzogchen does not contradict the Two Truths. Second, in Dzogchen there is no grasping at the view that a self exists. Third, the Dzogchenpa's conduct is not just going around doing whatever one wants at the moment. And fourth, there is no special apprehension of anything. [2]

As for the first point, according to the Sutras, it is well known that the Buddha taught the Two Truths: the Relative Truth and the Absolute Truth. They are without question the Buddha's teachings, and so when we understand Dzogchen, it is important not to speak against these Two Truths. However, Dzogchen, which represents the highest teaching of the Buddha, teaches that causality, that is to say, karmic causes and their consequences, is not the highest truth. In the Bonpo tradition, we find two methods for proceeding along the path. First, according to the highest way (Dzogchen) among the Nine Ways, the Nature of Mind is empty. Therefore, its essence has nothing to do with causality; it is in no way changed or modified by karmic causes and their consequences. It totally transcends them; it is beyond cause and effect, and so we say that it is primordially pure (ka-dag). A practitioner who has actually attained Buddhahood, remaining continuously in the Natural State, has nothing to realize as a cause for anything else. He does not expect any virtuous qualities to arise as the consequence of virtuous actions, nor does he fear any bad consequences of wrong actions. This is because the Natural State is beyond all karmic causality and its effects. That is why Dzogchen does not speak about karmic causes when referring to the Natural State. But otherwise, if the practitioner is not actually in the Natural State and this is one's usual ordinary Samsaric existence, then everything proceeds according to karmic causes. The actions we do will have their inevitable consequences, like the shadow following a body.

Second, there is the way of proceeding according to the eight other ways among the Nine Ways of Bon (theg-pa rim dgu) that are not Dzogchen in terms of their view and practice. Here matters are mostly understood in terms of Relative Truth and, therefore, we speak about karmic causes rather extensively. All results, whether good or bad, arise from causes. In the same way, the visions that arise in such practices as Thodgal and dark retreat belong to the sphere of Relative Truth (snang-lugs kun-rdzob bden-pa). But the contradiction is only apparent here. From the standpoint of the Natural State, we speak in terms of the Absolute Truth. Everything is empty and lacks any inherent existence. Dzogchen asserts that the Natural State is beyond causality, that it does not rely on any karmic causes. But it does assert that the system of appearances (snang-lugs) depends on causes. This is especially the case with our impure karmic vision, and one instance of such impure vision is our human karmic vision, our existence as a human being as we know it. Karmic vision is brought about by causes and all of us perceive this world as human karmic vision because we all possess the cause for that karmic vision. It is impure because it is caused by ignorance and the passions or emotional defilements.

Here we are speaking of two kinds of practitioner, ordinary persons and realized beings or adepts. We should remember that the content of the teachings, when expressed in words, depends on who is the audience listening to the teachings. The fundamental Dzogchen precepts were mainly revealed directly by the Primordial Buddha, the Dharmakaya Kuntu Zangpo (bon-sku kun tu bzang-po), and the Dharmakaya always spoke the Truth and never otherwise. [3] The Dharmakaya spoke from the standpoint of the Natural State. For this reason, Dzogchen does not accept as its ultimate view the Two Truths. It accepts only a single Truth or Source, called the Unique Essence (thig-le nyag-gcig). [4] This is the Natural State in which appearances and emptiness are inseparable. However, our ordinary vision or impure karmic vision arises from causes and Dzogchen agrees with that. Nonetheless, if we understand Dzogchen, then we do not find any inherent contradiction here. These Truths, the Two Truths and the Unique Essence, have different meanings. This is the first point.

As for the second point, Dzogchen does not grasp at or apprehend a view that a permanent self exists (bdag gi lta-ba). [5] In normal life, we are always thinking of ourselves. All of our thinking is tied up with this notion of a self as something real and abiding, and all of our emotional reactions are predicated on this self. The name for this process of constantly creating a self, whereas in reality there is none there, is grasping at a self (bdag 'dzin), or self-centeredness. Up until now this unconscious process has led us to accumulate negative karmic causes throughout countless lifetimes. This Dagdzin, or grasping at a self, represents ignorance, here meaning a lack of real knowledge and awareness (ma rig-pa). This ignorance has no absolute beginning in time; it has always been with us in each lifetime as an integral part of the habit of our existence. When we see something, immediately we accept or reject it. We judge the perceived object to be good or bad, and we have a corresponding emotional reaction of attachment or aversion. But if we do not have any grasping ('dzin-pa) at the object (that is, the mental process of apprehending and judging a perception), then we will not develop attachment to it.

For this reason, we must look back into ourselves and seek to find this so-called self (bdag). How do we think? We think that our perception exists externally to us and that it is objective and real. It is really there and so we grasp at it. But if we search into this, what is it that we grasp? Where is the grasper? It is like opening a series of Chinese boxes. Eventually we find that there is nothing there to grasp. Look at how we do this grasping or Dzinpa. For example, we have a headache, and so we think, "Oh, I have a headache!" Certainly there is the experience of a headache, yet this headache is not us. Nor is the head us. And yet we grasp and think, "I am sick!" But look more closely at this. There is no "I" existing here, only the experience of pain. It is the same with the other parts of the body. We can examine all of these parts, but where do we find any "I"? This identification process whereby we predicate an "I" to all of our experiences is what we meant by Dagdzin or grasping at a self. Yes, there are all of these parts belonging to our body, but when we pull them all apart, even down to the last cell, where do we find any "I"?

Then we conclude that, even though the self (bdag) is not the physical body, it must be our mind or consciousness. But we can proceed here with the mind in the same way as we did with the physical body, searching for a self or "I." We will not find any self. For example, there is eye consciousness. If that were not present, we would not see anything at all, even though the eye organ is present there and functional. A corpse may have its eye organs intact, but it does not see anything because there is no consciousness present. But is this eye consciousness the "I" or not? We can proceed to investigate in the same way all of the other sense consciousnesses in the current of our daily experience.

We have searched outside, through our perceptions and through the parts of our body and have found no "self" there. Now we search inside through our sense consciousnesses and find that there exists no "self" here either. But what of our mind? Is this the self or "I"? If we examine the mind, we discover that it is not a single unified entity or substance, rather, it is a process occurring in time, a succession of states of consciousness having varied mental contents. It is like a stream or a river that changes from moment to moment. It is never the same. Where in these states of consciousness and contents of consciousness do we find a self or "I"? We have searched outside and inside exhaustively and what do we find? Where is this "self" of which we speak so freely? All the things we see and experience are not this so-called "self." They are not us, and yet we grasp at them as if they were ourselves. [6]

Without there being any certain solid objective reality out there in space, still we grasp at perceptions of the world as if they are real. Perceived objects do not exist inherently, but we do perceive them as if they exist objectively. This is Relative Truth. External appearances do exist in terms of Relative Truth, but this is not the real truth. It is ignorance. This ignorance has existed from the very beginning until now and it is the source of our circulating in Samsara. We may think: "My conscious self grasps at an object, but there is no object there." But this is an illusion also. We habitually believe that external objects have an inherent existence, but this is not so. Nothing exists inherently. Otherwise, there would be no possibility of change in the world. Everything would be locked into its essence or inherent nature. But change is our experience all of the time.

Nevertheless, even though there is no inherent existence to phenomena our grasping at them persists. This consciousness which grasps is not reliable and leads us into error. There are perceptions; we see many beautiful and ugly things. We judge them as such and feel attachment or aversion towards them. But there is no real object out there that is beautiful or ugly because these judgments are created by our minds. And yet we grasp at these objects. In the dim light, we mistakenly perceive a pillar as our enemy and we hit it with our fist. This enemy did not exist independently; it was created by our minds. If we go into a totally dark room for a time, our imagination may create many strange effects which we see. They may look very real, but if we chase them, we hit our head against the wall because they are illusions. So there is no point in having desires for these phantoms and illusions which are as unreal as dreams. If we understand this point, our desires and our aversions will decrease.

Even though we cannot find anywhere an inherent existence to phenomena, still we cannot say that we do not exist because we are doing this grasping. We exist because we are engaged in this activity, the process of Dzinpa, or grasping at perceptions. But if we search on the inside for some inherent existence, we do not find anything either. However, this does not mean that we do not exist. For example, take the individual sitting here named "George." We can say that he is my son, or my friend, or my father, or my enemy, or whatever. Everyone in the room here has a different idea of who George really is, depending on our relationship to him. But who is the real George? If George is my son, he cannot be my father. Even if he is my son, "son" is not his real essence to the exclusion of anything else. To his own son, he is "my father." So George is created by our perception and our consciousness, and by our definition of him in relation to us. That determines what he is; it defines him. So on the object side, George has no inherent existence, but this does not mean that he is not sitting here right in front of us all. On the subject side, everything exists because we are conscious and are having perceptions. But on the object side, nothing exists as a solid, unchanging reality. Therefore, there is no point in feeling attachment or aversion towards these appearances. To understand this is the real Dharma.

It is not easy to stop the accumulating of negative actions without a strong antidote. But through practice, the antidote can become quite strong and in this way we can mitigate the influence of the passions. These negative emotions will become weaker and grow less because of our practice of meditation. Then we will do less harm to others and we will accumulate virtues. Just reciting mantras or circumambulating a stupa is not enough. It is bringing about a change in our consciousness that is most important.

The third point here means that we, as Dzogchen practitioners, do not go about acting on our momentary impulses, doing whatever we might feel like at that moment. At this present time, we have this human existence and this human body, and that is something not easy to get because it requires the accumulation of a great deal of meritorious karma over countless lifetimes. Even if we get a human existence, we may still encounter many difficult conditions, such as being born deaf and dumb, or being born in a country where there is no Dharma. So we need, not only a human rebirth, but the opportunity to come into contact with the teachings and the capacity to understand the teachings and practice them. We have to examine how we live our lives. Because life is impermanent, we should not postpone the Dharma until next month or next year, and we should not waste our capacities of body, speech and mind. We waste our opportunity in this life by not doing any virtuous actions. Thinking bad of others and speaking ill of them is wasting our minds and our speech. It is just stupid to waste our opportunities when we can use our body, speech and mind to practice, to grow and to develop. And so, in terms of Dzogchen, we must use every opportunity to do meditation practice in order to familiarize ourselves with the Natural State. No excuses! No saying that we have no time or that we are too busy. But what, and for how long, we practice depends on our capacity and our circumstances.

Very well and good. We are practicing Dzogchen. But the third point means that we cannot simply go about like a libertine, doing whatever we like and saying that there is no sin or consequence to our actions. Even though Dzogchen asserts that the Natural State is beyond cause and effect, and that karmic causality does not modify it in any way, this applies only to us, as practitioners of Dzogchen, when we are actually in the Natural State. Otherwise, our consciousness and our lives are totally under the rule of karma. Most of the time during the day we are not in the Natural State, and so karma applies very much to our normal daily thoughts and actions. We are living in the relative condition, save only when we actually find ourselves in the Natural State. So, to say we can do whatever we like is not the correct view of Dzogchen. These momentary desires and impulses we experience are conditioned things created by our unconscious karmic traces. To follow after them is not freedom, no matter how much we speak about Dzogchen. Only for the Natural State are there no rules or limitations, and only in the Natural State is there found total freedom.

As for the fourth point, in Dzogchen there is nothing special to be grasped or apprehended. In terms of our ordinary common vision and our daily life, we can say that everything is an illusion and created by our consciousness. If we really understand this, then there is no point in grasping strongly at anything, for example, as enemy or friend. We are not attached too much to anything; we do not grasp at wealth or possessions. Nothing is special. We come to understand that in terms of reality, everything is equal. All things are equally empty and all things are equally an illusion. If we understand that all things are in fact illusions, then there is no point in having negative emotions with regard to them. All of life is like a dream. We see it, yes, but in the end it dissolves and leaves no trace. But we, the Natural State, remain.

And so these are four essential points to remember according to the master Dranpa Namkha.

CHAPTER 4

The View of Shunyata found in Madhyamaka, Chittamatra and Dzogchen

According to Lopon Tenzin Namdak,
Bischofshofen, Vienna, Devon, Amsterdam,
March, April, May, June 1991.
Compiled and edited by John Myrdhin Reynolds.

The View of the Sutra System

Nowadays many Lamas say that the views and the results of the practice of Madhyamaka, Mahamudra and Dzogchen are all the same. [1] But this is not true. Why is that? Whenever we have a spiritual path, we can speak about it in terms of the Base, the Path, and the Fruit. When comparing two systems of practice, if their views of the Base are different, then their practice of the Path will be different, and therefore the results or the Fruit will be different. And so we must begin by making an examination of the views of these different systems.

Both the Buddhist and the Bonpo teachings are divided into Sutra, Tantra and Dzogchen. Each of these three systems has a different Base, a different Path, and thus they lead to a different Fruit or result. The method proper to the Sutra system is the path of renunciation (spong lam), the method proper to the Tantra system is the path of transformation (sgyur lam), and the method proper to Dzogchen is the path of self-liberation (grol lam). Madhyamaka belongs to the Sutra system, Mahamudra belongs to the Tantra system, and Dzogchen is just Dzogchen; it is neither Sutra nor Tantra. And so these systems are very different in their views of the Base. Since their views are not all the same, their practices do not all lead to the same result. That is only logical. [2]

Within the Sutra system, we have Hinayana and Mahayana. Hinayana has two subdivisions: the way of the Sravakas or Disciples (nyan-thos-pa) and the way of the Pratyekabuddhas (rang-rgyal-ba). These two types of practitioner think only of release for themselves from the suffering of Samsara. They are not concerned with the fate of others. They recognize the absence of any unchanging permanent self in individual persons (gang-zag gi bdag-med), but they think that dharmas or phenomena, the momentary physical and mental events that comprise our experiences as a stream of consciousness, are real. This is their view. But for Mahayana, on the contrary, compassion is fundamental. Here practitioners think not only of their own liberation from the suffering experienced in Samsara, but equally of the liberation of all sentient beings from Samsara. They recognize that there is no permanent and abiding self in individuals, just as Hinayana practitioners do but, equally, they recognize that these momentary events or dharmas are impermanent, unreal and insubstantial (chos kyi bdag-med). This is the view of Mahayana, and it is what we call Shunyata or emptiness.

The View of Madhyamaka

Within Mahayana, both in Buddhism and in Bon, we find two different systems of philosophy. The first is Madhyamaka, called Umapa (dbu-ma-pa) in Tibetan, meaning "the middle way" school. The second is Yogachara or Chittamatra, Semtsampa (sems-tsam-pa) in Tibetan, meaning "the mind-only" school. Although not as well known, the Bonpo tradition also possesses its Prajnaparamita Sutras, and the philosophical view and method expounded in these Sutras is known as Madhyamaka.

According to Tibetans generally, Madhyamaka represents the highest philosophy and Shunyata is the highest view found in Madhyamaka. Coming to an understanding of Shunyata, of the emptiness of all phenomena, their lack of any inherent existence, is the final goal. This is where the Sutra system takes us. This is also true of the Bonpos. Although the Bonpo tradition does not possess any independent Yogachara texts, such as those translated from Sanskrit in the Buddhist tradition, the Yogachara view, called Chittamatra, is well known and also its refutation by the Madhyamaka view is equally well known.

However, the Bonpo tradition does not regard the Madhyamaka view as the highest of all views. According to the view of Madhyamaka, even in the state of enlightenment there is something present there that is apprehended or grasped ('dzin-pa) by the intellect, and this situation, therefore, inherently involves duality. But there is a view which lies beyond the intellect and beyond all dualities. This is the view of Dzogchen, and so in the Bonpo system, it is Dzogchen and not Madhyamaka that is regarded as the highest teaching.

This does not mean that both Madhyamaka and Tantra were not taught by the Buddhas and are not perfect in themselves. They were taught by the Buddhas to certain students for specific reasons, to each according to his intellectual capacity and level of development. So within their specific context, each of these systems is complete and perfect in itself. It all depends upon the capacity of the student, and so we should not go around finding fault with other systems simply because we do not practice them. Moreover, it is necessary to have a clear understanding of the fundamental views of each of these systems. If we do not have a clear understanding of the view right from the very beginning then, no matter how much meditation practice we may do, our practice will be wrong.

In the Mahayana system generally, in both the Madhyamika school and Yogachara school, we speak of the Two Truths: the

Absolute Truth (dam-don bden-pa) and the Relative Truth (kun-rdzob bden-pa). Indeed, in the Sutra system and in the Tantra system also, we recognize these Two Truths as being the causes for realizing the Dharmakaya and Rupakaya respectively. The Dharmakaya, as the Ultimate Reality, has no form; it is empty. But in order to realize a fruit or result, we must first have a cause. And so, in order to realize the result which is the Dharmakaya, we must have the cause which is the understanding of the Absolute Truth, and the Absolute Truth means fully understanding Shunyata or emptiness. The Relative Truth is the cause for realizing the Rupakaya. Linking these respective causes and effects are the two accumulations. The accumulation of wisdom means the understanding of the emptiness and insubstantiality of all phenomena, internal as well as external, and the accumulation of merit means the practice of the Ten Perfections.

Sometimes six perfections are listed, but the Bonpo Sutra system speaks of Ten Perfections, namely, generosity (sbyin-pa), morality (tshul-khrims), patience (bzod-pa), vigor (btson-'grus), meditation (bsam-gtan), strength (stobs), compassion (snying-rje), aspiration (smon-lam), dedication (bsngo-ba) and wisdom (shes-rab).

Thus, according to the Sutra system, we have two bases or causes, two paths or methods, and two results:

(1) the cause is the Absolute Truth, the method is the accumulation of wisdom, and the fruit or result is the Dharmakaya and
(2) the cause is the Relative Truth, the method is the accumulation of merit, and the fruit or result is the Rupakaya.

Therefore, these Two Truths are necessary, just as two wings are necessary for a bird to fly. Where we practice according to Absolute Truth, we find that all things are empty or lack any inherent existence, and where we practice according to Relative

Truth we find that virtuous causes lead to good results. But we must practice them equally, for otherwise, we will not realize Buddhahood. This is because Buddhahood means both the Dharmakaya and the Rupakaya. The Rupakaya, or Form Body (gzugs sku), has two distinct manifestations: the Sambhogakaya and the Nirmanakaya. So we must complete and perfect the two accumulations in order to realize them.

The preparation for realizing the Dharmakaya is the practice of prajna, or discriminating wisdom (shes-rab). This discriminating wisdom entails a kind of philosophical analysis of all of our experiences, where we discover that, at bottom, they are empty, that they lack any substance or inherent existence. The essence of the Dharmakaya is just this emptiness or Shunyata. We practice the other perfections in order to realize the Sambhogakaya and the Nirmanakaya. These three aspects of Buddhahood are known as the Trikaya or the Three Bodies of the Buddha (sku gsum). Hinayana practitioners do not recognize the existence of this Trikaya. They only recognize the visible historical Buddha Shakyamuni, who disappeared long ago and is no more. However, they do recognize the existence of the Arhats or perfect saints who have eliminated all their kleshas (passions or negative emotions) and who, therefore, will be born no more in the lower realms of Samsara.

The principal view of Madhyamaka is Shunyavada, the view of emptiness. Madhyamaka asserts that all phenomena (all dharmas or momentary physical and mental events) lack any inherent existence. That is the meaning of Shunyata. If something existed independently, it would have its own inherent existence and nothing else could affect or change it. No karmic cause could give rise to it, because its inherent existence would be immutable and unchanging. If everything had an inherent existence, nothing could change into anything else, and all causality would be impossible. All change would be impossible because a thing would simply be its inherent nature, or essence, and not something else.

It would be locked into this nature and could not change into something else. But our experience tells us that things are changing all the time, and so everything must lack any inherent existence. All phenomena are empty. Thus we experience phenomena as impermanent and insubstantial. It is only our thinking that phenomena are somehow solid and permanent and real that is wrong-headed. We use the process of philosophical analysis or Prajna (shes-rab) as the method to correct this wrong way of looking at things.

For example, if we take a flower and pull off its petals, where do we find the flower? Wherein lies the essence or the inherent nature of this flower? Pulling off all of the petals, we find that there is nothing of the flower left behind. We search for the flower and we find nothing, only a pile of petals on the ground. But where is the flower? Each petal that we have pulled off is not the flower. All of the petals belong to the flower, but the "flower" in itself is nothing, only the sum of its parts. It has no independent existence, therefore, it is empty. So from the standpoint of the Absolute Truth, we say that it is empty. And "flower" is only a name and a concept imputed to a phenomenon, not something ultimately real. That which we name and conceptualize is called Relative Truth. We exhaustively analyze the phenomenon and ultimately we discover that there is nothing real there. There is no essence or inherent existence as "flower." There is only a name and a concept in our mind. This is at the level of Absolute Truth. But, of course, in the relative terms of everyday life, the flower does exist because we buy it, we smell its scent, and so on. This is at the level of Relative Truth. So we see and deal with everything from these two different perspectives, the absolute and the relative.

Everything in our world is known by way of our thoughts and we come to this knowledge through the applying of names. It is this process that gives rise to karmic causes. According to Madhyamaka, Shunyata means "no inherent existence." The example is the flower and its petals given previously. The concept "flower" is created by our minds. In this concept, the three times are joined in our mind; we have memories of flowers in the past and we anticipate seeing flowers in the future. But these objects do not have any inherent existence. We only find a collection or aggregate of parts; a pile of petals, but no flower. It is the same when we examine our body or our mind. We find an aggregate of parts, the skandhas, but we do not find any owner. There is no self or substance. If there is a person and he is our enemy, his nature as "enemy" would be unchanging. We would see him as an enemy, we could not see him as a friend. But this is not the case. Everything is created by thought and nothing exists inherently. By our becoming aware of this, the power held over us by karmic traces becomes less. Only the names exist, but they do not exist as real independent objects. Yet we become more and more involved with these fictitious objects and attached to them, and so we continue to revolve in Samsara.

Madhyamaka teaches that there is no inherent existence (rang-bzhin med), that things only exist interdependently (rten 'brel) and that, in fact, is the meaning of Shunyata. But without the mind, without thoughts, we cannot understand this Shunyata, this insubstantiality and interdependence of all phenomena. In understanding our experience, it is always necessary to grasp ('dzin-pa) and examine and judge thoughts and things with the mind. It is through the operation of the mind, in particular through the operation of this higher intellectual function called Prajna (shes-rab), or discriminating wisdom, that we come to understand the emptiness of all phenomena, external and internal. All phenomena have these two aspects of Absolute Truth and Relative Truth. They always occur together. Visible things represent Relative Truth; they appear to be real and solid, they appear to be really out there, but when we examine and analyze them, pulling them apart to find their actual essence, we find that they have no inherent nature. On the one hand, everything is without any inherent existence but, on the other hand, everything has a cause. Without a cause, a phenomenon does not exist. This is because it is dependent on other antecedent events, although in itself it does not have any inherent existence or nature. The appearance of phenomena depends on names and causes; this is the meaning of Relative Truth.

According to Madhyamaka, and the Sutra system generally, the understanding of Shunyata is the highest understanding. But this Shunyata is not a matter of being empty like a vase with nothing inside it. Rather, it is the culmination of a process whereby we examine a phenomenon in order to see whether it exists inherently or not. If we find that this phenomenon is not empty, if we examine it and discover that it has a precise inherent nature, then that cannot change. That nature is just what it is and not something else. It remains just what it is and cannot change into something else. This inherent existence of the phenomenon is fixed and immutable. Therefore, that phenomenon cannot change into anything else. So the method in Madhyamaka is to make this rather exhaustive philosophical analysis of objects to discover whether or not they have an inherent existence. Only by doing this habitually and for sufficient time, do we become convinced that all phenomena lack inherent existence.

The inherent existence of a phenomenon, as its immutable essence, is something that does not exist in fact. It cannot be found in a phenomenon, even in a single case. Rather, in each case there are these Two Truths. In the example of the flower, the flower is the Relative Truth and its emptiness is the Absolute Truth. According to Madhyamaka, this lack of any inherent nature (rang-bzhin med-pa) signifies emptiness (stong-pa nyid). In this sense, all phenomena are empty. Shunyata does not mean that there is nothing at all, rather, it means that all phenomena are contingent and interdependent. That is what makes all change and evolution and transformation from one thing into another possible. Otherwise the world would be static and dead, devoid of all change and growth.

Take the example of a table. We see the table and we know what it is. We say that it is really out there. But if we analyze it into its parts, where is the table? Whatever we can point to with our finger, that is not the table itself. In the same way, my head is not me. "My" and "me" are different. If we subtract every "my" where is the "me"? We may say and think: "I am here and it is there!" We are always thinking that somewhere in the world there is something solid and real. Everyone has this thinker or thought process but, according to Madhyamaka, that thought process represents ignorance. It is thinking in a substantialist way. We are habituated to this practice and trust it implicitly. We depend on this way of thinking and we are actually unaware that we are doing it. But there is no reality at all behind this process. It is all a complete fabrication made by our mind. We just assume that everything out there is solid and real. We implicitly trust this way of thinking.

But why is it deluded? We may grasp at something out there. We may think it is real and solid, but when we examine it, what do we find? In the same way, when we examine ourselves, each piece we find is "my," such as "my thought," "my idea," "my feeling," "my perception" and so on, but where do we find "me"? Our conventional way of thinking is lying to us; it falsifies reality. When we look into something, whether an external object or ourselves, we find that there is nothing solid and substantial left behind which we can grasp and hold on to. This is Shunyata and Shunyata is the Absolute Truth for us. We search for ourselves and we do not find anyone. But still we cannot say that I do not exist and this table does not exist. They both exist in a relative sense, but when we search for their essence, we do not find anything. All that is left behind is a name. For example, if we have a headache, the "head" is not us and the "ache" is not us, yet we say that we have a headache. The pain is there as experience, but where is the "I"?

Our thinking becomes the prisoner of our language. Relative Truth is this process of labeling or giving names to things as if they were concrete independent realities, separate things or entities independent of ourselves and our knowing them. When we utter the name "head", what exists here is only a name and a conception, and that is Relative Truth. All of this develops on the side of names, like karmic causes, but there is nothing real or substantial here. Karmic causality exists only on the relative side; it is not the Absolute Truth. According to the Madhyamaka view, nothing solid or substantial exists anywhere, and so everything is empty. Everything is Shunyata and that is the Absolute Truth.

Madhyamaka and Dzogchen on the Two Truths

Both Madhyamaka and Chittamatra recognize the Two Truths, although their understanding of the meaning of the Two Truths is different. Madhyamaka only recognizes the ultimate truth of Shunyata. Moreover, according to Madhyamaka, everything is related to the Two Truths because subject and object have no inherent existence, they are only "names" created by thoughts. Nothing exists here independently; everything in our experience is involved with the Two Truths and there is nothing beyond them.

Nowadays, in general, all the Tibetan schools, including the Gelugpas, assert that the Prasangika-Madhyamaka view of Shunyata, as expounded by Chandrakirti in his *Madhyamakavatara* (dBu-ma la 'jug-pa), is the highest of all possible views, and that there can be no view beyond it. They say that this was asserted by Je Tsongkhapa himself. Therefore, Shunyata is the final and ultimate view. There is nothing beyond this. So how can Dzogchen do any better than this? Many followers of Madhyamaka criticize Dzogchen, asserting that it denies the Two

Truths. Again, certain followers of Madhyamaka belonging to various Tibetan schools, who are scholars learned in the Sutras and the Shastras, have asserted that Dzogchen is not even real Buddhism, that it is some sort of Chinese Dharma like Ch'an, or that it comes from Advaita Vedanta or Kashmiri Shaivism in Hinduism. So how is it possible, they ask, to go beyond the view of Madhyamaka to something called Dzogchen? Why is Dzogchen then said to be the highest truth?

According to the two old schools of the Nyingmapas and the Bonpos, Dzogchen does indeed go beyond the view of Madhyamaka. "Highest" depends on our understanding. It is only the "highest truth" if we thoroughly understand the real meaning of the view. Otherwise, "highest" is just a word we say, but it has no meaning. A teaching becomes the highest because of our understanding of it. According to the Madhyamaka system, Shunyata means that all phenomena are empty (stong-pa) and that everything lacks an inherent existence (rang-bzhin med-pa), for otherwise no change would be possible. But this is not the final view of Dzogchen because the former is considered an incomplete view. It only gives half the picture. Madhyamaka speaks of the emptiness side of things (stong-cha), and does so correctly, but it does not speak of the clarity side (gsal-cha) or the awareness side (rig-cha).

According to Madhyamaka, there are two sources: the Absolute Truth and the Relative Truth. In terms of this first source, the Base is the Absolute Truth, the Path is the accumulation of wisdom through the understanding of the emptiness of all phenomena, and the Fruit is the realization of the Dharmakaya. And in terms of this second source, the Base is the Relative Truth, the Path is the accumulation of merit through the practice of the Ten Perfections, and the Fruit is the realization of the Rupakaya. Thus we have two Bases, two Paths, and two Fruits. Both of these methods of practice are necessary, as we have said, for the attaining of enlightenment, just as a bird needs two wings in order to fly. This is how Madhyamaka explains matters.

But Dzogchen does not recognize these Two Truths as being two sources; it recognizes only one source and One Truth, namely, the Thigley Nyagchik (thig-le nyag-gcig), the Unique Essence. There is only one Base, and not two. In a higher sense, the Two Truths are not necessary because the Base is unitary. Yet some great masters in their commentaries to the *Madhyamakavatara* of Chandrakirti criticize Dzogchen for not having these Two Truths. Dzogchen maintains that the final view is that there is only one nature. It does not claim that karmic causes and consequences are the ultimate reality. Dzogchen replies that if we recognize Two Truths, then we must have two minds in order to know them. Therefore, some scholars of the New Tantra tradition speak of an intelligence which knows Shunyata (stong-nyid rtogs-pa'i shes-rab) and a separate intelligence which imputes names (ming btags-pa'i shes-rab). Both of these are called intelligence (shes-rab), but they are two distinct types of intelligence and know different things. But in Dzogchen there is only this single Unique Essence (thig-le nyag-gcig), and not two minds. And according to Dzogchen, we only come to realize the Trikaya where we practice and realize inseparability (dbyer-med).

According to the Madhyamaka view, we can remain in total awareness of Shunyata by means of the state of contemplation or equipoise (mnyan-bzhag), but when we are in that state we cannot engage in any thoughts or actions of generosity and the other perfections and virtues. And so we must practice the two, the accumulation of wisdom and the accumulation of merit, alternately and separately. However, the Natural State in the view of Dzogchen is not only emptiness, it is equally spontaneous manifestation (lhun-grub). If we practice only on the side of emptiness (stong-cha), we will not realize the totality of Buddhahood.

Madhyamaka, Chittamatra and Tantra all recognize these Two Truths. Madhyamika asks how can we realize Buddhahood unless we have these Two Truths as the base, enabling us to practice the two accumulations? And we need these as the causes for realizing the Dharmakaya and the Rupakaya. Without such causes, we cannot realize Buddhahood. Dzogchen agrees that without causes as contributing factors we cannot attain Buddhahood. But if we are given a large piece of gold, we do not need to search for its qualities; they already inhere in it. If we just practice the Natural State, we will spontaneously realize the Dharmakaya and the Rupakaya because all the virtues of the Buddha already exist in the Natural State and, when the secondary causes are present, these virtues will spontaneously manifest. So here is the real contradiction between Madhyamaka and Dzogchen. [3]

According to Madhyamaka, the Buddha-nature at the core of every sentient being, also known as the Tathagatagarbha, is the conventional meaning (drang-don). It is provisional, whereas Shunyata is the real and ultimate meaning (nges-don). But according to the Nyingmapa master Longchenpa in his *Tshig-don mdzod*, it is said that the Buddha Shakyamuni himself taught Dzogchen in the Prajnaparamita Sutras. [4] This inherent Buddha-nature or Tathagatagarbha, when it is properly understood, is actually the Natural State referred to by Dzogchen. So here Longchenpa interprets Dzogchen as Prajnaparamita. Once we have discovered the real nature, the Natural State, we do not need to search for anything else.

If it is said that Dzogchen does not recognize the Two Truths, can we also say that it does not recognize the Ten Paramitas? And if this is so, how can there be any practice in terms of Dzogchen? If we do not practice, how can there be any accumulations of wisdom and merit and how can we then attain Buddhahood? But in Dzogchen it is never said that we should not practice the Ten Paramitas. It is simply said that the Natural State spontaneously contains these Ten Paramitas, so we do not need to practice them individually or separately. All the virtues of the Buddha spontaneously exist already within the Natural State. So, it is only necessary for Dzogchen to explain this single Natural State and that is enough.

The ordinary Sutra practitioner, on the other hand, when he no longer finds himself in the state of contemplation (mnyam-bzhag), thinks that his vision of the world is solid and real and substantial. Finding himself in that condition, he practices compassion and cultivates that motivation as a discursive thought. According to the Sutra system, compassion is a thought that must be cultivated and developed by way of other thoughts. But that sort of practice of compassion as thought is only a preparation, as far as Dzogchen is concerned. It is merely the thought of compassion, not the real compassion of a Buddha. Once we attain the Natural State and understand the view of Dzogchen, then we do not need to do any special compassion practice in which we try to generate and cultivate thoughts of compassion towards other living beings by means of the activities of the mind. Why is this? Because, when we enter into the Natural State, compassion for all sentient beings arises spontaneously and effortlessly; it does not need to be produced artificially by the discursive mind. It has been there from the very beginning, whole and complete, in the Natural State.

Sometimes it may say in a Dzogchen text that we do not even need to practice meditation. Why is that? There are Ten Perfections, or Paramitas, and generosity (sbyin-pa, Skt. dana) is the first among them. Since all of them are already fully contained within the Natural State from the very beginning, and their perfection or completion is also found in the Natural State, it is not necessary to generate generosity, or the other perfections, artificially by cultivating thoughts. If we practice the Natural State, generosity is already found there and it arises spontaneously. We then practice generosity naturally and spontaneously and we do not first have to meditate and to think that we should be generous to others. If we practice the Natural State, morality is already there and it arises spontaneously and effortlessly; it comes naturally and we do not need to think about it first. It is the same with all of the other perfections, including meditation. All of the virtues and powers attained through meditation are already fully contained in the Natural State. Therefore, it is not necessary to practice the perfections in any special way individually and separately from the Natural State since they are already fully present in the Natural State.

According to Madhyamaka, Shunyata can only be known by a thought. If something lacks inherent existence, that condition is Shunyata and this can only be known by a thought. If there is not a thought present, nothing at all can be known. All knowledge is by way of thoughts. So there is no other method for attaining the realization of Shunyata. This is a principal difference between Madhyamaka and Dzogchen. The former asserts that there must be a thought present which knows Shunyata. However, according to Dzogchen, from the very beginning, the Natural State has been beyond thought and cannot be grasped by the mind. In Dzogchen, if we try to grasp or apprehend something ('dzin-pa), this is mental activity, and so we find ourselves in the mind, and not in the Natural State. By this means we will never attain the Natural State. Thoughts always cut up and split apart objects. Otherwise, we would not be able to grasp them. We can only assimilate reality in pieces. With the activities of the intellect, we can practice a reductive analysis of some external object, like a blue flower, for example, in order to realize its emptiness. But this "emptiness" is only understood intellectually, it has been reached only by thoughts. However, we cannot proceed in Dzogchen by way of thoughts. Thoughts are always partial and one-sided; they never encompass the whole.

The great scholar Sakya Pandita complained about Dzogchen in his famous book, the *sDom gsum rab dbye*. He called it a Chinese Dharma or teaching (rgya nag gi chos), claiming that

Dzogchen simply teaches a state of "no thought" (mi rtog-pa), as does the Ch'an Buddhism of China. He also complained very much about the Kagyudpas, the followers of Lama Gampopa, claiming that all they do is practice rather than study and as a result they do not know anything. He claimed that if they just practice blindly like that, without thought and philosophical study, they will be reborn as animals. Sakya Pandita was especially critical of Gampopa's exposition of Mahamudra, claiming that it was in part based on Dzogchen. But in the Dzogchen system, "no thought" (mi rtog-pa) is not the goal. The condition of no thought is merely an experience (nyams); it is not Rigpa, or the Natural State. Dzogchen speaks of a state beyond cause and effect. The Natural State is this state beyond the mind. It does not matter to the Natural State whether thoughts arise or not because its nature is unaffected by them. The Natural State is like a mirror and thoughts are like the reflections in the mirror. The nature of the mirror is in no way changed or modified by the reflections. For this reason we say that the Natural State is primordially pure (ka-dag), pure from the very beginning.

Madhyamaka and Dzogchen contradict each other here. In the Madhyamaka system, we are always searching for an antidote to the kleshas or the passions. Dzogchen asks, how can we be doing this? The Klesha, the passion or negative emotion, is just a thought and the antidote to it is just another thought. This is like trying to wash away the blood on our hands with more blood. Thoughts will not eradicate thoughts. There is no end to thoughts. Thoughts have no limits; we can follow thoughts and we will never find the end to them. When we search for reality with thoughts, we will never find a final or ultimate truth, because thoughts inevitably lead to more thoughts. That is their nature. Only if we look for the source of all thoughts will we find the final truth.

So we cannot purify thoughts and eliminate them by applying yet more thoughts as antidotes. The whole process is circular.

This is not the method of Dzogchen. Rather, the right method, according to Dzogchen, is to remain in the Natural State as long as possible. Thoughts cannot be eliminated by thoughts. They will not disappear; they will only proliferate. But if left alone, they will dissolve into the Natural State. Self-liberation is the ultimate purification because no traces are left behind and thoughts do not give birth to new thoughts. But if our remaining in the Natural State is not stable, then we can easily be distracted by the arising of new thoughts.

In contrast to Madhyamaka, Dzogchen does not recognize the subject-object dichotomy as ultimate, nor does it recognize these Two Truths as sources of knowledge. The real view of Dzogchen is inseparability without partiality on the one side or the other. Emptiness and awareness are inseparable (rig stong dbyer-med). Therefore, there is only One Truth. And so, its view is beyond the view of the Two Truths. Dzogchen may be beyond this view, but this does not mean that the Buddha did not teach the Two Truths. What is meant here is that Dzogchen is beyond the Sutra definition of the Two Truths. [5]

According to the Madhyamaka system, it is said that there must be these two Truths, and that without them, including an intellectual comprehension of Shunyata, we cannot realize Buddhahood. To this assertion Dzogchen replies: If we practice only this single and unique Natural State, the Thigley Nyagchik (thig-le nyag-gcig), everything else, all of the virtuous qualities and powers of Buddhahood, are contained within it from the very beginning. That is sufficient. Therefore, Dzogchen can maintain that its view is the highest one.

The View of Chittamatra

The basis of the Chittamatra system of the Yogachara school is compassion and Bodhichitta. Chittamatra also recognizes a basic Kunzhi (kun-gzhi) or Alaya, as well as a self-awareness, or

Svasamvedana (rang-rig), that is inherent in each moment of consciousness. Chittamatra uses these concepts such as Rang-rig and Kunzhi but, according to Madhyamaka, Shunyata is the highest view. However, the Chittamatra position does not recognize the Shunyata known to and defined by the Madhyamaka school; the Chittamatra view of Shunyata is quite different from that of Madhyamaka. Madhyamaka asserts that if something had an inherent existence, then it could not change and disappear. Its essence would be immutable. But it is our experience that things change and disappear all of the time. So all of these consciousnesses (rnam-shes) are lacking in any inherent existence. In the Madhyamaka view, if we cannot find any inherent existence in phenomena, this is Shunyata. But Chittamatra asks, if this is so, how can there be any karmic traces?

The view of Madhyamaka is that everything is insubstantial (bdag-med) and lacks any inherent existence (rang-bzhin med-pa). Any self or substance (bdag) lacks inherent existence and does not exist independently. Everything is conditioned by causes and is constantly changing. Therefore, everything is empty. If there did exist an inherent nature, then the cause could not become a result which is different from it. It can only remain what it was originally and there would be absolutely no change. But Chittamatra asserts that mind (sems), the subject side, has an inherent existence (rang-bzhin gyi yod-pa), however external appearances, phenomena, do not exist independently. Everything is the result of karmic causes. An independent self (bdag) does not exist, but a self does exist in relative terms in a condition of dependence. The Kunzhi Namshe (kun-gzhi rnam-shes) is this self. What exists inherently here is the Kunzhi Namshe, the base consciousness, and this is the real "I", the principle that transmigrates from life to life. Each sentient being has this base consciousness. And this base consciousness is individual; we are not all "one mind." This is the Chittamatra view.

But Madhyamaka asserts that the self (bdag) is only a name. Absolutely nothing exists, whether dependent or independent; it is merely a name. Karmic causes and their consequences are only names. And the Madhyamaka system does not recognize a Kunzhi Namshe. There are only six consciousnesses and no storeroom for the karmic traces. There is no place to collect and store them. The Madhyamikas maintain that it is not necessary to store them anywhere. The owner just has them as baggage and does not need a particular place to put them. But in any event, this owner is only a name.

The Madhyamaka school teaches that everything is without an inherent existence but, according to Chittamatra, this view is insufficient. Chittamatra asserts that an inherent nature must exist (rang-bzhin gyi yod-pa) because, otherwise, there would be no basis for the existence of karmic causes. If we say that karmic causes are only names and concepts, they would produce no effects. We can say that we have a horn on our head, but this does not mean one exists there. We can say almost anything, but that does not mean that what we say exists. Therefore, there must exist something on its own as inherent nature. The Madhyamaka view is inadequate because it recognizes only the one side of Shunyata, the non-duality of subject and object.

Madhyamaka counters this argument. If we examine the eye, for example, we might say that it has an inherent existence. Its function is to see. Yet sometimes an eye may be defective or even blind and cannot see at all, even though we still give it the name "eye." Therefore, it lacks an inherent existence. All things lack an inherent existence because they are changing all the time. This represents their emptiness. For this reason, the Prajnaparamita Sutras say there is no eye, there is no ear, and so on. Their inherent nature (rang-bzhin) does not exist. So we must come to understand what Shunyata means in this context.

Chittamatra also recognizes Shunyata, but what is meant here by Shunyata is different from the Shunyata in Madhyamaka.

According to Chittamatra, it is a single karmic cause that gives rise to the two sides of subject and object. But these two sides are inseparable and this inseparability represents their emptiness. However, this is not the same as saying that there is nothing there at all. For example, when we see the blue color of the sky, we are aware of this blue color by means of our eye consciousness. So we have two things here: the blue color and our individual eye consciousness. But these two are inseparable because they arise from a single karmic cause. There is a single cause, but two effects, the object and the consciousness or subject. To try to separate them (subject and object) is like trying to cut an egg in half; we try to cut it in two, but there is only one egg. Subject and object are inseparable.

The Shunyata of the Chittamatra school means the non-duality of subject and object, that is, their interdependence. The blue color (the object) and the eye consciousness (the subject) are non-dual and interdependent because they arise from the same cause. They always occur together. If our consciousness is not present, there will be no blue color found out there. The blue color only exists in our act of perceiving it. It has no independent existence. Both arise from a single karmic cause. Consciousness and the object of perception are inseparable. The blue color does not exist until our consciousness is present to perceive it. For us, it exists only then. When we close our eyes, this blue color does not exist for us any more. This blue color and our consciousness are inseparable, and this is the meaning of Shunyata. They are empty or shunya (stong-pa) because they are not separate independent entities; they are interdependent and arise from a cause. This not existing independently is what Shunyata means. The blue color and our eye consciousness are merely two sides of the same coin.

So the meaning of Shunyata in the Yogachara system and the meaning in the Madhyamaka system are quite different. The Yogachara school is also called Chittamatra or Semtsampa (sems-tsam-pa) because the Yogacharins assert that everything is connected with mind (sems). If there is no consciousness present, then the object does not exist. For it to exist, the object and the consciousness must come together, embrace each other, and depart together. Their interdependence and their inseparability represent their emptiness. But this is not the same meaning as the Madhyamaka meaning of Shunyata.

Furthermore, according to Madhyamaka, the six consciousnesses lack any inherent nature. Chittamatra speaks of sixteen kinds of Shunyata, whereas Madhyamaka speaks of eighteen kinds of Shunyata. But whereas Chittamatra recognizes Shunyata, it is not the Shunyata of Madhyamaka which is the absence of any inherent existence. The cause is different in Madhyamaka and Chittamatra, that is to say, their understanding of Shunyata is different. Therefore, the path of practice is different and, therefore, the fruit will be different. Chittamatra recognizes Shunyata to mean the non-duality of subject and object and the followers of the Chittamatra view practice that Shunyata and not the Shunyata of Madhyamaka, that is, of no inherent existence. The practice follows from that view, and so the Madhyamaka Buddha will not logically be the same as the Chittamatra Buddha.

The Tantras may be interpreted according to either the Madhyamaka view or the Chittamatra view and in fact the texts of the Tantras allow for either interpretation. Although nowadays all the Tibetan schools are officially Prasangika Madhyamaka, and the Tantras are explained from that standpoint, in early days both in India and Tibet, many commentaries explained the Tantras from the Chittamatra standpoint and practitioners obtained results from practicing in that way.

There are many doctrines held in common by Madhyamaka and Chittamatra, such as the Ten Paramitas, compassion, and so on. They also have the five paths and the ten stages. Among the five paths, the path of accumulation (tshogs lam) is so-called because the practitioner practices accumulating (tshogs) merit and wisdom. The next path, the path of unification (sbyor lam) is so-called because the subject is unified (sbyor) with the object. The next, the path of vision (mthong lam) is when one sees (mthong) the first glimpse of reality. Here is found the first stage or bhumi. The remaining nine stages are found in the next path, the path of meditation (sgom-lam). Finally, there is the fifth path, the path beyond all training (mi slob lam).

But in Madhyamaka and Chittamatra, the practice of the Prajnaparamita, or the Perfection of Wisdom, is different, although the practice of the other Paramitas is the same, since both schools belong to Mahayana. Chittamatra says that all the world is an illusion, but it does not say that nothing exists. Madhyamaka asserts that everything is created by our thoughts. Chittamatra replies that if this were so, why is there any suffering experienced in the world? Everyone wants to be happy and enjoy pleasurable sensations. Since we do experience suffering, there must be some real existence apart from our thoughts and desires. We cannot just create everything in our minds. We do not want to suffer, and yet suffering exists. So it is not created by our minds. Chittamatra says there must be something real because otherwise there would be no practice and no attaining of Buddhahood. If it were all a matter of just creating it with our thoughts, we would not need to practice, but could just think that we are the Buddha and it would be so.

But Madhyamaka never claims that whatever we think is true. We can say: "My finger is like a car", but this is not a suitable statement. There is no reason there. In order to be able to give a name, there must be sufficient reason. Yes, everything is created by thoughts, but statements should be suitable. Our saying: "This ball is my head" is not a valid statement because there is no connection between this ball and my head. So there must be a basis for valid imputation. But Madhyamaka says even valid statements have no inherent existence. They are not sufficient. Dzogchen also says that everything is an illusion, but we must understand what that means. It is not enough to say it. We must realize it concretely in our experience.

According to Chittamatra, subject and object are inseparable, yet they are distinct. And this is true of consciousness, for there exists a self-awareness or an awareness of being aware. In this case, consciousness (rnam-shes) is the object side and self-awareness (rang-rig) is the subject side. This self-awareness or Rang-rig is a self-knowing or a self-seeing. In this Tibetan word, *rang* means "self" or "itself," and *rig* means "to know" or "to be aware." So it is an awareness which is aware of itself. For example, the flame of a butter lamp illuminates a dark room, but it also illuminates itself, that is, it is clear and luminous. Thus the lamp has two functions: externally to remove the darkness in the room and internally to illuminate itself. These two functions are inseparable in every moment of consciousness. We are aware of the object (gzhan rig) and we are aware that we are aware (rang rig). We know that we know. This is self-awareness. So what we actually see and know is not an autonomous external world at all. What we see is only our own consciousness. What we see is only ourselves. Every occasion of sense consciousness and of mind consciousness is a moment of self-awareness (rang-rig). And just at that moment, the subject knows itself without any thought; this is Rang-rig. This doctrine of Svasamvedana, that consciousness illuminates itself as well as its objects, is characteristic of the Chittamatra view and is rejected by the Madhyamaka view.

The Madhyamaka system only recognizes six operations of consciousness (tshogs drug), namely, the five sense consciousnesses and the mental consciousness, whereas the Yogachara system recognizes eight kinds of consciousness (tshogs brgyad). All of them are self-illuminated or Rang-rig. The previous example of the lamp light illuminating itself, as well as illuminating the objects in a dark room, illustrates this. Thus, consciousness and Rang-rig are always inseparable. Besides the five sense consciousnesses of sight, hearing, smell, taste, and touch, and the sixth, mind consciousness or Manovijnana (yid kyi rnam-shes), there are two further types of consciousness: the defiled mind consciousness or Klishta-manovijnana (nyon-shes), and the base consciousness known as Alayavijnana or Kunzhi Namshe (kun-gzhi rnam-shes). Defiled mind consciousness means the operation of the mind (Skt. manas) has become defiled (Skt. klishta) and distorted by the presence of the passions or negative emotions (Skt. klesha). Therefore, our mind does not work properly, but it sees everything in a distorted fashion, colored by the presence of passion.

In the Chittamatra system, this Kunzhi is the basis of everything, that is, it is the container of all karmic traces. The relationships among these eight operations of consciousness are explained by way of an example. The Kunzhi Namshe, or Alayavijnana, is like a treasure house and the Manovijnana, or mind consciousness, is like a husband. The five sense consciousnesses are like his servants. They constantly go about in the world, searching for wealth to bring back to their master. And the Klishtamanas is like his wife; it is she who keeps and enjoys all the wealth her husband and servants collect in the world. Moreover, she is very vain and has little sense of economy. This Kunzhi is the basis for collecting and preserving karmic traces, but when the individual attains Nirvana, this Kunzhi Namshe is dissolved because there are no more karmic traces remaining and no new ones are accumulated. Its operation ceases. Until then, each sentient being possesses an individual, own Kunzhi. It is the basis of our individuality. And each of these eight consciousnesses are Rang-rig, that is, self-knowing and self-clarity. Consciousness and the Rang-rig are always inseparable.

The Kunzhi Namshe serves as the medium for the transmission of karmic traces, or vasanas (bag-chags), from one lifetime to another. Every action of free will leaves behind a karmic trace in our stream of consciousness at its deepest level. These traces or residues are like seeds which are stored here and when in the future the proper configuration of secondary causes exists, these seeds germinate and we experience the fruit of our past karma. Because these karmic traces are stored in the Kunzhi Namshe, it is also known as the storehouse consciousness. In Tibetan, it is called Kunzhi Namshe (kun-gzhi rnam-shes), where *kun* means all, that is, all karmic traces both good and bad, *gzhi* means base, the receptacle where the traces are kept, and *rnam-shes* means consciousness.

However, although Chittamatra does not say that the Kunzhi and the karmic traces are the same, it does say that both have an inherent existence. The example is that the Kunzhi is like a grain storehouse and the karmic traces are like the seed grains contained in it. On the other hand, Madhyamaka counters this argument and asserts that they must be the same. In that case, if we purify the Kunzhi, it will only be the same as before. If we merely wash our house on the outside, it will make no difference on the inside. But according to the Madhyamaka, if we dissolve our karmic traces, the Kunzhi will also dissolve. Through the practice of Shunyata and the practice of Bodhichitta, these karmic traces are purified.

Generally, there are two Tibetan words for karmic traces: *sa-bon* (Skt. bija, seed) and *bag-chags* (Skt. vasana, residue, trace). In the Chittamatra system, these two terms have the same meaning. But according to Madhyamaka, *sa-bon* is much coarser and easier to purify and remove, whereas the *bag-chags* are much more subtle and difficult to purify. The Tenth Bhumi, or stage of Bodhisattva practice, is the antidote for all of them.

In conclusion, we can say that there is a fundamental difference between the view of Madhyamaka and the view of Chittamatra. The Chittamatra system may use concepts like Rang-rig and Kunzhi, but in the Madhyamaka system, which rejects these characteristic ideas of Chittamatra, Shunyata is the highest view. Chittamatra also conceives of Shunyata but in a quite different way from Madhyamaka. We have seen that Madhyamaka denies the self-aware nature of consciousness (rang-rig). And it does not recognize the existence of the Kunzhi Nanshe, or base consciousness, as a storehouse for karmic traces.

These are some of the principal differences between the two philosophical systems, and it is important to understand them. Furthermore, Dzogchen also speaks of Kunzhi and Rang-rig but understands the meaning of these terms quite differently.

Chittamatra and Dzogchen

The followers of Chittamatra assert that everything depends on mind (sems) and that there is nothing beyond mind. According to the Chittamatra view, everything that exists is connected with mind. It is mind-created; that is their real view. According to them, if we see a blue color, the eye consciousness (the subject side) and the blue color (the object side) are inseparable, that is, they both arise from the same single karmic cause. Therefore, anything that is perceived is connected with mind, although it is not made out of a mind-stuff or substance. If consciousness were not there, the object would not be there. Nothing exists without this connection with consciousness; it cannot exist independently. Thus, the Chittamatrins ask, how can Dzogchen do better than this? How can Dzogchen have a higher view? That is to say, how can it go beyond thoughts and consciousness to a state that transcends mind? It is not possible that there is anything beyond mind.

There are some similarities in the languages of Dzogchen and Chittamatra, and so some people have confused the two views, whereas actually they are quite distinct. Dzogchen is always speaking about "mind" (sems) and, therefore, people commonly think that "mind" here has the same meaning as in Chittamatra (sems-tsam, "mind only"). But in the context of Dzogchen, "mind" is not part of the system of the eight consciousnesses (rnam-shes brgyad); the word refers to the Nature of Mind (sems-nyid), that is, what we usually call the Natural State. The essence of this Natural State is emptiness (stong-pa nyid) and immediate awareness (rig-pa), and they are always found together. They are inseparable (dbyer-med). So there does not have to be any separate thought or consciousness present to know emptiness because a pure immediate awareness (rig-pa) is equally present in this state of emptiness. But according to Chittamatra, whatever we see or experience is interdependent, and its "emptiness" lies in that fact. A perception depends on the presence of consciousness and this consciousness exists inherently, although the objects perceived do not. But Dzogchen does not say that the Natural State has an inherent existence; it lacks any inherent existence because it is emptiness itself, a pure potentiality.

What is the difference between Rigpa, or the Natural State, and consciousness? The Natural State is totally pure, pure from the very beginning (ka-dag), whereas the eight consciousnesses are not pure and represent the vehicle for the karmic traces. When we attain enlightenment, they are absorbed into the Natural State, and then they manifest as wisdom, or primal cognition (ye-shes), rather than as consciousness (rnam-shes). But although the Kunzhi Namshe, in particular, is the medium for the transmission of the karmic traces, they in no way disturb or defile the Natural State. A distinction is made between Kunzhi in the Dzogchen usage of the term and Kunzhi Namshe in the Chittamatra usage; they are quite different.

Like Chittamatra, Dzogchen also speaks of Rang-rig and Kunzhi, but it understands these terms in quite a different way. According to Chittamatra, consciousness (rnam-shes) and its self-illuminated quality (rang-rig) are always found together. Furthermore, subject and object are inseparable, yet they are distinct. At the primary level, sense consciousness represents the subject side and the external object the object side. But at the secondary level, consciousness (rnam-shes) itself represents the object side and Rang-rig the subject side. In the Chittamatra view, this Rang-rig is a self-knowing of itself by consciousness, that is to say, consciousness is self-illuminated. Each of the eight consciousnesses (rnam-shes) has two functions: it illuminates an object (gzhan-rig) and it illuminates itself (rang-rig). An example of this, cited previously, is a lamp flame in a dark room; it illuminates the objects in the room and it illuminates itself. It is this second function that makes memory possible.

So, according to Chittamatra, Rang-rig is a secondary subtle consciousness which knows the primary sense consciousness it accompanies. Chittamatra asserts that if there was not this self-aware quality, this Rang-rig, we would not be able to remember anything. And since we do have memories, this Rang-rig must exist. Madhyamaka replies to this argument that we can remember without this hypothetical Rang-rig. When we see an object, it simply reminds us. We only remember it by name; it has no inherent existence. So, this is the meaning of Rang-rig here in the Chittamatra system, but in Dzogchen the term Rang-rig has a different meaning.

According to Dzogchen, Rang-rig is the awareness which knows the Natural State. It is not something separate from the Natural State. The Natural State is aware of itself; it is self-aware and self-illuminated. In the Chittamatra system, however, this term only applies to the eight relative consciousnesses. Chittamatra has no knowledge of the Natural State; in its view, there is nothing beyond consciousness. So, here we find the same word, but a different meaning. Such a consciousness is always dualistic in its operation, there being a bifurcation into subject and object, and it is always something conditioned by antecedent causes. In contrast, the Natural State is non-dual, there is no duality of subject and object, and it is unconditioned and outside time. It is not something brought about by causes. It is totally beyond cause and effect. Although we may speak of Rang-rig as the subject side of the Natural State, it is not something which originates among the eight consciousnesses, as in the case of the Chittamatra view.

Chittamatra does not know of this primordially pure Natural State which transcends totally the Kunzhi Namshe. This Kunzhi Namshe of the Chittamatrins is still something which is defiled by the passions and conditioned by past karma.

In Dzogchen, the same word is used but it has a different meaning. What is seen on the object side is the empty nature, but the awareness (rig-pa) in Dzogchen is different from the consciousness (rnam-shes) in Chittamatra on the subject side. In analyzing the Tibetan term, *rang* normally means "self", but here, in the Dzogchen context, it refers to emptiness or Kunzhi, whereas *rig* refers to awareness or Rigpa. What we see is the empty nature, on the emptiness side (stong-cha), and *rig* is the seeing, on the clarity side (gsal-cha). The reference is to immediate awareness (rig-pa) and not to consciousness (rnam-shes). And according to Dzogchen, these two are inseparable (rig stong dbyer-med); the subject side and the object side are not distinct and separate. We can speak of Rang-rig representing the subject side of the Natural State and Kunzhi representing the object side. But this Rang-rig did not originate among the eight consciousnesses, nor is it what originates from consciousness (sems byung). According to Dzogchen, Kunzhi and Rang-rig are inseparable. They always go together like fire and warmth, or like water and wetness. We can speak of these different qualities but, in actuality, they are always inseparable. Rigpa is a synonym for clarity (gsal-ba). What is clear is the Kunzhi. The way in which it is clear lies in their inseparability. They are inseparable in the same way as the sky (i.e. Kunzhi) and the sunlight (i.e. Rigpa) which illuminates the sky are inseparable.

The other key term is Kunzhi. But Kunzhi has a different meaning in Chittamatra from that in Dzogchen. In the Chittamatra system, Kunzhi Namshe is one of the eight relative and conditioned consciousnesses (rnam-shes), and it functions as the container of the karmic traces (bag-chags). It is called Kunzhi because all (kun) karmic traces, both good and bad, are contained within this base (gzhi) as a receptacle. It is the base consciousness or Kunzhi Namshe and this consciousness knows these karmic traces.

According to the Chittamatra view, when Nirvana is attained, the Kunzhi Namshe dissolves. The Dzogchen view is different. All of existence is contained in the Kunzhi because it is the Base of both Samsara and Nirvana. Therefore, it does not dissolve. The Kunzhi is emptiness itself, it represents the matrix out of which can manifest all possible forms. Therefore, it is compared to the sky, or to infinite space. It is not just a container or storage place for the baggage of karmic traces. It does not serve as the basis for these karmic traces because it is primordially pure (ka-dag). But according to Chittamatra, the Kunzhi Namshe is impure because it is mixed up with karmic traces. When these karmic traces are finally purified, the Kunzhi disappears. The ordinary mind or consciousness (rnam-shes), which is soiled with karmic traces, is now transformed into Buddha-mind, or primordial awareness (ye-shes), which is clean in itself and without karmic traces. It is like washing the hands. When all the dirt has been washed off, the hands are still there. What remains is only this pristine awareness or knowledge (ye-shes). So we say that when the Kunzhi Namshe has been purified of all karmic traces, it becomes the knowledge of the Dharmadhatu (bon-dbyings ye-shes).

In Dzogchen, the Kunzhi is the basis (gzhi) of everything (kun) in both Samsara and Nirvana. In the Dzogchen context, Kunzhi means the empty, unchanging Natural State. In it all things exist spontaneously and potentially. But in terms of the Natural State, there is nothing to be purified or changed or transformed. Thus we speak of it as being primordially pure (ka-dag); it has never been sullied or adulterated by the karmic traces of Samsara. Nevertheless, it remains the basis of everything. Whatever arises, arises in the Natural State and whatever liberates, is liberated in the Natural State.

On the other hand, the Kunzhi Namshe of Chittamatra contains only the karmic traces of Samsara. It is only the base for these karmic traces and not the base for Nirvana. According to Dzogchen, there are no karmic traces to be found in the Natural State. It is like trying to write something in space, or like clouds passing across the sky; there are no traces left behind. No traces remain because the Natural State is primordially pure (ka-dag). The reflections in a mirror leave no trace behind. The Natural State is always pure, uncontaminated by the passions or their traces. It is the basis of everything; whatever arises, arises in the Natural State. They abide in the Natural State and they liberate into the Natural State. Thus, the Natural State is called the Dharmakaya.

In Dzogchen, we speak of the Kunzhi as being the Dharmakaya of the Base (gzhi'i bon-sku), but this is not the real Dharmakaya, that is to say, the Dharmakaya in manifestation, for that is the Fruit. And here we are only speaking of the Base. The Trikaya are fully present in the Base as its Essence, Nature and Energy (ngo-bo rang-bzhin thugs-rje gsum), but for the Trikaya to become fully visible and manifest as the Fruit, certain secondary causes are required, namely, purification of the two-fold obscurations, which are emotional and intellectual. To behold the face of the sun, the clouds in the sky must first dissipate, even though the sun has been there in the sky all of the time.

CHAPTER 5

The Views of Tantra, Mahamudra and Dzogchen

Talk by Lopon Tenzin Namdak,
Bischofshofen, March 1991.
Compiled and edited by John Myrdhin Reynolds.

The View of Tantra

Nowadays there are two principal philosophical traditions in Tibet. The first is found among the Sarmapas or Newer Schools, which employ the Prasangika-Madhyamaka view not only in explaining the real meaning of the Sutras but also in their interpretations of the Tantras as well. The second is found among the two Old Schools, Nyingmapa and Bonpo, which emphasize the Dzogchen view in explaining the Higher Tantras. [1] However, in both cases the fundamental principle upon which Tantra rests is Shunyata, or the state of emptiness. And here, especially in early times before the eleventh century, it did not matter whether we practiced Shunyata according to the Madhyamaka school or according to the Yogachara school.

Visualization practice according to the Tantras, unlike ordinary visualizations, always begins with the three contemplations. The first of these, the contemplation of reality, represents the state of Shunyata. This is followed by the second contemplation, compassion which is everywhere manifest. The third contemplation is of their unification, emptiness and compassion, and represents the contemplation of the cause in the form of visualizing the seed syllable from which the visualization of the deity arises. So, in Tantric visualization practice, the deity and its mandala always arise out of the potentiality of the state of Shunyata. In the same way, at the conclusion of meditation practice, the visualization of the Yidam or deity is always dissolved again into the state of even contemplation (mnyam-bzhag), which is Shunyata. So, Shunyata is basic here in the practice of Tantra.

In general, the Sutra system of the Gelugpa school, as well as the other Tibetan schools, is based on the Madhyamika tradition as expounded, for example, in the *Bhavanakrama* of Kamalashila and in the *Bodhipathapradipa* of Atisha. This Sutra system became fully elaborated in Je Tsongkhapa's great work, the *Lam-rim chen-mo*. After the eleventh century, all the schools of Tibetan Buddhism came to adhere to the Prasangika Madhyamaka system of Chandrakirti as their official philosophy, in the same way as the Gelugpas did later. Even the Nyingmapas and the Bonpos adopted Prasangika Madhyamaka for their understanding of Shunyata in relation to the Sutra system. However, their descriptions of the path according to the Sutra system may differ in some details. The great Tsongkhapa discussed his understanding of Shunyata in his commentaries on the Sutra system as well as in his *Legs-bshad snying-po*, and elsewhere.

Although nowadays all the Tibetan schools use only the Prasangika Madhyamaka interpretation of Shunyata, in the early days it was quite a different situation for one could alternatively use the Chittamatra interpretation of Shunyata. Whichever view was adopted was up to the individual practitioner. Shantirakshita, the first abbot of Samye Monastery in the eighth century, accepted the doctrines of Kunzhi and Rang-rig from Chittamatra, although he rejected the Yogachara teachings in general. His subschool of Madhyamaka was known as Svatantrika-Yogachara-Madhyamika (rang-rgyud rnal-'byor spyod-pa'i dbu-ma-pa) and this was the original Madhyamika tradition in Tibet. Only after the eleventh century were the writings of Chandrakirti translated into Tibetan by Patsab Lotsawa and then his interpretation, known as Prasangika-Madhyamaka (thal-'gyur dbu-ma-pa), gradually became the fashion among all the schools of Tibet, as far as explication of the Sutras is concerned. [2] As said, this was true even for the Nyingmapas and the Bonpos. However, the interpretation of the Tantras in the two Old Schools is a different matter.

In terms of the Tantra system, the Gelugpas follow the system of the *Guhyasamaja Tantra*, the chief of the Father Tantras and, in particular, the commentary of Je Tsongkhapa on that Tantra, as well as his famous *sNgags-rim chen-mo* which is a treatise on the New Tantra system generally. [3] However, in terms of the interpretation of the Tantra system, the Sakyapa school emphasizes the *Hevajra Tantra* and the Kagyudpa school emphasizes the *Chakrashamvara Tantra*. According to all these schools, both the Sutras and the Tantras are recognized as the authoritative word of the Buddha. However, the Gelugpas interpret the Tantras in terms of the Sutras and when these scholars explain the view of Tantra, the foundation for their interpretation is the *Guhyasamaja Tantra*. This is the principal Tantra practiced by the followers of that school and they rely upon the view of the great master Tsongkhapa. In his commentaries he makes much use of, and has many quotations from, Marpa the translator, especially from the latter's commentary on the *Naro chos drug*, or the Six Doctrines of Naropa. He did this because Marpa wrote from the *Guhyasamaja Tantra* point of view. But this view is not the same as that of Dzogchen.

Nowadays, there are some Lamas who assert that the Madhyamaka view, the Mahamudra view, and the Dzogchen view are all the same. But this is not true, because Madhyamaka belongs to the Sutra system and Mahamudra belongs to the Tantra system. Both Sutra and Tantra rely on the mind and its operations, such as the thought process. Hence, Sutra and Tantra apprehend and grasp at thoughts. But Dzogchen says that we must go beyond all grasping ('dzin-pa), which is the apprehending of an object by the subject, even when this is just a thought. This Dzinpa or grasping represents a working of the discursive mind, an agitation of thoughts, even though this movement of thoughts may be very subtle, perhaps only an unobserved undercurrent. Yet it is agitation nonetheless, and so it represents delusion ('khrul-pa). Therefore, according to Dzogchen, the practitioner must go beyond this Dzinpa, no matter how subtle it may be.

Moreover, if this Dzinpa, or grasping at an object by a subject, is present, then that practice is not Dzogchen. The capacity of the Natural State to be aware intrinsically is called Rigpa and that Rigpa is not thought (rnam-rtog). Some Lamas assert that there must always be some subtle Dzinpa, or thought process present, for otherwise there could be no knowing or apprehending of anything whatsoever. If there is no Dzinpa, they maintain, there is nothing because everything is known by thoughts. Therefore, the Dzogchenpas are "know-nothings"; they aim at a state of "no mind," like the followers of the Hwashang who attempted to teach Ch'an Buddhism in Tibet. [4]

Furthermore, when the Anuttara Tantras are explained in terms of Madhyamaka, some grasping is still found ('dzin-pa) to be present. According to some interpretations, there is a subtle mind present which needs the support of prana to exist. In Tantra, we speak of Detong Yeshe (bde stong ye-shes), where *stong* (stong-pa nyid) or emptiness has the same meaning as it does in Madhyamaka. But the Natural State in Dzogchen is inexpressible and inconceivable, so that we cannot get at it through mental constructions and doctrinal formulations. Nevertheless, according to some Lamas, we can only understand something by way of thoughts.

The great scholar Sakya Pandita also maintained that, even in the state of Mahamudra, there must be some Dzinpa or thought present, otherwise the state is devoid of all apprehending ('dzin-pa med-pa) and it knows nothing whatsoever. Gampopa in his writings did not directly state that Dzinpa must be present in the state of Mahamudra, but the philosophical background of his Mahamudra indicates this. Marpa followed the view of the *Guhyasamaja Tantra*, and the view of this Tantra is the same as that of Madhyamaka, so Dzinpa must be present there in the state of contemplation (mnyam-bzhag).

According to the *Guhyasamaja Tantra* as explained by Je Tsongkhapa in his commentary and elsewhere, there are two things that must be united in our meditation practice, namely, bliss and emptiness. This is called Detong Zungjug (bde stong zung-'jug), that is, the unification of bliss and emptiness. Here, emptiness (stong=stong-pa nyid) refers to the object side of our experience and bliss or pleasurable sensation (bde=bde-ba) refers to the subject side. When these two aspects or sides are united, this is known as the pristine knowledge of the unification of bliss and emptiness, or Detong Yeshe (bde stong ye-shes). This knowledge, or primal awareness (ye-shes), is the very foundation of the view of Tantra and Mahamudra. Here Tongpanyid (stong-pa nyid) or emptiness is the same as the Shunyata or emptiness referred to in the Madhyamaka philosophy. Therefore, in his explication of the *Guhyasamaja Tantra*, Tsongkhapa also gives many quotations from such authorities as Nagarjuna, Chandrakirti, Aryadeva, and so on.

The notion that the subject, that is, *bde-ba*, knows the object, that is, *stong-pa nyid*, is taken mainly from Marpa's commentary on the *Naro chos-drug*, the six doctrines of Naropa. According to this commentarial tradition, Shunyata or emptiness is the same as the Shunyata in the view of Nagarjuna. Following this line of thought, some Lamas maintain that Detong Yeshe is the same as the Dzogchen view. However, according to Tsongkhapa, the Dewa (bde-ba) or subject very strongly grasps or apprehends ('dzin-pa) the object which is emptiness (stong-pa nyid). This occurs not only on the path of practice, but at the very moment of realization as well. In this context Dewa represents a kind of subtle consciousness. And so here in this experience of an immediate primal knowledge (ye-shes) we have the unification of subject and object. This is Detong Yeshe and it is the basis of Mahamudra in the Tantra system.

Now, there are many different methods, including physical procedures such as consort practice and methods of visualization, which aim to produce this experience of bliss or pleasurable sensation (bde-ba). But in every case, there is a subject that grasps or apprehends and an object that is grasped or apprehended (bzung-ba). And so this view found here cannot go beyond grasping. But Dzogchen, on the contrary, goes beyond all grasping at anything whatsoever. The state of Dzogchen does not unite two different things, whether bliss and emptiness or subject and object but, rather, it transcends them from the very beginning. This state, known as Rigpa, or intrinsic awareness, is prior to any distinctions or unifications, both of which would be functions or operations of the mind. Dzogchen is beyond the mind. So, we must realize the distinctions being made here.

When we do Tantric practice, we visualize ourselves as the deity and find ourselves as that deity, in total identification with all of that deity's feelings, emotions and thoughts. We are that deity. In the Sutra system, there is the taking of Refuge by means of visualizing the Buddha in front of us. But we are separate from the Buddha and we are in our ordinary karmic body. So simply visualizing a deity is not the definitive characteristic here. Dewa is the feeling or sensation of being that deity. Here the object side, that is, emptiness, is the same as in Sutra, but the subject side, which is bliss, is different.

But according to Tantra, Dewa as our practice must not be mixed up with ordinary desire or attachment ('dod-chags). It must be without any discursive thoughts (mi rtog-pa). If Dewa were just an ordinary feeling, and that feeling was mixed with desire, then that would be a klesha or emotional defilement. But if the feeling is suffused with Shunyata, then we can make use of it in Tantra as a means. Our actual physical union with a consort can produce this Dewa, as can also visualization in meditation.

According to this interpretation, Shunyata here is the same as the Shunyata of the Madhyamaka view of Nagarjuna. Therefore, some Tibetan scholars say that Detong Yeshe is the same as the Dzogchen view. But this is not so. According to Marpa the translator and Je Tsongkhapa, Dewa, the subject, very strongly grasps Shunyata, the object. Dewa represents a kind of consciousness, so here in this Yeshe, or knowledge, we have subject and object united. They are now non-dual, although they were not so in the beginning. This unification is Detong Yeshe and its realization is the goal of Tantra and Mahamudra. In fact, its realization is what is meant by Mahamudra in the context of the Tantra system.

In Dzogchen, we may also speak of Detong (bde-stong), but the meaning here is not the same as in Tantra. In Dzogchen, it is not necessary to develop any Dewa or Tongpa as it is in Tantra. The Dewa is not something coerced or brought into existence by way of some special practice, sexual or otherwise. Rather it simply arises naturally and spontaneously. Here, the Dewa, or bliss, is Lhundrub (lhun-grub), spontaneously self-perfected, and the Tongpanyid, or emptiness, is Kadak (ka-dag), primordial purity. The experience arises spontaneously and without deliberate effort as both Kadak and Lhundrub, because it is beyond the mind or thought process. Here also in Dzogchen, there is no unifying of Wisdom and Means (thabs-shes) as is done in the Sutra system. Everything is already contained and fully present within the Natural State. When the practitioner realizes the Natural State, then there is no longer any question of the necessity to practice Kyerim (bskyed-rim), the generation process, and Dzogrim (rdzogs-rim), the perfection process. Although the practice of these two processes is necessary for the realization of Mahamudra according to the Tantra system, in Dzogchen there is no need to practice them as antidotes. Rather, the practitioner proceeds directly to the Natural State.

The proper method of Tantra is the Path of Transformation (sgyur lam). Thus, in the Tantra system, the energies of the emotional defilements or kleshas are used in our practice and they are transformed. Klesha, or passion, is transformed into Jnana, or wisdom (ye-shes). Transformation is the method belonging to the Higher Tantras. However, pleasurable sexual sensation (bde-ba), used as the object in our practice, must be unmixed with desire or attachment. It must exist in a state of non-discursiveness or no thought. Dewa in itself is just a feeling, a feeling of pleasurable sensation; but if that feeling becomes mixed with desire and attachment, it is a klesha, a defilement or passion. On the other hand, if this original feeling, this pure sensation, is mixed with Shunyata, then it can be used in Tantra as part of the meditation practice. The physical union with a consort produces this pleasurable sensation. Or the visualization of a consort may be used. Now, it is possible to attain the enlightenment of Buddhahood through either the methods of Sutra or of Tantra but, according to the Tantra system, the realization of a Buddha by way of the Sutra system is not complete, not fully realized, and so further steps must be taken.

Of course, when we are speaking about Dzogchen as a teaching, rather than as the primordial Natural State, then we do make distinctions. We speak of the side of emptiness (stong-cha), on the one hand, and of the side of clarity (gsal-cha) or awareness (rig-cha), on the other hand. But these distinctions are only linguistic and logical; they are not found in the Natural State itself. However, even when we speak of this distinction of clarity and emptiness in the context of Dzogchen, it is not the same as the unification of bliss and emptiness (bde stong zung-'jug) in the method of Tantra.

A thought or concept arising in the mind has a kind of picture accompanying it. For example, when we think of

Frankfurt, a picture of that place comes into our mind. Thoughts are always grasping at something and are mixed up with such pictures. This is the way thoughts interact with the Manas, or the discursive mind (yid), the bio-computer in the human brain. The technical term "clear" (gsal-ba) means that these computer-generated pictures never cover over our consciousness; on the contrary, our awareness (rig-pa) remains in its own original condition, like a mirror reflecting an object set before it. The mirror is not changed or modified by whatever object, good or bad, beautiful or ugly, is set before it. It clearly reflects all of them, whatever their nature may be. Rigpa is this capacity of the Nature of Mind, that is to say, it clearly reflects everything. But the Nature of Mind (sems-nyid) is in no way changed or modified by whatever is reflected. This is clarity. So, in terms of Dzogchen, when we speak of the inseparability of clarity and emptiness (gsal stong dbyer-med), comparing the Nature of Mind to a clear empty mirror, we do not mean that some sort of mixture occurs, or that there is a uniting of subject and object. The word Yermed (dbyer-med), inseparable, means that they have never been separate, so there is nothing to unite.

Dzogchen is also different on the object side. Dzogchen recognizes Shunyata as being the same as in Madhyamaka, but this is not the Absolute Truth or the goal of Dzogchen. It is only a part of the view; it is not the complete view in itself. The Natural State is the inseparability of clarity and emptiness; they have always been together from the very beginning. There is only the Natural State as it is; there is nothing to add to it, nothing more to be unified with. We just have to become familiar with it and continue in that state. So there are no paths or stages (sa lam) to be gone through here; there is only the single stage (sa gcig) of the Natural State.

In Dzogchen, we speak of the inseparability of clarity or awareness, on the one hand, and emptiness, on the other. But here we are not unifying or bringing anything together (zung-

'jug). Clarity and emptiness have never been separated, so they do not need to be brought together. Therefore, their inseparability is not the same as the unification of bliss and emptiness spoken of in Tantra. The practice of Dzogrim requires that we apprehend or grasp something, namely, Detong Yeshe, the knowledge of bliss and emptiness united. Some people say that Dzogchen, Tantra and Mahamudra are the same, but this is not so, according to this understanding of Tantra, because Dzogchen has no grasping, no apprehending of anything, not even emptiness.

In Tantra, there is the practice of Dzogrim, and here the subtle mind (sems) and the prana, or vital energy (rlung), are united and this unification persists in the Bardo, after the death of the physical body, as a subtle body. And because he has practiced during his lifetime, when the Tantric practitioner dies, he finds that his consciousness now inhabits this subtle body or Gyulu (sgyu-lus), illusion body, produced from the unification of mind and prana. His mind has been transformed into his Yidam's mind. The mind which inhabits this subtle body is realized by way of Yidam practice according to Tantra, and this experience is known as Detong Yeshe. Until the Yogi leaves behind his physical body, there are actually two beings dwelling inside him like a mother and a child. Then at the time of death, the link between the physical body and the mind is severed, and the former dissolves into its constituent elements, whereas his consciousness (rnam-shes) enters the Bardo. Now he is only left with this Gyulu or Illusion Body, which is the product of the unification of mind and prana energy by way of Dzogrim practice. This Gyulu already possesses Detong Yeshe. Here there are two possibilities — pure Gyulu and impure Gyulu. But still this attainment is not Buddhahood. Moreover, this is still grasping or Dzinpa; it is not the Natural State or the realization of Buddhahood. In Dzogchen, however, there is no grasping and no transforming. When we practice Dzogchen, we do not have to check what is the emptiness side and what is the clarity side.

Now inhabiting this subtle body or Gyulu, which has the form of the Yidam, one must continue to practice, but in an exalted status ('phags-pa'i sa) and one need not return to human rebirth. One is no longer controlled by karmic causes and can project Trulpas (sprul-pa), or emanations of oneself in whatever form, when and where one chooses. One can choose where one will be reborn and under what circumstances. The procedure of how to produce a Gyulu is explained in the Dzogrim section of the Anuttara Tantras. And in the Bonpo tradition, in particular, this means the *Ma rgyud* or Mother Tantra. [5]

In the Bonpo Tantras, the subject side is more like that in Dzogchen, namely, an inherent unchanging nature just as it is (mi 'gyur rang lugs ji-lta-ba). This is the Bonpo interpretation of Tantra. In the Bonpo Tantra, the object (Shunyata), is taken from the downside, namely, Sutra, and the subject (self-awareness) is taken from the upside, namely, Dzogchen. Nevertheless, these two have been inseparable from the very beginning. They are the two sides of the Natural State. Only self-awareness, or Rang-rig can see it. This self-awareness illuminates itself like the flame of a lamp. The lamp flame not only illuminates the dark room; it illuminates itself. Each individual sentient being has this individual Natural State, so there is individual continuity from life to life. However, the Natural State in itself is unchanging, even though individual awareness (rang-rig) is changeable. Yet these two are always inseparable. So, the practice of Dzogchen and Tantra do not necessarily exclude each other. But if we are practitioners of Dzogchen, as well as of Tantra, we should be aware of the differences in the views of Dzogchen and Tantra.

Mahamudra and Dzogchen

Mahamudra and Dzogchen, in terms of their respective definitions of the Base, the Path and the Fruit, are not the same. Mahamudra belongs to the Tantra system; indeed, it represents the culmination of the Tantric process of transformation where the practitioner becomes totally identified with the meditation deity or Yidam. That is the meaning of Mahamudra in the Tantra system, total (maha, chen-po) identification (mudra, phyag-rgya). Moreover, Tantra speaks of Detong Yeshe, the unification of two things, bliss and emptiness, whereas Dzogchen has been non-dual from the very beginning. In Sutra we have the intelligence which understands emptiness (stong-nyid rtogs-pa'i shes-rab). In Tantra we have the knowledge of the unification of bliss and emptiness (bde stong ye-shes). And in Dzogchen we have the Unique Essence (thig-le nyag-gcig), which is non-dual from the very beginning. So the goal of each of these paths is defined differently.

Nowadays, there are some Lamas who say: "*Phyag-chen rdzog-chen dbu-ma chen-po gcig-pa red*", that is, Mahamudra, Dzogchen and the Great Madhyamaka are all the same. [6] This statement may be useful to promote non-sectarianism, but it is not true philosophically. Mahamudra, although possessed by all Tantric schools, is especially associated with the Kagyudpas, whereas Dzogchen is especially associated with the Nyingmapas and the Bonpos. The great Madhyamaka is what the Gelugpas call their view. We have already pointed out how the view of Madhyamaka clearly differs from Dzogchen, and here we are considering how the view of Mahamudra differs from Dzogchen. [7] They differ in terms of their Base (view), their Path (meditation) and their Fruit (result). The results are not the same because the view and the meditation are different.

According to Madhyamaka, on the Path of Vision at the First Bhumi, [8] we come to realize the unification (zung-'jug) of emptiness and clarity. But according to Dzogchen, emptiness and clarity have been inseparable from the very beginning (ye nas dbyer-med). Attaining Buddhahood, therefore, depends on recognizing the Nature of Mind and not on uniting two different things. According to Madhyamaka, which belongs to the Sutra system, it takes three immeasurable kalpas to attain Buddhahood, whereas if we practice according to the Tantras, we will attain enlightenment in at least seven lifetimes. The difference is that Tantra and Mahamudra unite bliss with Shunyata or emptiness, while Madhyamaka knows only Shunyata. Tantra has access to the additional methods of Kyerim and Dzogrim which are unknown in the Sutra system. Dzogchen, however, does not need any sort of visualization process as preparation, but seeks immediately to discover the Natural State as it is in itself. We do not need to do anything special. So, with the practice of Dzogchen, if we have the capacity, we can realize Buddhahood within a single lifetime. When there are different views and different paths, they lead to different results. This is only logical. If we plant a seed of barley in the earth, it will not produce wheat. So the Buddhahood, which is the Fruit according to Madhyamaka and also according to Mahamudra, will not be the same as the Fruit according to Dzogchen. [9]

So, if we recognize the Nature of Mind, there is no reason to make a postponement. In the Sutra system, we purify our mind through applying antidotes. In the Tantra system, we use visualization to transform our vision and make a unification of Shunyata and Bodhichitta. This is the method of transformation, not that of applying antidotes. But in Dzogchen we have the method of self-liberation. Because their methods are different, Sutra is known as the Path of Renunciation (spong lam), Tantra is known as the Path of Transformation (sgyur lam), and Dzogchen is known as the Path of Self-Liberation (grol lam). [10] If they are different paths, how can we get the same result? Thus each system here has its own distinct Base, Path and Fruit. [11]

In Mahamudra, which also represents the culmination of the Tantra system, there is the unification of bliss and emptiness (bde-stong zung-'jug) and this is the experience of Detong Yeshe, the knowledge of bliss and emptiness, as we have pointed out before. And here "emptiness" is conceived as being the same as that in

Madhyamaka because it was explained in this way by Marpa the translator. There is the unification (zung-'jug) of feeling (bde-ba) and emptiness (stong-pa nyid) and these two become knowledge (ye-shes). This Detong Yeshe (bde-stong ye-shes) is what distinguishes Tantra from Sutra. Shunyata is always the object side, and so in this system, Dewa and Yeshe are on the subject side. Thus the Sutras speak of the intelligence which understands emptiness (stong-nyid rtogs-pa'i shes-rab) and the Tantras speak of the knowledge which is bliss and emptiness (bde-stong ye-shes). But in Dzogchen, when we refer to the Natural State, we do not speak of thoughts (rnam-rtog) or consciousness (rnam-shes), but of clarity (gsal-ba) and awareness (rig-pa). So, we do not find here in Dzogchen the same way of speaking that we find in Madhyamaka, for example. The Natural State has its emptiness side (stong-cha), but it equally has its clarity side (gsal-cha). These two are inseparable, like fire and heat, or water and wetness. However, in Madhyamaka and in Mahamudra, there is always some subtle grasping by a thought ('dzin-pa), that is, a catching or seizing or apprehending of something, even if this something is just emptiness. There must be a thought present there that knows the emptiness. But this is not true of the Natural State. There is no thought present that knows the Natural State, because the Natural State is self-aware and knows itself from the very beginning. Just as a lamp flame illuminates a dark room, so simultaneously it also illuminates itself. There is no need for a second thought or consciousness to know it. It simply knows itself. In Dzogchen everything is open and there is no grasping ('dzin-med).

The various Tibetan schools agree that we can attain Buddhahood either through the path of Sutra or the path of Tantra. But according to Tantra, the Buddhahood attained through the Sutra method is not complete and not fully realized. There are some further stages or bhumis that must be gone through and these are described in the Tantras.

In the Sutra system, the Paramitas are according to Relative Truth and Shunyata is according to Absolute Truth. Like Madhyamaka and the Sutra system, Thodgal practice in Dzogchen teaches us the illusory nature of all things. We come to realize that all appearances are illusions created by mind. But when we are in the Natural State, we do not make judgments, such as thinking: "It is only an illusion!." In Dzogchen, the Trikaya has to be attained simultaneously, not successively. But according to Madhyamaka, without the Two Truths, there can be no attaining of Buddhahood. In the Sutra system, we find these two ideas. First, that the knowledge which knows emptiness is the cause of the Dharmakaya and, second, the practice of the accumulation of the Paramitas is the cause of the Rupakaya. But this Sutra practice takes a very long time to realize the result. They practice Shunyata only, not the visualization of the visible forms of the deities. But in Tantra, we begin by assuming the state of emptiness, and then practice the visualization of the deities from the very beginning. Thus, this method is much quicker. Sutra possesses only the cause for the Dharmakaya, the practice of Shunyata. It knows only this; it does not know the real cause of the Rupakaya. So the Sutra system is like planting charcoal in the ground and watering it regularly; no tree will grow from this. Tantra practices Shunyata, but also the visualization of the deities, so this provides a cause for the manifestation of the Rupakaya and the method works much quicker. [12]

But when Sutra and Tantra look at Dzogchen, they see no causes for producing the Rupakaya. There is no visualization practice. There is nothing done that might be the cause of the Rupakaya. They ask: Dzogchen does not recognize the Two Truths, so how can Dzogchen lead to the attaining of Buddhahood? In answer, Dzogchen has the Natural State which is not at all the same as the Shunyata of Madhyamaka. Emptiness means a lack of inherent existence. It is a condition which is merely empty, passive and negative. But according to Dzogchen, all visible things spontaneously exist (lhun-grub) as manifestations of the inherent energy (rang rtsal) of the Natural State. For example, when we look at a mustard seed, we see no oil. But when we press the seeds, oil comes out. So this oil spontaneously exists in the seed, but the secondary cause of pressing the seed is required for the oil to manifest. If Buddhahood did not already spontaneously exist in the Natural State, no matter what practices we did, and no matter for how long, nothing would come out of it. The Natural State has the potentiality of the Ten Paramitas already fully present within it. Dzogchen possesses all the causes of Buddhahood because everything already spontaneously exists within the Natural State. Therefore, we need practice only this single truth, and not two.

According to Dzogchen, Tantra cannot attain complete Buddhahood because it turns to one road and then to another. We cannot go simultaneously on two roads. All of the forms of the Tantric deities, the Zhitro, or Peaceful and Wrathful Deities, are inherent in the Natural State. According to the Jonangpas, the Natural State has these forms of the deities in potential, so each sentient being is a potential Buddha, but as yet this Buddhahood is not visible. [13] So everything can come out of the Natural State. But for this potentiality to manifest, there must be secondary causes; it is not like a Buddha image enshrined in a temple with the door open. Thodgal practice links us with the secondary causes for the manifestation. But these are only secondary; the real cause and source of the visions is the Natural State.

In Dzogchen, we only practice the one path of remaining in the Natural State, and everything else manifests out of that spontaneously, which is Lhundrub, whereas in the Sutra system, we are expected to practice the two accumulations equally. But how can we take two roads at one time? We must neglect the one while we pursue the other. However, all the Buddhas, all their virtuous qualities and all their activities, already exist in the

Natural State. This single Natural State is the basis of everything in Samsara and Nirvana. Therefore, we call it the Kunzhi, the basis of everything. At this present moment, our Natural State is only the basis of Samsara, and it is not now acting as the basis of Nirvana. At present for us it is only the basis of delusion ('khrul-gzhi) and not the basis of liberation (grol-gzhi). But the Natural State is also the basis of Nirvana, and when we find ourselves in the state of enlightenment then it is no longer the basis of the delusion of Samsara, but the basis of Liberation (grol-gzhi). This is the case for a particular individual; when speaking in general, it is the basis of both. This teaching is profound (zab) because it teaches in individual and particular terms, and it is also vast (rgyas) because it teaches in general and universal terms. All of the Ten Paramitas and all the other virtues of a Buddha already spontaneously exist in the Natural State. It is as if everything has already been placed there in the temple, but the doors are closed. We must open these doors by way of secondary causes and practice and then the contents will be visible. It has all been there right from the very beginning, but access to it depends on our knowing the qualities of the Natural State. But we do not make any examination or research into this while we are in the Natural State; we just let it be. This one truth is enough; we do not need the Two Truths.

The Rimed Movement of Jamyang Khyentse Wangpo and Jamgon Kongtrul in eastern Tibet, in the present and in the last century, was very much influenced by the Dzogchen view and, basically, it adopted the Dzogchen view. Thus, many Lamas who come from eastern Tibet, especially Kagyudpas, now explain Mahamudra as if it were Dzogchen. They say again and again: *rDzogs-chen phyag-chen gcig-pa red*! "Dzogchen and Mahamudra are the same." Generally they are speaking about the Mahamudra of Gampopa, which had been so severely criticized by Sakya Pandita and other scholars.

However, the traditional explanation of Mahamudra is made according to the Tantra system and it is quite different from Dzogchen. For example, we can find this explanation of traditional Indian Mahamudra in the Lamdre (lam 'bras) system of the Sakyapas and in the Dohas of Virupa. And there it is explained according to Dzinpa or the apprehending of something. Tsongkhapa asserts that without Dzinpa there is no recognition of what is subject and what is object. In the Natural State there is no knowing or recognizing of an object by a subject, but here in Mahamudra there is still this separation of subject and object. In Tantra also, there must still be something present on the subject side and on the object side. When some Lamas say that Dzogchen and Mahamudra are the same, this cannot be so, because in Dzogchen there is no Dzinpa, whereas in Dzogrim there is Dzinpa, that is to say, the knowing of Detong Yeshe. And if the view is different, then the path will be different, and correspondingly the fruit will be different.

According to some Lamas, in Sutra and in Tantra the object, namely, Shunyata is the same, while the subject is different. In Sutra the subject is the ordinary discursive mind, whereas in Tantra it is the purified mind in the thigleys or energy drops (bindus). [14] However, in both cases, whether a gross discursive mind or a purified subtle mind, there is Dzinpa, the apprehending of something, whereas in the Natural State of Dzogchen, there is no duality of subject and object and there is no Dzinpa present from the very beginning. So, here we find some fundamental differences in the views held by Sutra, Tantra and Dzogchen. As practitioners, we should be aware of them.

CHAPTER 6

The View of Dzogchen

Taught by Lopon Tenzin Namdak,
Devon and Amsterdam, Spring 1991.
Compiled and edited by John Myrdhin Reynolds.

Dzogchen as the Highest Teaching

Within the Bonpo tradition, there are nine successive ways (theg-pa rim dgu) to enlightenment and Dzogchen is the highest of these. But it is not enough to say Dzogchen is the highest. We must know and understand the reasons why it is the highest. If we understand the reasons precisely, then no one will be able to destroy our devotion to the Dzogchen teachings. The source of the Dzogchen teachings is the Dharmakaya Samantabhadra, or Kuntu Zangpo (kun tu bzang-po) as he is known in Tibetan, and Dzogchen has had an uninterrupted and continuous lineage from the Dharmakaya down until the present time. For example, we can find this lineage in the Zhang-zhung Nyan-gyud. [1]

When we come to Dzogchen, there are two methods of practicing the teachings: (1) We do the preliminary practices, and then go to a master who introduces us to the Natural State (rig-pa ngo-sprod), after which we go on to practice retreat in isolation in the wilderness for years until we attain some realization. (2) At Menri Monastery in Tibet, we had an educational system whereby students thoroughly studied Sutra, Tantra and Dzogchen. However, this also meant that there was little time for practice. It was mostly a matter of intellectual study, and at the end of their course of studies, having passed the oral examinations, students received a Geshe degree. [2]

For what reasons is Dzogchen the highest view? In all of the nine successive ways or vehicles we search for the Natural State (gnas-lugs). But this depends on the capacity of the individual. Each of these nine successive ways has a different view. In general, the method of Sutra is the path of renunciation (spong lam), the method of Tantra is the path of transformation (sgyur lam), and the method of Dzogchen is the path of self-liberation (grol lam). So we say that Dzogchen is the final or ultimate way. Self-liberation (rang grol) is the definitive view and method of Thekchod (khregs-chod).

The text we have here is entitled the *Theg-pa'i rim-pa mngon du bshad-pa'i mdo rgyud*, "The Sutra and Tantra of the Clear Explanation of the Nine Successive Ways." This text is from the collection of Central Treasures, or U-Ter (dbu-gter), so-called because they were found at Samye Monastery and at other places in central Tibet. [3] It deals with the view of Dzogchen, contrasting it with the views found in Madhyamaka, Yogachara and Tantra.

If we depend on intellectual speculation alone, however, we shall be very far away from the Dzogchen view. It is not a matter of thinking "Maybe Dzogchen is like this or like that." That is something artificial; it is not direct experience. What is required at first is a direct introduction to the Natural State (rig-pa ngo-sprod). This Natural State is the view of Thekchod. The introduction is very simple: we just look inward, we look back at ourselves. It is like looking at our own face in a mirror, not looking out at the external world through eye-glasses. Every one of us has the possibility of realizing it for ourselves. It is not very far, but it must be pointed out to us. So it is not a matter of collecting different teachings. As such, it only becomes more remote. No, it is a matter of direct personal experience. The watcher and what is watched both dissolve at the same time and we just leave them as they are. We just continue in the Natural State; that is the view of Thekchod.

But a direct introduction is necessary because, even though it is near at hand, due to our obscurations, we do not recognize it. We get this direct introduction from a master who has had his own personal experience of the Natural State. He knows what it is and can point it out to us. This makes for clarity and understanding and dispels disturbances. The Dzogchen teachings were transmitted from the Dharmakaya Kuntu Zangpo down to the master Tapihritsa who, in the eighth century, transmitted them to his disciple Gyerpung Nangzher Lodpo (Gyer-spungs sNang-bzher lod-po) in the country of Zhang-zhung, and the latter wrote them down. These teachings have been transmitted from then until the present day in a continuous lineage. For this reason, in the tradition of the Zhang-zhung Nyan-gyud, "the oral transmission (snyan-rgyud) from the country of Zhang-zhung", Tapihritsa is the principal figure in the Guru Yoga practice. From him as the Nirmanakaya Guru, all blessings, all the powers of knowledge and inspiration (byin-rlabs), come to us. He attained the enlightenment of a Buddha through the practice of Dzogchen and realized the Rainbow Body of Light ('ja'-lus-pa). Then at a later time he appeared in the guise of a small child and bestowed the Dzogchen precepts upon the master Gyerpungpa. [4]

The Base

In the Dzogchen teachings, the Base (gzhi) is the state of total primordial purity (ka-dag chen-po). This state of primordial purity may, in some respects, resemble unconsciousness, but it is not at all unconsciousness as such because it is characterized by the presence of Awareness (rig-pa). It is often compared to the sky, but this is only an example, because the sky is not aware. But just as the sky is not changed by the presence of the clouds in it, so in the Base there is no change or addition in response to whatever we think or do. There is nothing new to be added to it, nor is it in need of any correction or modification (ma bcos-pa). It is naturally pure and never otherwise; that is its quality. The Natural State has never been defiled or modified by the events of Samsara. It is like a mirror which is in no way changed or modified by whatever it reflects.

Nonetheless, in this Base, which is the Natural State of the Nature of Mind (sems-nyid gnas-lugs), manifestations spontaneously appear, just as clouds appear in the sky or reflections appear in a mirror. This is its quality of spontaneous manifestation (lhun-grub), and these manifestations represent the creative potentiality or energy (rtsal) of the Natural State. All things, all that we think and perceive as individual sentient beings, are manifestations of the inherent energy (rang rtsal) of the Natural State. In the end they return again to the Natural State. There is nothing in Samsara or Nirvana that goes beyond the Natural State. It is the primordial Base (ye gzhi) of both Samsara and Nirvana. Everything that appears, exists as spontaneous self-perfection (lhun-grub) and yet it is empty. The emptiness side (stong-cha) of everything is called primordial purity (ka-dag) and the clarity side (gsal-cha) is called spontaneous perfection (lhun-grub). And although we differentiate between these two aspects when speaking, in reality they are inseparable (dbyer-med). So there is nothing special here. Everything is present in the Base. The quality of the Natural State is the inseparability of clarity and emptiness (gsal stong dbyer-med). If this is not our view, than that view is not Dzogchen.

But when we are actually practicing the Natural State, we do not analyze and examine matters in this way intellectually. We leave everything in the state of being just as it is (ji-bzhin-pa). If we think or examine or judge, we disturb and lose our contemplation; we fall out of the Natural State and enter into the workings of the mind. In the Natural State, everything is fine just as it is; we do not have to think about it or evaluate it.

In Dzogchen, we speak of three series of teachings: the Semde or Mind Series (sems-sde), the Longde or Space Series (klon-sde), and the Manngagide or Secret Instruction Series (man-ngag gi sde). [5] The Longde emphasizes the emptiness side, whereas the Semde emphasizes the clarity or awareness side. The Manngagide, or Dzogchen Upadesha, emphasizes the inseparability (dbyer-med) of these two sides. If we go along only with Shunyata on the emptiness side, that is not Dzogchen. Semde and Longde are mainly just names referring to a matter of emphasis. The ultimate point in both is Yermed (dbyer-med), or inseparability; otherwise they would not be Dzogchen. Their difference is only a matter of how they bring the practitioner to the understanding of Yermed. The Dzogchen Upadesha begins immediately with Yermed. It assumes that we already understand Yermed, at least to some degree. It is Yermed that is most important, and without it there is no basis for Dzogchen.

Commitment to the Dzogchen View

If this is all clear to the practitioner, then there is a commitment (dam-tshig). Although there are no vows and rules to be found in Dzogchen, as there are in Sutra and Tantra, nevertheless, there is a commitment to the view of Dzogchen, if we would be practitioners of Dzogchen. This Damtsik or commitment is fourfold:

1. singularity (gcig-po),
2. spontaneous perfection (lhun-grub),
3. negation (med-pa), and
4. abiding naturally in purity (rang-bzhin gnas dag).

The Tibetan word *gcig-po* means "single, singular, unique, singularity, uniqueness." The Dzogchen view is singular and unique because we do not fall onto the one side or onto the other, but remain always with Yermed. In the view of Dzogchen, all appearances are spontaneously perfected (lhun-grub). The word *med-pa* means negation: "it is not." But in the context here, we are not thinking that something does not exist. The Dzogchen Semde text entitled the *Nam-mkha' 'phrul mdzod* clearly explains this negative way of speaking: no refuge, no compassion, and so on. This negation has reference only to the Natural State. It means that in the Natural State, there is nothing but the Natural State. On the side of manifestation, however, everything exists, including all practices and virtues, but on the side of the Natural State, nothing exists independently because all things, including refuge, compassion, the Ten Paramitas, and so on, are already there, present in their full potentiality, and so there is nothing to realize. Everything is already there. If we grasp at anything, then that is not Dzogchen; we have gone beyond the Dzogchen view and fallen into a lesser view. And so we speak in a negative way (med-pa). Abiding naturally in purity means we continue in Yermed, we continue in the Natural State which is primordially pure.

The Dzogchen View

If we grasp at something or try to do something, we lose the Natural State and deviate from the view of Dzogchen. To leave everything just as it is without trying to correct or modify anything is the view of Dzogchen. The Natural State has no partiality or divisions. In it, there is nothing to affirm or negate. This is what it means to be without accepting or rejecting anything (spang blang med-pa). But if we think: "I must be in a state of Yermed", then this is grasping at a concept and it represents a wrong view. Thoughts and concepts are not the Natural State. This awareness (rig-pa) is self-aware (rang-rig); it is not divided into subject and object. So if we try to do anything in terms of thinking and judging, we bifurcate it into two parts and we are no longer in the Natural State.

The Lower Ways speak of the Two Truths, but in Dzogchen, we do not do that. We speak only of a single source or Base (gzhi). Thus Dzogchen is also known as Thigley Nyagchik (thig-le nyag-gcig), the Unique Essence. In the Tibetan language, the word dzogpa (rdzogs-pa) means two things: (1) something is completed, finished, exhausted, and (2) everything is full, perfect and complete. The Sambhogakaya is called Dzogku (rdzogs-sku) in Tibetan because it is effulgent, complete, and perfect. It is the actual form or visible manifestation (sku) of perfection (rdzogs-pa). But this does not mean that it is finished or ended. In the Dzogchen view, everything is perfect because it is Lhundrub.

Everything exists in potential in the Natural State. But things manifest according to secondary causes. In the Dzogchen view, this also applies to the Ten Paramitas and other virtues. The entire accumulations of merit and wisdom are already present in the Natural State. There is nothing more to be added or developed. So if we practice in just this single way by remaining in Rigpa, all virtues will manifest in their entirety because they are already fully contained in the Natural State. Everything is encompassed by the Natural State; there is no "external" or "internal" in relation to it. Yet the Natural State in each sentient being is individual, while it has the same quality and level. The Natural States in an enlightened Buddha and in an ignorant insect are the same. One is not bigger and the other smaller. The differences between an enlightened being and an ignorant being are in terms of the Path and the Fruit, but in both cases the Base is the same. And the Base is the Natural State. But the Natural State is individual with each sentient being. We are not all "One Mind." Otherwise, if there was only one single Natural State, or One Mind, then when the Buddha attained enlightenment, all sentient beings would have become enlightened. But that is not our experience.

However, the eight Lower Ways or vehicles (yanas) contradict this Dzogchen view. The text we have here, the *Theg-rim*, deals with four contradictions or objections brought against Dzogchen and refutes each of them in turn.

First Contradiction – Chittamatra

According to the Chittamatra (sems-tsam-pa) view, everything that exists is connected with mind. It is created by the mind. That is the real view of Chittamatra, the philosophy of the Yogachara school. When we see the blue color of the sky, this means that the eye consciousness, which is the subject doing the apprehending, and the blue color, which is the object apprehended, are inseparable. This is because they arise from the same karmic cause. This is true of all perceptions of appearances, and so we can say that everything is connected with mind, even though they are not made out of some sort of mind-stuff. Nothing exists independently without this connection with consciousness.

The Chittamatra view of the Yogachara school asserts that everything depends on mind (sems) and that there is nothing beyond mind. Thus, the Chittamatrin asks: So how can you Dzogchenpas do any better than this? That is to say, how can you go beyond thoughts to a state beyond mind? It is not possible that there is anything beyond mind.

Dzogchen is always talking about "mind" (sems), so some people think that Dzogchen has the same view as Chittamatra. But "mind" (sems) has a different meaning in the context of Dzogchen where it means, not "mind"(sems) in the sense of the thought process or in the sense of consciousness (rnam-shes), but "mind" in the sense of the Nature of Mind (sems-nyid). In Dzogchen, Sem (sems) means Semnyid (sems-nyid), and it is not part of the system of eight consciousnesses (tshogs brgyad). This Nature of Mind is characterized by awareness (rig-pa); it is inseparable from the Base. But this Base is unknown to Chittamatra, which knows nothing beyond the Kunzhi Namshe (kun-gzhi rnam-shes), the storehouse consciousness, that is, the receptacle for karmic traces (bag-chags). When Dzogchen speaks about the Kunzhi, the basis of everything in both Samsara and Nirvana, this has a very different meaning from the Kunzhi Namshe in Chittamatra where it is only the basis for karmic traces.

Dzogchen falls outside their view. To the objection raised by the Chittamatrin, the Dzogchenpa replies: You say that consciousness is real and exists independently. But we do not recognize this. We do not recognize all these phenomena as real or the thoughts that know them as real. According to Chittamatra, the consciousness of whatever we see or experience is inherently existing, but Dzogchen does not claim that the Natural State exists inherently. So our view goes beyond yours.

Second Contradiction – Madhyamaka

The second contradiction represents the Madhyamaka criticism of Dzogchen. Both Chittamatra and Madhyamaka recognize the Two Truths, the Relative Truth, which is appearances, and the Absolute Truth, which is Shunyata. Madhyamaka asserts that everything is related to these Two Truths and that there is nothing beyond them. Subject and object have no independent existence; they exist only as names created by thoughts. Nothing has any independent existence. Shunyata is the final or ultimate reality and there is nothing beyond this. So the followers of Madhyamaka ask: How can you Dzogchenpas do better than this? Your Dzogchen is not even Buddhism!

To this, the Dzogchenpa replies: We do not recognize the subject/object dichotomy and the Two Truths. Our view is inseparability (dbyer-med) without any partiality. There is only one Truth, which we call Thigley Nyagchik (thig-le nyag-gcig), the Unique Essence. So our view is beyond your view of the Two Truths. Dzogchen is beyond your Madhyamaka view, but this does not mean that Dzogchen is not the Buddha's teaching. It simply means that it is beyond your definition of the Two Truths. [6]

Some authors in their commentaries on the *Madhyamakavatara* of Chandrakirti criticize Dzogchen for not asserting the Two Truths. Dzogchen asserts that the final view pertains to only a single nature, a state beyond cause and effect. It does not say that karmic causes and consequences are ultimate. If there are two truths, then we must have two minds in order to know them. These critics speak of two kinds of cognition: (1) a discriminating intelligence (the subject side) that understands Shunyata (the object side) and (2) a discursive intellect that knows names and concepts, imputing them to phenomena. Both of these represent "wisdom" or "intelligence" (shes-rab), but here we have two minds, not one. According to Dzogchen there is only one cognition, the Thigley Nyagchik, and not two minds.

Again, the Madhyamaka practitioner objects: If Dzogchen does not have the Two Truths, then it does not recognize the Ten Paramitas. How then can you Dzogchenpas do any practice? And if you do not do any practice, how can you accumulate any virtues? And if you do not have the two accumulations of merit and wisdom, how can you attain Buddhahood? The sources of the two accumulations are the Two Truths and the result of the two accumulations is realization of the Two Bodies, the Dharmakaya and the Rupakaya. So you cannot realize Buddhahood unless you have these Two Truths. They are required as causes for the Dharmakaya and the Rupakaya. Without such a cause, you cannot realize Buddhahood.

The Dzogchenpa replies: Dzogchen agrees that without a cause we cannot realize Buddhahood. But if we are given a piece of gold, we do not have to search for its qualities, they are inherent in it from the very beginning. Dzogchen never says that we should not practice the Ten Paramitas; it only asserts that the Natural State already contains the Ten Paramitas and, when we realize the Natural State, they will manifest spontaneously. So we do not need to practice them separately, one after the other. The Ten Paramitas are spontaneously present within the Natural State. Thus Dzogchen only explains the Thigley Nyagchik, or Natural State, and that is sufficient. If we practice the Natural State, we will realize the Dharmakaya and the Rupakaya because all things are present already in the Natural State, and when the secondary causes arise, they will manifest spontaneously. If we practice the one Natural State, everything is present there already, and so that is enough.

According to the Sutra system in general, if we do not recognize the Two Truths, then there is no cause for the realization of the Two Bodies. The Lamas, in this tradition in particular, rely upon the exposition of Chandrakirti in his *Madhyamakavatara*. They take his Prasangika view as being the highest view and assert that there can be nothing beyond that. They follow Chandrakirti in this. According to Madhyamaka, the Buddha-nature is the conventional meaning, whereas Shunyata is the ultimate meaning. However, according to Dzogchen, once we discover our real nature, the Natural State, we do not need to search for anything else. Everything is present there already, all of the Paramitas, and will manifest spontaneously. But in Dzogchen, we do need secondary causes for the manifestation of the Trikaya. So, Dzogchen can justly claim that its view is the higher.

Third Contradiction – the Lower Tantra

Along with Chittamatra and Madhyamaka, the Tantras recognize the Two Truths. But here the emphasis and the method are different. According to Kriya Tantra, the practice involves two kind of beings, the Wisdom Being (ye-shes sems-dpa') and the Symbolic Being (dam-tshig sems-dpa'). The Symbolic Being is the visualization of the deity in the sky in front of us; it is created by our mind, and then the Knowledge Being is the blessing and energy invoked into it from a higher source. Then the two of them are united into one and that unification is called the Action Being (las kyi sems-dpa'). In Kriya Tantra, this Knowledge Being is like a king and the Symbolic Being is like a servant. The king gives siddhis and blessings to the servant. Thereby the latter becomes much more powerful and wise, and then this power can overflow into the practitioner.

The Kriya Tantra practitioner asserts: We visualize that the entire universe has become a celestial palace and that all beings become the deities in this palace. How can you do better than this point of view? We invoke the wisdoms of the deity, and uniting the Symbolic Being and the Knowledge Being, we receive siddhis from this Action Being. How can you Dzogchenpas explain anything better than this? There is no better view or practice!

To this the Dzogchenpa replies: You do not actually understand the real nature of things. You are unable to go beyond visualization (dmigs-med). You create one being with your mind and invoke the wisdoms as another being, and then try to mix them together. But you cannot make them into one. You do not know Nyamnyid (mnyam-nyid), the state of sameness or self-identity, and so you make one the lord and the other the servant. You are like a child with its parent. You do not know real unification, and so our view is beyond yours. Our view is spacious and unlimited; our conduct has no negative rules, and so our view is the higher. The "highest" view means getting near to the real nature. And we do not use thoughts to do that. You cannot practice the Two Truths simultaneously, but only consecutively. You must alternate one with the other. But in Dzogchen, we have gone beyond that.

Fourth Contradiction – the Higher Tantra

In the Bonpo system, there are four kinds of Tantra. The two Lower Tantras are the Kriya Tantra (bya-ba'i rgyud) and Charya Tantra (spyod-pa'i rgyud). The two Higher Tantras are called Yeshen gyi Gyud (ye-gshen gyi rgyud) and Yeshen Chenpo Gyud (ye-gshen chen-po'i rgyud). The distinction here is somewhat similar to the distinction between Mahayoga Tantra and Anuyoga Tantra in the Nyingmapa system, and the distinction between Father Tantra and Mother Tantra in the Sarmapa system.

The practitioner of the Higher Tantras asserts that we know both awareness (rig-pa) and contemplation or equipoise (mnyam-bzhag, samadhi). All the deities spontaneously exist; this is the view of Yeshen gyi Gyud. Therefore, the Knowledge Being and the Symbolic Being are like brothers, and what we unify here is bliss (bde-ba) and emptiness (bde stong zung-'jug). All the deities and the universe itself are visualized as arising from the dimension of space (dbyings), that is to say, Shunyata. Everything is connected with Shunyata and is a manifestation arising out of Shunyata. We meditate on these visualizations and discover that everything arises from this cycle of Dimension and Primordial Awareness (dbyings dang ye-shes). So there can be no better view than this!

To this the Dzogchenpa replies: You Tantrikas are still grasping ('dzin-pa) at knowing Shunyata as an object. But our Dzogchen view is beyond all grasping at anything. We do not create anything whatsoever with the mind, such as visualizations of deities and mandalas. We do not come to any conclusions or create anything, but we go directly to the Natural State. Therefore, our Dzogchen view is the higher. You Tantrikas are always playing happily like children, that is, playing with discursive thoughts. You are always trying to create or to dissolve something. And this mind-created cycle is never finished. But Dzogchen is not bounded by thoughts. All of the lower vehicles are bounded by this sickness or obsession with discursive thoughts, but the Natural State is primordially beyond all thoughts and actions. In the Higher Tantras, you assert that all the deities are reflections or manifestations (rtsal) of the state of emptiness and that they are not created by thoughts. You say that Dzogrim represents reality! They are not just mind-made visualizations, as is the case with Kyerim practice. Everything exists spontaneously. Yet you have to visualize deities and mandalas. You are perpetually creating things with the mind, and so you are always limited by thoughts. You are tied up with thoughts. This is not at all compatible with Dzogchen. Dzogchen is primordially liberated from all thoughts and deliberate actions. In it, there is nothing artificial or contrived. Therefore, it represents the highest view.

These replies found in the text clearly indicate why Dzogchen is the deepest and highest view (lta-ba zab rgyas). We should know these reasons why Dzogchen represents the highest view, otherwise the assertion means nothing. For the practice of Dzogchen, it is necessary to understand the Natural State, but it is not necessary to create anything intellectually or experientially in order to find ourselves in the Natural State.

Inseparability

Inseparability (dbyer-med) is what is emphasized in Dzogchen. This term Yermed does not mean bringing two different things together and making them one. That is unification or coalescence (zung-'jug). Inseparability means that they have never been separate. We may speak about them being separate qualities or aspects, but in reality they have never been otherwise than perfectly unified, like water and wetness, or fire and heat. Dzogchen asserts that primordial purity (ka-dag), that is to say, Shunyata and spontaneous manifestation have been inseparable from the very beginning (ye-nas ka-dag lhun-grub dbyer-med), and never otherwise.

So as practitioners of the view of Dzogchen, we do not fall on the one side or on the other. The emphasis may be different in the three series of Dzogchen teachings. The Longde emphasizes the emptiness side (stong-cha) and the Semde emphasizes the clarity or awareness side (gsal-cha), but even here, what is basic and fundamental is to realize their unity or inseparability. Dzogchen Upadesha or Manngagide at the very outset stresses Yermed; it begins with inseparability and it does not first need to go through emptiness or clarity to get at it. The real nature of Dzogchen is beyond expression in words; we can only discover it within ourselves. For this, the experiences of the calm state (gnas-pa), the movement of thoughts ('gyu-ba), and immediate awareness (rig-pa) can be used as a direct introduction to the Natural State. However, if we just play around with discursive thoughts, like children playing with their toys, we will fall away from the Natural State. So, philosophies and intellectual speculations are not enough on their own to discover Reality.

CHAPTER 7

The Practice of Dzogchen

Teachings by Lopon Tenzin Namdak,
Amherst College, October 1991.
Transcribed and edited by John Myrdhin Reynolds.

View

Dzogchen is an especially valuable teaching for this time in the West. It goes directly to the essence of the matter. All of us as sentient beings (sems-can) possess mind (sems). So this teaching about mind and its nature is very useful to us in practical terms and not just theoretically. The benefit is that Dzogchen can bring us peace of mind and happiness in our lives. In the practice of Dzogchen, there are no complicated visualizations, no difficult yoga positions, no monotonous chanting of mantras; there is only an examination of our condition and a discovery of the Nature of Mind. We need to discover what really exists. Our mind is nearer to us than anything else, yet it is invisible and we do not see it. We do not immediately recognize its nature. For this reason, we need to hear the teachings and then put them into practice. This will not only bring us a calm and contented life in the present but, in the future, it will bring the circumstances of a better rebirth. However, in order to understand this, we first look at our own condition before we can discover and recognize this Nature of Mind.

The Dzogchen teachings look very simple, but in the Tibetan texts they are made much more complicated. Usually in a Dzogchen text, it will say that it is not necessary to practice

Kyerim and Dzogrim as in Tantra, or to practice virtues like Bodhichitta, generosity and so on, as in Sutra. Dzogchen asserts that we do not need to do anything except enter into, and continue in, the Natural State (rig-pa). Other than this, we do not need to do anything in particular. There is no question of karmic traces or of practicing virtues. It will even say in a Dzogchen text that there is no need for view or meditation. What does this mean and why does it say this in some texts? Some explanations given in Dzogchen are direct, while others are indirect. Some critics in Tibet even asserted that Dzogchen is some sort of nihilism and not even Buddhism. But this is not so, and many wrong ideas have been given out over the centuries by the critics of Dzogchen. Traditionally, Dzogchen is taught within a specific cultural and intellectual context, and we need to know what this context is, otherwise we can develop many wrong ideas about Dzogchen.

This intellectual context is principally represented by the teachings of Sutra and Tantra in both Buddhism and Bon. The Bardo teachings of the famous Tibetan Book of the Dead are also included here. In both Tibetan Buddhism and Yungdrung Bon, Dzogchen is regarded as the highest and most esoteric teaching of the Buddhas. The Nyingmapa school of Tibet also asserts this. The Dzogchen teachings and terminology in the Nyingmapa texts and in the Bonpo texts are essentially the same; the principal difference between Nyingmapa Dzogchen and Bonpo Dzogchen is that of lineage. The Nyingmapas claim that their lineage of transmission comes from India and Uddiyana and the Bonpos claim that theirs comes from Zhang-zhung and Tazik. [1] Otherwise, the meaning of Dzogchen in both traditions is the same.

In presenting the view and practice of Dzogchen here, we are following a collection of Bonpo Dzogchen texts known as the *Nam-mkha' 'phrul mdzod*, "the magical treasury of the sky." They are connected with the master Lung-ton Lha-nyen (Lung-ston Lha-gnyan, b.1088) and the teachings of this cycle were transmitted to him orally by Tsewang Rigdzin (Tshe-dbang rig-

'dzin), an ancient sage who was disguised as an Indian sadhu. [2] The texts are from the Dzogchen teachings of the latter's father, Dranpa Namkha (Dran-pa nam-mkha'), and they present a more philosophical view of Dzogchen.

Basically, in the Bonpo tradition of Tibet, we have two different approaches to the practice of Dzogchen. In the first, we find for ourselves a suitable Lama who is a master of Dzogchen, and we request teachings from him. Then, in a retreat, we carry out the preliminary practices according to his instructions. These are known as the Ngondro (sngon-'gro) and consist of nine practices which are done a hundred thousand times each. [3] Thus they are called the Bum-gu ('bum dgu) or nine Bum, "Bum" meaning a hundred thousand. When these preliminaries are completed, we then return to our Lama and request the Dzogchen teachings. Thereupon he gives us a direct introduction to Rigpa or the Natural State (rig-pa ngo-sprod). There are many different ways of doing this. We then go into a long retreat in some isolated place and practice, continuing in the Natural State as much as possible. Since we have been introduced to it by the master, we now know what Rigpa is. But this knowledge is not enough. We must practice remaining in that state.` We must develop our capacity to do so. Otherwise, because of a lack of familiarity with it, we may begin to develop doubts. At this point, it is only necessary to go occasionally to our Lama to have him check our understanding of the Natural State. We continue in this way until we attain enlightenment. [4]

The second approach is much more intellectual. In Tibet, formal education was only to be had in monasteries. In the larger Bonpo monasteries there was a traditional curriculum of scholarly studies, beginning with Sutra, then proceeding on to Tantra, and finally culminating in Dzogchen. [5] The Bonpos cherished this tradition of profound scholarship and there was a dialectical system connected with the study of Dzogchen. Nowadays, at the Bonpo monastery at Dolanji in India, this involves a nine-year program of studies for the Geshe degree. But when one is a student in the philosophy college at the monastery, one does not have much time for practice, or for making retreats. It is up to the individual student to practice after he has finished his course of studies and obtained his degree. Shardza Rinpoche instituted a reform at his monastery in eastern Tibet and inaugurated a three-year retreat system like the Nyingmapas. First one completed all the philosophical studies and then the student went into a three-year retreat to practice Tantra and Dzogchen. This Shardza tradition was much influenced by the Nyingmapas and the Kagyudpas of eastern Tibet or Kham, and so we find the same sort of preliminary practices here. Of course, we are talking about practicing until one attains realization or enlightenment, so practice is not just limited to a three-year retreat.

What is Dzogchen and what is the purpose of practicing Dzogchen? We must know this and have a clear understanding of what Dzogchen is all about, not only for our view and practice, but also because people will ask us about Dzogchen. We do not want to give them any mistaken ideas because this will be bad for them and bad for the reputation of the Dzogchen teachings. So we must understand what Dzogchen is, how one practices it, and what the results of this are. To understand what Dzogchen is, we need a direct introduction to it from someone who knows what it is, not only intellectually, but from his or her personal experience. It is like being introduced to an old friend from years ago. Although at the present time we do not recognize him, once introduced we then have this flash of recognition. What is introduced here is Rigpa or the Natural State. There are many ways to do this, to make a direct introduction to Rigpa; one method is fixation on the white Tibetan letter A.

Fixating the mind on an object of meditation involves concentration. It does not matter what object we use as long as we do not keep changing it because this leads to distraction. A stick or a small pebble in front of us can be used but, traditionally, as an introduction to Dzogchen, the white Tibetan letter A is used. If one does not know what that looks like, the English letter A can be used, or even a small white dot. This white letter is drawn on black or dark blue paper and that piece of paper is affixed to a wall, or to a stick which is stuck into the earth so that it stands upright before us when we are sitting in meditation position. Located in front of us, the letter A is not too high or too low. Our eyes remain fixed on this letter A, and so our mind is also fixated on it. The eye is the servant of the mind, and the mind as the king depends on this servant to bring him provisions. So this is one method to control the mind which, otherwise, is very difficult to control.

When we fixate our gaze on the white letter A, the mind then concentrates on it. If the eyes do not move, the mind does not move. We meditate with our eyes open in Dzogchen (or half closed) but the gaze is unmoving and, if possible, there is no blinking. The principle involved here is one-pointed concentration of mind, and when this is the case, there is no space for discursive thoughts to arise and distract us. We can do this by making our fixation of attention very acute and sharp, and then relaxing this fixation a little. But, on the other hand, maintaining acute fixation for too long can give rise to problems. So, in the beginning, it is best to meditate only for short periods of time. Then take a short break and begin again. We must use our judgment here. This process is not the same as repressing thoughts; there is just no space for them to manifest. This gives us control of the mind by a more indirect means. It is like aiming an arrow at the center of a target. The white A is this target for our full and total attention, and so this is a method for controlling the mind.

When the mind is agitated, thoughts are incessantly arising, and so we become easily distracted and our attention wanders. Then, suddenly, we recall that we have lost our focus. So again we fixate on the white A. If the mind is too agitated, it is best to take a break and try again later. Forcing ourselves can also cause problems. If the white A appears dull and not clear, then we must fixate our attention more sharply. In general, we can have problems with agitation (rgod-pa) or dullness (rmug-pa), but we can also have a problem with lack of energy or drowsiness (bying-ba). There are various methods we can employ as antidotes to these problems, and these we have discussed elsewhere when giving meditation instruction.

If we continue to practice in this way, we will come to experience a feeling of happiness in the mind and a pleasurable sensation in the body. This is known as dewa (bde-ba). And continuing to practice, we develop Shamatha or zhine (zhi-gnas), a calm state of mind. [6] Our mind is concentrated; it becomes calm like the surface of a lake when there is no wind, and we are no longer disturbed by negative thoughts. But do not think this is the Natural State; it is only an experience (nyams), that is, an experience of a calm state and an experience of a state without thoughts (mi rtog-pa). That is not yet Rigpa. This concentration is something created by the mind; it is not the Nature of Mind or the Natural State. But it is a useful method because it makes it easier to recognize the Natural State. Even an advanced practitioner may find that his practice has become stale, and so we can use these Semdzin practices (sems-'dzin), which means fixating the mind, such as fixating on the white Tibetan letter A, in order to freshen up our practice of continuing in the Natural State. [7]

Now, when we are fixating on the white A and find ourselves in this state of calm, undistracted by whatever thoughts arise, then at that time we look back into ourselves and observe what the mind is doing. This is how we begin researching our real nature. When a thought (rnam-rtog) arises, simply observe this thought, without judging it and without trying to change or modify it in any way. Does it have any color or shape? Does it have any location in space, either inside or outside the body? Does it come from anywhere? Does it stay anywhere? Does it go

The Practice of Dzogchen ~ 129

anywhere? What is the difference between the calm state and the movements of thought? Do this for a little while.

Observing the calm state created by fixation as well as the movements of thoughts, what can we say about the mind? Look again inward. Who is it who looks at this thought that arises? Where is the watcher and where is the watched? We must observe and examine our mind. We have spoken of the mind and the Nature of Mind. Who is this watcher of thoughts arising? Where is the watcher? Research this. What can we say? Look and see what it is like. We may say "look", but we do not really mean here that there is a subject and an object. We look and search and we cannot find anything. We cannot separate the watcher and the watched. They have the same nature. We look back and find nothing. We realize this and leave things just as they are.

It is at this moment that we begin to find out what is the Nature of Mind. We remain in that moment. This is the beginning of the recognition of the Natural State. If we cut down one bamboo stick and realize that it is hollow, we do not need to cut down the rest of the bamboo forest to see if they are all hollow. Whether there is a calm state or the movement of thoughts, there is a sense of presence or immediate awareness there and this is Rigpa. That is the quality of the Natural State Even if there are no thoughts arising, we are very present and aware; we are not unconscious. This presence is very bright and clear. It is just there; there is no duality of subject and object. If this intrinsic awareness were not present, we would be asleep. But we are not. We just leave it as it is; there is nothing to change, or correct or modify. It is just what it is and nothing else, but it is something inexpressible. We cannot explain it, even though we call it clarity (gsal-ba) and awareness (rig-pa). This clarity or awareness is the characteristic quality of the Nature of Mind, the Natural State, and yet, at the same time, it is empty because we have found nothing there. So this clarity and this emptiness are inseparable. But none of this was created by the activity of the mind. This state was not created by the mind, as calmness and concentration were created; it is not something created at all. Rather, it is unconditioned and primordial. It is the basis and context for mind and the activities of mind, but it is not mind (sems); it is the Nature of Mind (sems-nyid).

We have searched for the mind by way of fixating on the white A. But this white A is something created by the mind. So also are the calm state and the movement of thoughts. When we look and search for this mind that creates the white A, where is the watcher and the thing watched? They disappear when we look, but they do not go anywhere. They dissolve and liberate, leaving no trace behind. Where do these thoughts come from? Where do they stay? And where do they go? We search and find nothing and this "unfindability" (mi rnyed) is what is there; it is the final source. We call this Shunyata or emptiness. Modern science has always been searching for the ultimate particles, but has never found them. Why? Because there is no limit. When we follow after thoughts, they lead us on endlessly. We never come to an ultimate source, or ultimate particle, or absolute beginning. We are looking in the wrong place. This is just circulating in Samsara. All states of consciousness are conditioned; they are created by our thoughts. But these same thoughts liberate of themselves and leave no trace. What is their source? Where do they go? They arise in the Natural State and they dissolve again into the Natural State. This Natural State is empty but, on the other hand, it has the potentiality for all manifestations to arise. It is the Nature of Mind, and as such it is like a mirror which has the capacity to reflect whatever is set before it, but is itself in no way changed by what it reflects, whether beautiful or ugly. That is the state of Dzogchen, the Great Perfection.

There are many methods that can be used to bring us to recognition of the Natural State. It does not matter which one we use. The waters of all rivers flow into the great ocean. So we can use fixation, visualization, breathing, sound, whatever in order to bring about this recognition. Here we use concentration. At university, we must constantly create many thoughts and the mind never stays quiet. It is quite the opposite here. We just focus our attention one-pointedly and do not allow any space for extraneous thoughts. We do not go about in our usual manner because there is no limit to the creating of discursive thoughts. We fixate on the white A in order to stop this creating of thoughts. Sometimes we can sound "A" long and low, and fixate on that sound without distraction. We can also use the humming sound of "HUM" with an open mouth. There is the same point to all of these Semdzin methods.

Can children practice Dzogchen? Young children have fewer discursive thoughts; their habits are not so set. But when people grow up, they think about different things all of the time. Their thoughts are always circulating and there is no time to rest the mind. It does not matter whether these are good thoughts or bad thoughts. Whether the clouds are white or black, they equally cover the sky and obscure the face of the sun. A person must work and think all day; there is no time just to practice concentration and discover our real nature. The working person and the university student do not even try to discover their real natures because they are continuously caught up in the creating of thoughts. But children have not yet gone so far from their original nature. Nevertheless, they also need to be introduced to the Natural State in order to recognize it. The child may be more familiar with it, depending on the capacity of the individual, but still not know what it is.

Whether we study the texts or not, we must understand what the Natural State is. We can approach this intellectually or experientially or both, depending on the individual. Results come whichever approach we adopt. For example Shardza Rinpoche was a great scholar and an intellectual. He attained the Rainbow Body in 1933 and left some physical remains behind. He had a disciple who mainly practiced the preliminaries and did not study very much in an intellectual sense. But when that disciple attained the Rainbow Body, he dissolved completely his physical body and there were no remains left behind.

Can we use Vipashyana (Pali: vipassana) in order to realize Rigpa? Shamatha (zhi-gnas) and Vipashyana (lhag-mthong) are rather general terms and much used in the Sutra system. In Dzogchen, we can use any methods which are appropriate for the circumstances. There are no limitations. In Dzogchen, there is no special way to train with only Shamatha and Vipashyana. But what is important in Dzogchen is Yermed, or inseparability, and this can develop naturally. The practice of Vipashyana brings us bliss in terms of body, speech and mind, and unites this feeling with emptiness. The Tibetan term Lhagtong (lhag-mthong) for the Sanskrit Vipashyana means "bright" or "clear." When we build a house, we begin with the foundation, and if this is made of bricks, the bricks must all be of the same quality. So if we begin with the Natural State, as is the case in Dzogchen, then our practice of Shamatha and Vipashyana must be in accord with the view of Dzogchen. If we begin practicing Vipashyana according to the Sutra system, we must then proceed with an understanding of Shunyata or emptiness as presented in Madhyamaka. We cannot mix all of these distinct views together to make some sort of stew.

In our practice, we must proceed consistently. Shunyata is understood quite differently in Dzogchen and in Madhyamaka. In terms of Madhyamaka, the state in which we find ourselves is empty only but, according to Dzogchen, this state is not only empty, it is equally clear and present (gsal-le-ba hrig-ge-ba). So, in Dzogchen practice, we must have this bright clear awareness, together with the Shunyata or emptiness. The Sutra system does not speak this way. If things are only on the side of emptiness (stong-cha), this is not Dzogchen. Only when we have an understanding of the inseparability of awareness and emptiness (rig stong dbyer-med) from the very outset, can we speak of Dzogchen.

This is really a very important question: How do we link awareness and emptiness? In the Sutra system we find two different philosophies, Madhyamaka and Chittamatra, and each understands Shunyata differently. Chittamatra speaks of consciousness (rnam-shes) as being self-aware (rang-rig, Skt. svasamvedana), but there is a different meaning when Dzogchen speaks of the Natural State being self-aware. So do not confuse the two usages. The Vedanta philosophy also has its own formulation of these matters. There are many resemblances between Dzogchen and the philosophies of Madhyamaka, Chittamatra and Vedanta, but there are also precise differences. Not all the views are the same. The views found in the other eight ways (yanas) are not the same as the Dzogchen view. So we must understand properly the similarities and the differences before we can make comparisons. Characteristic of Dzogchen is that it is always talking about Yermed.

We say that Dzogchen is the highest and the most esoteric view, but why? While the view of Dzogchen asserts Yermed, this is not the view of Madhyamaka and Chittamatra. In particular, many people confuse the view of Dzogchen with that of Chittamatra. Although a number of the same technical terms are used in both systems, they hold different meanings. Generally, Dzogchen exists in the context of Buddhism, and so we need to know something about other Buddhist views. It is like being a blind man in a mountain cave. We tell the blind man not to move about because he will fall off the mountainside. He has to be very careful because he cannot see, and so he has to listen to what others tell him. If we do not know why Dzogchen is the highest teaching, we can say "highest" as much as we want, but we are just like that blind man. It's easy to fall down when we do not know the reasons for what we say and believe.

Each text describes different ways and methods. Chittamatra teaches Rang-rig, "self-awareness", but here the term holds a meaning different from that in Dzogchen. According to the former, all living beings have Namshe or consciousness (rnam-shes) and each consciousness possesses Rang-rig or self-awareness. If we did not have that, we would not be able to remember anything. For example, we saw a blue flower yesterday, and when we see it again today, we remember. The experience of seeing it today and the experience of seeing it yesterday are linked; mind links together memory and eye consciousness. When we see the blue flower with our eye consciousness, our Rang-rig is the witness that has tasted the sensation. This experience leaves an imprint or trace in the Kunzhi or base. Therefore, we have a second very subtle consciousness accompanying the eye consciousness. This second consciousness has access to these traces or memories. Normally, at the moment of perception, we do not distinguish eye consciousness and Rang-rig; they appear to occur simultaneously. And even where a perception does not occur, the Rang-rig can remember and link the impression from yesterday with that of today. But whereas eye consciousness has a visible phenomenon as its object, Rang-rig takes consciousness itself as its object. And this Rang-rig and sense consciousness are inseparable.

The Chittamatra view unites self-awareness (rang-rig) and consciousness (rnam-shes). The first is very subtle, the second is coarse and gross. Now, Dzogchen also speaks of inseparability, but according to a different meaning. Dzogchen does not speak about consciousness (rnam-shes) which is something conditioned and inherently dualistic. It speaks about Rigpa, the intrinsic awareness that is the inherent quality of the Natural State. Here it is awareness and emptiness that are inseparable (rig stong dbyer-med). The Natural State and its intrinsic quality, Rigpa, are unconditioned and outside of time. They are not brought into being by causes, as is the case with consciousness. This immediate intrinsic awareness called Rigpa is primordial and beyond dualistic consciousness and the workings of the mind. If Dzogchen consisted of only the Chittamatra view, it would not be something special and would easily be refuted by Madhyamaka.

Meditation

Once we have realized the Dzogchen view, then the next question is how to practice. We need to practice because this is how we can develop the view, make it more concrete, and remove all doubts. In any session of practice, we begin with Guru Yoga; we have explained how to do Guru Yoga in some detail elsewhere. Then we dissolve the visualization and all thoughts created by the Guru Yoga practice. [8] Even this discursive thought, the Guru Yoga visualization, cannot stand on its own and it dissolves. We just let everything be and keep in this Natural State for as long as possible. Very soon other discursive thoughts arise and disturb us, but if we just relax and let them go, they will self-liberate. At the same time, we look and see who it is that sees this thought. We just allow the thought to dissolve and we come back to the source.

But when we are in the Natural State, even if thoughts arise, we are not thinking about anything. We have no expectations or doubts. Nor do we search for secondary causes or check whether or not we are experiencing Rigpa. We just leave everything as it is without interference or correction or examination, like a mirror reflecting whatever is set before it. When we are in the Natural State, we do not need to know anything beyond this Natural State. We just let all thoughts that arise liberate by themselves. So there is no recognition, or attention, or analysis, or name-giving here; there is no work at all that is done by the mind. At that time, we do not check or examine anything. If we try to do anything with thoughts or change things, or if we start thinking, examining, or recognizing something, then we lose it; we fall out of the Natural State.

But outside the Natural State, when the session of meditation practice is completed, it is a different matter. At this later time, it is necessary to know with the mind what the qualities of the Natural State are. We must know that it is Yermed. Otherwise, we will become confused and develop wrong views. In the Natural State there is a clear awareness; we are not asleep. While we remain in the Natural State, it is bright and clear, like a mirror. That clarity is awareness (rig-pa) and what is clear is the dimension of Shunyata. These two, clarity and emptiness, are never separated; they are always together. If we really understand this, then we have the Dzogchen view. This inseparability is not something merely invented at the moment. We just realize the view and remain in it. In fact, it was there from the very beginning as the very basis of our existence. So now we have merely rediscovered it.

This Natural State, which was there from the very beginning, is our real nature; it is unproduced and uncreated and does not undergo change or evolution. It always was and always will be. It is unchanging, whereas mind and consciousness are changing and evolving all the time. They exist in time and are conditioned, but the Natural State is like space; it does not change. Discursive thoughts pass through it like birds passing across the sky leaving no trace behind. Whether these thoughts are good or bad, beautiful or ugly, they do not change the Nature of the Mind and, when they dissolve, they leave no trace behind.

But if this is so, why do we practice? Why are we not enlightened already? All sentient beings possess this Natural State, so why are they not Buddhas at this very moment? Consciousness is always with us, so why are we not enlightened? The Natural State is primordially liberated (ye grol), so why are we not liberated? If the Natural State never changes, if it never falls or gets any better, why are we not already enlightened? What is the difference between Samsara and Nirvana? Both of them come from the same source, and yet they are different.

To understand these questions, we must go back to the Base. Whether we have knowledge of something or do not have it, the Natural State remains unchanged. The Natural State is not changed by any events that occur in time, just as a mirror is not changed by whatever objects it may reflect. The Natural State is the same in all beings from the Primordial Buddha down to the lowest insect; it does not get any bigger or get any smaller. It is the same in all beings, but it is individual for each being. It is not all just "One Mind." Otherwise, if one individual attained enlightenment, all the other beings would simultaneously attain enlightenment. Or if one individual thought of Bodhichitta, all the other beings would think of Bodhichitta. This is not our experience. Each individual has a different mind or stream of consciousness. Yet the Natural State is the same in everyone; it has the same quality. The Yermed in all beings is the same. But this is not just One Mind occurring everywhere. The qualities of the human mind and the insect mind are different, but their respective individual Natural States have the same quality of Yermed. This is not like the assertion in Vedanta that only one Brahman exists. The attaining of Nirvana is not like a drop of rain falling into the sea. Whether we find ourselves in Samsara or Nirvana, there exists individuality.

If so, how is it that Samsara and Nirvana began? They have the same source and the same base. The Natural State is the basis of both Samsara and Nirvana. Although there is no absolute beginning for them in time, we can still explain things in logical terms. When we die, our Namshe, or consciousness, becomes unconscious. Our mind stops functioning when our internal breathing ceases to operate. The time when this actually occurs varies with the individual. When our external breathing stops, we look unconscious to others and our physical body becomes rigid and begins to deteriorate. Internally, we experience the various signs of the elements (our energies) dissolving. The elements begin to dissolve and cease to be the support of consciousness. When our internal breathing ceases, we black out. It is the same with all beings. At that time our Natural State as the Clear Light dawns, whether the individual is aware of it or not. The presence of the Natural State is Clear Light. All beings experience this; the difference lies in whether we recognize it or not. If we are practitioners of Dzogchen, it is much more likely that we will recognize the Clear Light as the manifestation of our own Nature of Mind at this time. Later, visions will arise. These manifestations are principally of three kinds: sounds, lights and rays. Various visions arise depending on the practice carried out in our previous life, especially if we have done Thodgal and dark retreats. In that case, we will recognize the visions as Thodgal visions, such as we experienced when we were alive. They come from inside us; they are not of external origin. And we recognize them because we have done practice.

When these manifestations arise, there are two possibilities. An accomplished practitioner will recognize that these sounds, lights, and rays represent Tsel (rtsal), the creative energy or inherent potentiality of the Nature of Mind and, having been recognized intuitively, they will liberate into the Natural State. The individual can become enlightened at that point, at that very moment. Then Nirvana will begin. But if one does not recognize them, then more visions will come. If these are related to the pure vision of Nirvana, then one will see the visions of the Zhitro (zhi-khro), the Peaceful and Wrathful Deities, their mandalas and retinues, and so on. At that point also, one may recognize that they are merely manifestations of the Nature of Mind and one will attain enlightenment soon afterwards in the Bardo. This is how Nirvana begins.

But if we have done no Dzogchen practice previously, then more and more visions will arise, and they will no longer be the pure visions of the Zhitro, but the impure karmic visions associated with the various destinies of rebirth. What they are specifically depends on our individual karmic traces inherited from the past. They are like our dreams. Not recognizing them as manifestations of mind, we think that the sounds, lights and rays have an inherent existence and, having an objective reality, exist independently of us. "Sounds" (sgra) mean vibrations (invisible), "lights" ('od) mean luminosity (visible colors), and "rays" (zer) mean shapes and forms. If we do not recognize that they are merely visions, then we think that they are real and have an inherent existence, just as we do in dreams before waking up. Ignorance starts at precisely that point, and this is the beginning of Samsara in the relative sense. Progressively the visions become coarser and more developed. They seem more and more real, solid and opaque. Then the passions arise and this is how Samsara evolves. Speaking in general, we can say that the Base for Samsara and the Base for Nirvana are the same. But when speaking of a specific individual in his present condition right now, it is the Base for his Samsara alone and not the Base for Nirvana. In the Dzogchen texts, we find explanations in general of the Base, but for us as individuals at present, the Base is specific, that is, it is the Base for Samsara only.

Every sentient being equally possesses the Natural State. The difference comes in the Bardo when the visions arise. We either recognize their nature or we do not. However, we do not have to wait until we die and find ourselves in the Bardo. Right now we can do dark retreat or Thodgal practice as preparation for the after-death experience.

The Natural State is like a great ocean; all beings are equally encompassed by it. There is no difference in this Base; it is the same everywhere because it transcends time and conditioning. So it is present with us now and we can have access to it. We can practice fixation on the white Tibetan letter A and look back at the watcher and the watched and they dissolve. Then at that moment we have the opportunity to recognize the Natural State.

This is the moment of recognition. We look back at thoughts and they dissolve. But where do they dissolve? They arise in the Natural State and they dissolve into the Natural State. We simply realize and understand this without creating thoughts about it. At the moment of understanding, there is awareness and this awareness is very clear and fresh. It is like being in a channel that is leading our boat to the sea. The channel represents our practice, whereas the great ocean is the Natural State itself. We have a proverb in Tibetan: If I am too close, I cannot see me; if it is too bright, I cannot see it. The Natural State is something that is always connected with us, but we do not see it. So this awareness (rig-pa) is only found just after a thought has liberated. When the clouds are cleared away, then we can see the luminous sky. Our practice removes the clouds. The examples are that of a channel of water leading to the sea or that of an only child returning to its mother. So that is why we need to practice.

This awareness developed in practice represents Tsel, the energy of the Base (rig-pa'i rtsal). How does this develop? It arises from the Base which is the Natural State. In the Dzogchen texts, for example, the Zhang-zhung Nyan-gyud (Zhang-zhung snyan-rgyud), there is a complicated explanation given of this process of evolution, and contradictions of other views are found here. [9] The Base is the source that creates everything, whether good or bad. Is this the same view as Vedanta? Sometimes the same words may be used, but the meanings are different. Tsel (rtsal) means potentiality, the potentiality of the energy of the Nature of Mind, which is not yet visible to the senses, whereas Rolpa (rol-pa) means a visible manifestation of energy. It is kinetic. Rolpa is like looking into water and seeing a reflection. If we look at a rock, we do not see any reflection; this reflection would be Rolpa.

What is the purpose of looking back and observing thoughts? To find if there is anything there. That discovery that there is nothing to find (mi rnyed) is the whole point. We have already spoken about what the Natural State is, and how we observe thoughts and how they dissolve. We just remain in this Natural State without changing anything. We keep in it continuously as long as we can. That is the practice. But if our remaining in the Natural State is not stable, then thoughts can arise and we are easily distracted. Then suddenly we remember to go back. Here three points are relevant: (1) In order to remain in the Natural State, we must have the energy to do so. If we are too loose, we can easily lose it. (2) There is no particular way to think, but we must recognize when agitation arises to disturb us. (3) We may be in the Natural State, but our experience may become dull and lack clarity and presence. So we need to be aware of these three points. If we try to do anything special, we will lose the Natural State. Beginners especially should practice only for short sessions, and then gradually extend the time of practice. If we try to force ourselves to practice for too long, more distractions will come.

Sometimes we can have a problem with agitation. New discursive thoughts arise spontaneously; we are not creating them deliberately. But if we are successful in remaining in the Natural State, whether discursive thoughts arise or not, they do not disturb us. We do not follow after them and become distracted. Agitation is of two kinds. Rough agitation is very easy to recognize, whereas subtle agitation is not because it is almost subliminal. Nonetheless, it becomes just as much a distraction. If we do not immediately recognize distraction, it will soon lead us astray. We can apply various methods here. When rough agitation disturbs us, we find that we cannot stop thoughts arising and control the mind. If we try to stop the thoughts, generally this will not work. It is very difficult to control the mind under any circumstances. If we have kept our energy and our clarity from the very beginning, then distractions will fall away. But when agitation becomes rough, then it is best just to stop practice for a while. There can be any number of causes for agitation, including bad health. As a countermeasure, we should take heavy, nutritious food and keep warm. Subtle agitation is much more difficult to recognize and counteract. We should try to stay in a room with less light, lower our gaze and the object of meditation, do some deep breathing and movement, put on warmer clothes, eat heavier foods, and so on.

If we lose energy, not during the session but afterwards, then we need to do exercises and other practices to increase our energy. If we lose strength or energy during a session, we should not add too much energy because this will cause agitation. When we lose a lot of energy, we experience drowsiness. This all depends on the individual. When we are drowsy we will go for a long time without clarity. Practitioners can lose much time and opportunity because of drowsiness. It is just like sleep, but it is not just a matter of taking a rest. If we find that our clarity is weak, we must apply antidotes. What can we do? First we must examine to see whether it is a health problem or simply a loss of energy. In the latter case, just take a break and get some fresh air. Try practicing in a high place, such as on a mountainside, and in a place which is not dark but well lit. We must judge these external circumstances for ourselves. For drowsiness, we can raise higher the object of meditation, take off some clothes, open a window for fresh air, do deep breathing and hold the breath, shake the body, eat lighter foods, and so on. But in general, especially at the beginning, it is better to practice in many short sessions, taking breaks in between. Then gradually we can extend the time of the sessions. Again, we can practice Guru Yoga and take initiations and receive the blessings from our Lama. We have to judge for ourselves what is best for our individual body and our circumstances.

When the body and the mind unite, we experience a pleasurable sensation, so when we realize Shamatha, or the calm state of mind, then physical problems will become less. Our minds will be happier and our bodies more comfortable. We can then easily bear the problems that go on around us. In general,

Guru Yoga practice can restore our energy. Also reciting prayers, so that we feel the actual presence of the Lama, can be helpful.

The principal practice here is to keep ourselves in the Natural State. In the beginning, it is best to practice for short sessions. If one can develop capacity in these short sessions, then the sessions can be gradually lengthened, and finally the advanced practitioner will be able to bring his practice into daily life. One will be able to walk, sit, eat, sleep, and so on, and yet remain in the Natural State. One will eventually be able even to think and talk while being in the Natural State. Then keeping practice to discrete sessions will not be very important. But for the beginner, discrete sessions are important.

In our meditation practice, it is important to understand that Shamatha or Zhine (zhi-gnas), the calm state of mind devoid of thoughts, is not Rigpa, the Natural State. The former is just an experience (nyams), the experience of no thoughts (mi rtog-pa'i nyams), whereas Rigpa is beyond the mind and beyond thoughts. But Shamatha practice may help us to get into Rigpa, the Natural State. In Dzogchen generally, it is not necessary to first practice Shamatha. If we practice contemplation in the Natural State, then Shamatha is present there naturally. We can do Shamatha practice according to the Sutra system without any reference to Dzogchen and the Natural State. We just select an appropriate object of meditation and concentrate our mind on it. We can have Shamatha without clarity or Rigpa, and we can then apprehend the empty state. That is the experience of being without thoughts. But for our practice to be Dzogchen, clarity and awareness must be equally present with this empty state. Emptiness alone is not sufficient. If we just practice Shamatha alone, then it is quite possible that we will be reborn in the higher mental realms of the Devas. [10] It is crucial to understand that Shamatha alone is not Dzogchen practice.

In early Tibetan texts, we also find these contradictions between Dzogchen and Shamatha. The Dzogchen texts insist that clarity and awareness must be inseparably present with the empty state; Shunyata alone is not Dzogchen. Not understanding this is a cause of confusing the two, Dzogchen and Shamatha. This is a key difference between Dzogchen and Ch'an Buddhism, which is usually expounded in accordance with the Sutra system. [11] In the empty state, there is nothing special there in terms of focusing, but with Dzogchen, clarity must be present. Shamatha maintains that it is sufficient just to stop the arising of discursive thoughts and to refrain from creating new thoughts. We simply remain in that gap between thoughts and expand the gap. What is the characteristic of this gap? It is just an empty space where no thoughts are present Shamatha has stopped the past thought and impeded the arising of the next thought. The mind then grasps that empty space and dwells in it. So there is a perception here, the result of grasping.

But in Dzogchen, there is no grasping at anything. Nor is there any special searching for an awareness or clarity. The awareness is already there, present from the very beginning, so there is no necessity to grasp or apprehend it. There is no perception created by the work of the mind. No mind work done at all; there is just presence. But in the case of ordinary Shamatha practice as defined by the Sutra system, there must be a perception there, that is, an apprehending of an empty state devoid of thoughts. There must be a thought present that knows that there exists a state without thoughts. This thought thinks: "This is Shamatha!" or "This is an empty state without thoughts!" So here the mind is functioning even where there are supposedly no thoughts. That is not Dzogchen. Nevertheless, through the realization and the perfecting of Shamatha practice, we can attain psychic powers such as clairvoyance (mngon-shes) and telekinesis (rdzu-'phrul). These develop because we have learned how to control the mind.

How do we verify that we are in the Natural State? How do we know when we are in it and when we have fallen out of it?

We can use methods here such as Guru Yoga and fixation on the white A. When we have been introduced to the Natural State, we know what it is from our direct experience. Then we can focus on the white A and look back into our mind and find nothing there. Then we continue in that state of presence. We know what the Natural State is because we have been introduced to it previously. If we are in the Natural State or Rigpa, it is just present there, and there is no problem or doubt. We do not need to examine it to see whether it is actually Rigpa or not. If we begin to examine, that is the work of the mind and we have gone beyond the Natural State. We are again caught up in thoughts. We are creating something. The Natural State is Rang-rig, or self-awareness as such; it knows itself without having recourse to any secondary thoughts or cognitions. Once we know its true condition, we can enter into it in the same way each time. It is just itself and knows itself. We do not have to verify it each time.

What can we do about subtle thoughts that arise? When a discursive thought dissolves, we have a moment of clarity. We are in a state of clear awareness. But if this clarity is not fully present, then subtle thoughts can arise. However, if we do not interfere with them or elaborate them, they will dissolve. Then just dwell in that moment when the thought dissolves. Do not try to do or change anything, but gently intensify the sense of awareness. The perception which apprehends the gap between thoughts is an experience; it is not what we mean by Rigpa. Shamatha, as we have explained, apprehends this gap, this empty space, and this apprehending thought is subtle. Dzogchen allows even that subtle thought or apprehension to dissolve and self-liberate. Then we leave everything just as it is. There is no thinking or apprehending. If we try to do something like perceive or apprehend an empty space, we fall out of the Natural State. Rather, in Dzogchen that empty state itself is awareness and knows itself because emptiness and awareness are inseparable.

The Natural State is just itself and nothing else, whether thoughts are arising or not. Having no thoughts (mi rtog-pa) is not the essential practice of Dzogchen. There is nothing wrong with having thoughts; it is natural for thoughts to arise. They represent the creative potentiality or dynamism (rtsal) of the Nature of Mind. When we are in the Natural State, there are no special thoughts associated with it. The Natural State is always there whether thoughts are present or not. The problem is to recognize this Natural State without being distracted by thoughts. Watching thoughts arise and dissolve again is one way to discover this for ourselves. It is like having an open window. There is no special apprehending or grasping involved. And if we are familiar with this practice of continuing in the Natural State, then when we find ourselves in the Bardo after death, we will also be able to enter into the Natural State. This will be like an only son who comes home to his mother's lap.

However, although we have been introduced to the Natural State, it is still possible for doubts to arise subsequently. In terms of doing practice, different people have different capacities. So even though we have been directly introduced, we may develop doubts where we think: "It is like this or that." Individuals have differing notions and understanding. We may possess a memory of having once been in the Natural State. But we have no reference point for this Natural State in our memory because memory is dualistic. Memories are thoughts and thoughts represent the working of the mind; they are not the Natural State. Memories, however, may help us to come back to the practice once we have lost it. When we enter the Natural State again, this memory, being a thought, dissolves. We are totally present; we do not live in the memory. If doubts arise, they are just thoughts. Just look back at this doubt and it dissolves.

The Natural State is beyond all thoughts and words. It just is, and it is inconceivable and inexpressible. But we must have our own personal experience of thoughts dissolving, and not just hear an explanation in words alone. How can we introduce the moon to a child? We point at the moon; the child looks at our finger and listens to our description and explanation. Our finger does not need to touch the moon, yet the moon is introduced to the child. So an explanation in words may be helpful by way of an introduction, but Dzogchen in itself is beyond thought and speech.

What is the benefit derived from realizing this Dzogchen nature? What is the purpose of all this? When we practice according to Sutra and Tantra, we cultivate Bodhichitta as our intention and we think of releasing other beings from the prison of Samsara. Now when we practice being in the Natural State, this is certainly of benefit to us and our happiness and peace of mind, but what of the benefit to other beings? Is this not like the Arhat of the Hinayana Sutra system who is thinking only of his own benefit and release from Samsara? If this is so, how can we then say that Dzogchen is the highest teaching? We can justly say that it is the highest because all virtuous qualities are already inherent in the Natural State from the very beginning. They spontaneously exist there, and include Bodhichitta, the perfections of Dana (generosity) and the rest, as well as the Shilas (moral precepts) of the Vinaya.

So if we practice the Natural State, this alone, all of these many virtuous qualities will manifest in us spontaneously and effortlessly. It is like a panacea, the one medicine that cures all ills. The potential exists there all the time. Therefore, we do not need to practice these virtues individually and cultivate them by means of discursive thoughts. It is like the butter inherent in milk; it is there all the time, even though we do not see it. All of the virtues of the Path are inherent in the Natural State, and we do not need to develop them individually one after the other. The Natural State encompasses all good things But we must know this first, for without the knowledge we can stray into wrong actions. This knowledge is the secondary cause for the manifestation of virtues.

It is like churning milk in order to bring out the butter. The butter is there all the time in the milk, but it is invisible; the churning is the secondary cause for its visible manifestation.

In practical terms, in order to realize these virtues, we should also pray to maintain the connection with the lineage of Dzogchen masters. This means practicing Guru Yoga regularly and offering puja to the Guardians and the Dakinis. Of course, this is on the relative level. It is not that the Natural State needs any of these activities; it is we ourselves who need them. Because all negative thoughts progressively dissolve into the Natural State, we find that our minds become much happier. Virtuous thoughts arise spontaneously and effortlessly.

Nevertheless, Dzogchen does not grasp at anything, even at virtuous things. In Dzogchen, we do not even grasp at the presence of awareness. We find no grasping there and no watcher. Both the watcher and the watched dissolve into the Natural State. Both the subject side and the object side simultaneously dissolve. But other schools are not satisfied to let thoughts dissolve and then find nothing there, no trace at all. They maintain that there must be a thought or a perception present that knows this state. Such a thought or perception, however, no matter how subtle, still represents grasping. This is not Dzogchen.

They assert that a subtle thought that knows this Shunyata must be present there, for otherwise we can know nothing at all. Only the presence of such a thought makes knowledge possible. When we practice Shamatha, we must have the presence of some object, whether a visible object like a white A, or a sound, or our breathing, etc. Then we find the gap between thoughts and focus on that empty space. We apprehend something, this empty space, and so there is a thought present there which knows that empty space. It knows this gap; it knows that there is a state devoid of thoughts. In other words, there is a thought which knows non-thought.

But this is not what Dzogchen asserts. According to Dzogchen, the Natural State is awareness as such; it is Rang-rig or self-aware; it does not need some other thought or perception to know it. Dzogchen says to let thoughts liberate of themselves and then just let everything be. It is just being in itself, and not the presence of some thought which knows "Just being." So this self-aware state is beyond thought. Thoughts arise and if we are in the state of presence (rig-pa), then there will be no interference with these thoughts. Thoughts come and go and the state is just as it is (ji bzhin-pa).

Action

How are we to connect our Dzogchen practice in meditation with the activities of our ordinary worldly life? Meditation (sgom-pa) is only one side, whereas the activities of daily life (spyod-pa) are the other. How can we link and connect them? And what benefit will we find in this? We experience the ill effects of the passions or negative emotions in our lives. and it is very difficult to stop them from doing this. It seems at times as if these negative emotions rule our lives. What antidotes can we apply to them?

The principal Dzogchen practice is to develop our capacity to continue in the Natural State. The more familiar we become with contemplation, the greater becomes its strength. We become calmer and disturbances grow less. The presence of the Natural State reduces the power of the passions and we manifest many virtuous qualities. We come to understand that external phenomena are not real, that they lack any inherent existence. Having understood this, we become less attracted to objects and it becomes easier to control the passions.

In our meditation sessions, we may practice keeping in the Natural State, even for long periods of time, but it is not so easy to apply this to our worldly life. Madhyamaka may be used to counter our belief in the inherent existence of external things, but what about the situation when a robber faces us on the road? Do we just think "He has no inherent existence" and he will just go away? When we meet something that is not according to our wishes, we have an emotional reaction of anger. This is because of our ingrained habit of thought, thinking that things exist inherently. Our meditation may not make the robber go away, but it can undermine the power of our emotional reaction to him, so that our mind is perfectly calm and clear, and we can make an appropriate response to our circumstances.

What is this inherent existence? We see a blue flower and we think that it really exists out there as an object, that it exists inherently. But this represents ignorance. We see things and think that they exist independently. And then we react to them emotionally. This basic and fundamental ignorance that falsely assumes the inherent existence of phenomena is the root cause of our negative emotions or passions. Everything else represents a secondary cause or occasion for the manifesting of these passions. To eliminate them categorically and comprehensively, we must go to their root cause. Otherwise, we simply attack the symptoms and not the cause. Ignorance means a lack of awareness; we see things in a false way. We think things have an inherent existence and so we grasp at them, and we experience attachment or aversion towards them. Then we have an emotional reaction of one, or the other, of the passions. Once this process starts, it is almost automatic and very difficult to stop. So we go to the cause. We can lessen attachments by means of meditating on Shunyata.

How can we understand Shunyata? Take again the example of the blue flower. Pull apart the petals and where is the flower? We find that there is nothing left behind. The flower is only a name for a phenomenon that we create with our minds and then use for purposes of communication. But it is nothing in itself. However, the naming misleads us because we think that what we name must exist and be real, whereas it is only a name. Language has come to dominate our consciousness and we think things actually exist because we name them and speak about them. We falsely think that language mirrors reality. We give the world a structure according to our use of language. But we mislead ourselves. We should understand that this whole system of phenomena has been created by ourselves. Not understanding this, ignorance gives rise to the passions. But meditation can weaken the force of the passions by attacking this link, this fundamental belief in the inherent existence of things.

In the same way, when we practice being in the Natural State, we come to understand experientially that thoughts may arise but they leave no trace behind. So, for the Natural State, there are no karmic traces left behind. It is totally free of them, intrinsically free. Thus we find here no bad seeds deposited as causes for negative thoughts or consequences in the future. But remember, this is only true when we are actually in the Natural State; for the ordinary everyday condition of our mind, everything works in terms of karmic causality.

How do we understand our worldly life and integrate the Natural State into it? What we have discussed above is one method. All phenomena are empty and created by our minds. With an understanding of this we lessen the power of attachments and passions and their hold over us grows weaker. We no longer grasp so strongly at anything. Madhyamaka tells us that everything is made up of our thoughts, that is, of names. But actually there is a different notion in Dzogchen; everything is a reflection or a projection of mind (sems kyi snang-ba). If we look into a calm pool of water, we see our entire world reflected, that is, sky, sun, moon, stars, mountains, trees, everything. But if we search, we do not find any of them there. There is nothing there, but we see everything reflected in the water. If we touch the reflection, we find only water. In the same way, all appearances arise in the Natural State and they dissolve again into the Natural State.

We can say that there is no inherent existence, but it is difficult to understand this in concrete terms because we are so habituated to think otherwise. However, engaging in this examination of phenomena, and meditating on the emptiness of all phenomena, helps us to become less attached to the things of everyday life. Dzogchen asserts that not only is everything empty, but that everything is a projection, a manifestation of energy (rtsal).

That is the first point here. Second, we should make an examination of the phenomena of our daily life. If we practice Thodgal, we will get visions. After the sessions of practice, we should compare these visions with the vision which is our daily life, our everyday karmic vision of human existence. The experiences of the Thodgal visions in sunlight or dark retreat provide us with an example of how visions arise and develop from the Natural State. When we do practice in a dark retreat, we will see visions with colors and shapes, and even though they may seem to be very real, we know that they do not have any inherent existence. If they did have an inherent existence, how would we be able to see them in a totally dark room when our physical eye cannot function? We may see a wild yak in our dark retreat room, although we know that this room is much too small to hold such a huge beast. We can see visions of the whole world in this room, although we know that the whole world could not fit inside it. Everything looks bright and clear and real, yet they are only projections. These are not real trees and mountains and yaks that we see in the room. Yet we see them and they look solid and real. These visions or appearances (snang-ba) are not seen by the physical eye or the eye consciousness; they are seen by Rigpa and they represent the energy or potentiality of Rigpa (rig-pa'i rtsal). Then they dissolve. They are liberated into the source out of which they have come in the first place.

If we examine matters, we discover that these Thodgal visions and the visions we call ordinary life share the same quality. Our vision of everyday normal life also arises from the Natural State, dwells in the Natural State, and dissolves into the Natural State. However, do not make these comparisons with ordinary life while in the Natural State, only afterwards.

Another comparison we can make is with dreams. The visions we call everyday life arise from our minds as projections. They are like dreams. They both seem real, these visions in the dream state and these visions in the waking state. But if we follow after a dream, what do we find? When we wake up, we find that nothing remains. Comparing them, we find that the dream state and the waking state, both being composed of our visions, that is, our projections, are equally unreal. Therefore, there is no point in grasping at these delusions and having emotional reactions to them.

Normally when we see phenomena we like, we desire them, and when we see phenomena we do not like, we become angry. But they are just phenomena or appearances. We must understand this, not just intellectually, but experientially. We can get intellectual understanding from reading a book or from hearing a lecture, but we get experiential understanding from practice. So practicing this comparison is useful to make us calm and less attached.

Fruit

Now that we know what the Natural State is, how to continue in the practice of the Natural State, and how take it into everyday life, we need to know what the results of practice are and what the ultimate goal is. This knowledge provides us with the reasons why we do practice. If we do not have this basic background, then we will not last very long in a Dzogchen retreat. But if we have a solid foundation, then the results will surely come.

We must consider the benefits of practicing Dzogchen. These benefits are both immediate and ultimate. The immediate benefit is that our mind becomes calmer and less disturbed by external circumstances and the unfavorable conditions of life. And since we experience less attachment and aversion towards things, our passions or negative emotions grow less and less, and we create less negative karma for ourselves. The ultimate benefit is that we realize liberation from Samsara and attain the enlightenment of a Buddha, manifesting the Rainbow Body of Light. That is to say, through the practice of Thekchod, we come to realize the primordially pure state of the Dharmakaya itself, which is the Fruit, and through the practice of Thodgal we come to realize the spontaneous manifestation of the Rainbow Body, both the Sambhogakaya and the Nirmanakaya, which is also the Fruit. [12]

But what about other sentient beings? Our perceptions of them are ultimately illusions. Are they empty phenomena and lacking any inherent existence? Yet all of them also possess the Natural State and are as equally caught up in their unreal projections as we are, depending on their individual and collective karmic causes. What can we do to help to liberate them from their suffering in Samsara?

If we actually realize experientially that all phenomena are illusion and then progress through the four stages in the development of vision (snang-ba bzhi), we will find that our entire vision of the world will become like rainbow light. The very solidity of reality will dissolve before us spontaneously and, in return, be reabsorbed back into its source. Even our own physical body, which is the result of karmic causes and a manifestation of human karmic vision, will dissolve into rainbow light and vanish into space. [13] All our visions will dissolve, and for us reality itself is exhausted (bon-nyid zad-pa) and vanishes, including the vision of our own material body. It has dissolved progressively into rainbow light and then into empty space.

But all other sentient beings, who are still caught up in their ignorance, remain behind in Samsara. However, we have not abandoned them. Because we are now fully and permanently in the Natural State, the virtuous quality of the great compassion for all sentient beings, which is inherent in it, manifests spontaneously and without limitations. This compassion is total, the great compassion, because it is extended to all sentient beings impartially. And by virtue of the power of this spontaneous compassion, we reappear to Samsaric beings as a Body of Light in order to teach them and help guide them along the path to liberation and enlightenment. This is the natural and spontaneous activity of a Buddha.

Conclusion

If we understand the real meaning and nature of Dzogchen, then it is not necessary for us to do anything special. If people slander us, it will make no difference because it will only be like an echo in a cave. Whether people say good things or bad things about us, it is the same empty sound. The point is that we have come to an understanding and can apply that understanding in our lives. All virtuous qualities already spontaneously exist in the Natural State. We do not need to seek anything else beyond the Natural State.

At the end of a session of practice, we should recite the dedication and prayers to send away any external and internal disturbances. This is how we practice Dzogchen on a daily basis. If we realize the Natural State and, having practiced it for some time, find that we are not ready to attain the Rainbow Body, then we must make a proper connection with regard to our next life. This is one primary reason for practicing in our present life. Thus we can do Bardo practice and Phowa practice before we actually die, and thereby we can gain some first-hand experience of what to do when the time does come to die, and thereafter in the

Bardo. This is making preparation before doing the actual practice at the time of death. In this way, we can prepare ourselves for realizing enlightenment in the Bardo after death or in our future life. These Bardo and Phowa practices have been explained elsewhere. [14]

CHAPTER 8

Rushans: The Preliminary Practices of Dzogchen

Talks by Lopon Tenzin Namdak,
Coos Bay, Oregon, November 1991.
Transcribed and edited by John Myrdhin Reynolds

Rushan Exercises

Here we shall briefly introduce the Rushan practices of Dzogchen. Rushans are the main preparation for entering into Dzogchen and for discovering "the Nature of Mind" (sems-nyid) as opposed to "mind" or the thought process (sems). This distinction is very important for Dzogchen. Rushans represent the real Ngondro (sngon-'gro) or preliminary practices for Dzogchen. Generally, we speak of external Rushans, internal Rushans, and secret Rushans. In the Bonpo tradition, these three kinds of Rushans are found, and it is customary to practice certain of the exercises for forty-nine days in a retreat. In these preparatory exercises, there is much visualization practice, really quite similar to the Tantra system. But these are not Dzogchen as such. The actual Rushans representing the real preliminary practices for Dzogchen introduce us to the Nature of Mind.

Impermanence of Life

But first we must say something about preliminary practices (sngon-'gro) in general. These preliminaries are very important and very necessary in both Buddhism and Bon. They represent the gateway or entrance to the practice of both Tantra and Dzogchen. They serve as a guide instructing us in what to do and what to think when we do practice. [1]

In general, we realize that our normal everyday life is impermanent and that death will eventually come to us. But we do not know when the hour of death will come. Among the preliminary practices there is a meditation on the impermanence of life in order to make this knowledge concrete for us. Death can come to us at any moment and it is sheer delusion to think otherwise. And if death were to suddenly come upon us, what could we do? Therefore, in the spiritual life generally, as found in all religious traditions, and also in Bon, there is much emphasis on considering what happens after death and in the future life. This is very important. According to Buddhism and Bon, it is karmic causes, what we have done in the past, that will bring future consequences, both good and bad. So we should not lose ourselves in the vain pursuit of wealth and worldly success because these will be of no help or benefit to us after we die. All sentient beings desire happiness and to avoid suffering, yet most of them do not know how to realize this. It is karmic causes that bring about future happiness or sorrow.

Karmic Causes and Consciousness

Karmic causes are discussed very much in the texts of both Buddhism and Bon. But how do we accumulate them? Virtuous actions such as generosity, not harming others, and so on, create positive karmic causes and in the future they bring about happy results. But it is not enough just to talk about doing good deeds and avoiding bad deeds. In our present life here and now, we are experiencing the fruits of what we have done in past lives. These past causes are not changed or modified by our actions in this present life because they have already been accumulated and their consequences will inevitably come in the same way as the shadow follows a body. But we can affect future consequences and future lives by our actions in the present that create new karmic causes. Therefore, in the present we can make a preparation for our future life. This begins by cultivating a good motivation.

Each of us, as an individual sentient being, has our body, speech and mind. Now, how do we develop a good motivation in terms of these three? First we must understand how we accumulate positive and negative karmic causes. We have eight kinds of consciousness and among them the most fundamental is the Kunzhi Namshe (kun-gzhi rnam-shes) or base consciousness. We call it the basis of everything (kun-gzhi) because it is the basis for the transmission of all karmic traces or bagchaks (bag-chags). It is called Alayavijnana in Sanskrit, and all of the other consciousnesses evolve out of it. Second, there is the defiled mind consciousness or Klishta-manovijnana (nyon-shes) and, third, there is the mind consciousness or Manovijnana (yid-shes). Finally there are the five sense consciousnesses, and this makes a total of eight Namshes or consciousnesses. The Madhyamaka philosophy asserts that there are only six consciousnesses: the five sense consciousnesses and the mental consciousness. According to Madhyamaka, ignorance, here meaning the defiled mental consciousness (klishta-manovijnana), is not a special consciousness, and so there are only six, whereas the Chittamatra philosophy, as well as Tantra and Dzogchen, explains the working of consciousness and the transmission of karmic causes in terms of these eight kinds.

How do these eight work? The five sense consciousnesses operate in conjunction with the corresponding sense organs and sense objects. All three, that is, the sense organ, the sense object, and the sense consciousness, must be present for there to be a sense perception. But then, this raw sense data must be correlated with memories (dran-pa) and with mind (yid) in order for this raw sense data to be organized into a recognizable object, which is then identified by a name. This work is done by the mental consciousness, and so the five sense consciousnesses act like servants continually collecting data, and are controlled by the mental consciousness which is like their lord or king. If the mind is a powerful ruler, he sends his five loyal servants out to engage in different kinds of activities appropriate to their capacities. The eye consciousness captures forms, shapes, colors, and so on, and brings these back to his master. The ear consciousness, and the rest, act in a similar way.

This is rather like bees going everywhere to take nectar from flowers and returning with it to the hive so that it can be made into honey. Our perceptions are like this honey; the raw sense data of the senses must be transformed into perceptions by the mind. Then at the end of this process, we are aware of the perception, but not the actual material, the raw sense data, out of which it was constructed. The sense consciousnesses, like the worker bees, do not make any evaluation of the perception as being good or bad; they do not judge. It is the mental consciousness that makes the decision good or bad. And then the perception mixed with this judgment is imprinted on the Kunzhi, or base consciousness, like making an impression on soft clay. That reaction to the original perception made by the mental consciousness is stored there and, in our ignorance, we do not focus on our actual immediate external experience, but we focus on this data stored in the Kunzhi and think "self", that is, we appropriate it or think it is "mine", and thus grasp at it and become attached to it.

So the focus of attention is on the stored data in the Kunzhi and not on reality. Thus the five sense consciousness are like the servants who run about everywhere in the world collecting wealth to bring back to the house of their master, the mental consciousness, who is like the king. He gathers together and tallies all this wealth of the senses, and then he deposits it in his treasury or storage hall; this is the Kunzhi. But he does not enjoy this treasure; that is done by his wife, the Klishta-manovijnana, or defiled mental consciousness. It is she who thinks "All this treasure is mine! I love it!" So this is how we collect karmic causes, and these are retained in the Kunzhi. But karmic causes are not something material, so there is always surplus room in the Kunzhi storehouse for more. There is no limit here, for we have been accumulating karmic causes over an infinity of past lives from time without beginning.

When we go to sleep at night, the five sense consciousnesses dissolve into the Kunzhi. During the waking state, the five senses are focused on the external world, but during sleep they return to the Kunzhi, like a turtle drawing his limbs into his shell when he is frightened. During dreamless sleep, there is only the Kunzhi present, but during sleep there are also periods when we have dreams. At that time, mental consciousness comes back into operation, but the five senses are still dormant. The material of dreams arises from inside, from the Kunzhi, rather than from outside as with the senses. Most of our dreams during the night are connected with recent daytime memories because that material was freshly stored in the Kunzhi. But at deeper levels, there are also memory traces left from previous lives. Everything is there in the Kunzhi, our entire past history over countless lives; nothing has been lost. So dreams arise from these causes deposited in the Kunzhi.

Also, the after-death experience of the Bardo is quite similar to the dream state. The Kunzhi is there all the time; it is not destroyed by an individual death. All of the past karmic traces are there in the Kunzhi Namshe and they are causes for the arising of karmic visions in the Bardo of Existence, the Sidpa Bardo (srid-pa bar-do). In the Bonpo tradition, we find Sutra, Tantra and Dzogchen, and in all three the existence of the Bardo between death and rebirth is taught. When our mind experiences death and leaves behind the lifeless physical body, our mind-stream continues to have experiences because the karmic causes still remain in the Kunzhi Namshe. We can have rough thoughts linked to the passions, as well as subtle thoughts linked to movements of subtle psychic energy (rlung, Skt. prana), and both of these can have effects. There is a union of mind and subtle prana which occurs, and this unification is necessary for rebirth to occur. Some schools maintain that it is the Kunshe Namshe itself, the storehouse or base consciousness, that takes rebirth, but Madhyamaka denies this and asserts that it is the mental consciousness (manovijnana) that undergoes rebirth. In any event, this mental consciousness is functioning in the Bardo. We see and feel just as we do in normal life or in a dream. We feel that we are inside a body with all its senses operating, even though it is not a material body, but a mind-made subtle body (yid lus). When we wake up from a dream, we know that the dream was unreal and not true. We realize that it was only a dream. But actually, we find ourselves in the same condition with the same feelings, whether we are in the dream state or the waking state. The same occurs in the intermediate state of the Bardo.

There is no precise time limit for the Bardo experience; forty-nine days is only a convention. We have the same feeling in the Bardo that we have in the dream state. At this moment, we think that the dream state is unreal and not true, whereas the waking state is real and true. Yet they are both the same condition and arise from karmic causes. Karmic causes give rise to our karmic visions, whether in the dream state, in the waking state, or in the Bardo. And they condition our future rebirth. So we need to be aware and scrupulous about accumulating positive karmic causes.

The accumulating of karmic causes by the mind (yid, Skt. manas) is fundamental and crucial. The mind is the great collector. For example, we may have a perception, the mind judges this, and we have an emotional reaction of anger. The mind then collects this thought complex and deposits it in the Kunzhi Namshe. It is imprinted and retained there in the vast Kunzhi storehouse. But how can we stop this process? How can we stop this linking up with the emotional defilements and with ignorance? Ignorance is the most difficult of all to stop because we have been habituated to ignorance for a long period of time. And it distorts everything; it distorts how we see reality, like a yellow dye on the glass of our spectacles that colors yellow everything we see. So, it is very difficult to see things clearly. This distortion is the result of ignorance and the passions.

All of our different kinds of consciousness are mixed up with this habit of ignorance; only just before we attain Buddhahood do we finally purify this radical and fundamental ignorance. But otherwise, it is extremely hard to purify ourselves of it. When we look out at the world, we do not see what is really there, rather, we perceive what has already been deposited within us, our karmic causes. Our vision of the external world is really a projection of our own internal condition; the external forms we perceive are influenced and distorted by our mind. The external object that we perceive does not exist inherently, so it is our ignorance that looks backward at itself and grasps at the object as being substantial and real.

As the result of this mistaken assessment, the passions come into existence as emotional reactions and impulses. In this way all the passions or negative emotions are created. If ignorance was not present there at the very beginning, the passions would not arise. Just look back into ourselves and observe how this ignorance functions. For example, if we intend to go to war, we must first know who is our enemy and what are his capabilities. We do not just jump into battle immediately. So we must recognize what the emotional defilements are and how they work, for it is by means of these defilements that we accumulate negative karmic causes. But there is also the possibility of accumulating positive karmic causes through acts of generosity, meditating on the Buddha image, and so on.

There are two principal types of karmic causes: collective and individual. For example, all human beings possess the same karmic cause for a human rebirth and for human karmic vision.

That is why we, as human beings, see the world in the same way. But the Devas and the Asuras and the Pretas see the world very differently from the way we humans do because they possess different collective karmic causes. We humans all see the ocean in the same way, but the ocean looks quite different to a fish or a Naga living in its dimension of water.

We also have our individual karmic causes which bring about our individual existence and circumstances. For example, there is a man and some people see him as a friend, while others see him as an enemy even though he is the same man. This is according to individual karmic causes. In himself, he is none of these things. Nothing has an inherent existence, but everything depends on the causes of perception. When an individual human being dies, his share of the collective vision possessed by humanity dissolves, just as when the sun finally sets in the west, all of its rays are gone, but the sky remains. So even though the individual cause dissolves, the collective cause remains because all other humans still participate in it.

Even though it is said that in Dzogchen there are no rules, it is not a matter of just going about everywhere and doing as we please. This is because, unless we are actually in the Natural State, karmic causality continues to operate as long as the mind operates. Some teachings have a direct meaning, whereas others have an indirect meaning. So when we hear the statements made in Dzogchen texts, it is very important to understand their context. It is important not to confuse and mix up these different types of meaning.

So, the principal thing here is for us to collect the ten virtues in terms of our activities of body, speech and mind. In terms of the body, we do not kill or steal or rape. In terms of speech, we do not lie, slander, use harsh speech, or gossip. And in terms of the mind, we do not have ill will, covetous thoughts, or wrong views. These ten virtues accumulate good karmic causes, whereas the ten vices do the opposite. But if we have bad karmic causes, then we need to release and purify them. We require methods to accomplish this, and this represents the spiritual path.

Methods of Purification

Even the Buddha himself was once an ordinary human being like us. But how did he attain realization? He followed the teachings of the previous Buddhas and practiced these teachings. Thereby he realized enlightenment and liberation from Samsara and, in turn, he gave the teachings to others. Anyone who follows the teachings of the Buddhas will most certainly attain results and purify negative karmic causes. Then that person will be like a man who has caught smallpox in the past; he will never catch it again because he is immune. The sickness of Samsara will never come back. And this is the purpose of following the teachings.

In the Bon tradition we have three principal methods for accomplishing release from the karmic causes of the passions or emotional defilements: Sutra, Tantra and Dzogchen. Take the example of finding a poisonous plant blocking our path. According to the Sutra method, we must avoid it, or else burn and destroy it utterly. The methods employed by the Sutras represent the path of renunciation (spong lam). But it is not necessary to destroy the poisonous plant because, if we know the proper method, we can transform the poison into medicine. That is the method of the Tantras and it represents the path of transformation (sgyur lam). But if we do not touch the plant and just leave it be, the poison will not harm us. This is the method of Dzogchen which represents the path of self-liberation (rang grol lam).

The Sutra system employs various antidotes in order to control the passions, whereas the Tantra system uses visualization to transform negative karmic vision into positive pure vision in our imagination. This is done with the mind, but the method in Dzogchen is different because Dzogchen goes beyond the mind. When the emotional defilements arise, we do not follow after them or give them support in any way. Nor is there any searching for antidotes or transformations. When they arise, we just leave them as they are and they will dissolve of themselves. Their energy will dissipate. They go away and do us no harm. In Dzogchen, we leave everything just as it is and it self-liberates. Thoughts can do no harm and they leave no traces behind. These are the principal methods for purifying the kleshas or passions and for purifying negative karmic causes.

The Outer Rushans

Now, having understood something about the inter-relationship of karmic causes and consciousness, we can see the purpose of preparation in Dzogchen. Here there are the preliminary practices known as Khorde Rushan Chewa ('khor 'das ru-shan dbye-ba), which means distinguishing between Samsara and Nirvana. We first have to know what is good about Nirvana and what is bad about Samsara. It is always imperative to know clearly the purpose of our practice, otherwise we may not persist in it. Nirvana means a state where all negative karmic causes and all obscurations have been purified. Samsara is cyclical existence, the beginningless cycle of death and rebirth, where in each lifetime we experience suffering.

Principally we speak of six realms or destinies ('gro-ba drug) and each has its characteristic forms of suffering. If we are reborn in the hell realms, for example, then we experience great suffering of heat and cold. When we are experiencing such intense suffering, how is it then possible to do any practice? The Rushan exercises, however, can give us some experience of what it is like there. If we are reborn in the Preta realm, then we experience intense hunger and thirst. But we do not die from this suffering until the energy of the karmic cause for Preta rebirth is exhausted. Reborn in the animal world, whether as a wild animal or as a domestic animal, we experience suffering. Even in the most pleasant realm of the Devas, where we possess great powers and long life, when our good karma for Deva rebirth is exhausted, we will suffer death and rebirth elsewhere. So there is no refuge from suffering anywhere in Samsara.

Now it is possible for us to accumulate karmic causes and then act on them, and it is also possible to accumulate karmic causes and not act on them. For example, we may become angry and kill someone, but we may become angry and not kill anyone. It is also possible to kill someone when we are not angry, such as soldiers do in a war. They just shoot other soldiers and do not even know the names of those they kill. In all of these cases, we are collecting karmic causes. However, at the time when the fruits ripen, we will experience different results depending on the precise causes. Sometimes the results come immediately, and at other times only after a long while, perhaps in a future life. This is because, in order for a karmic cause to manifest its result, certain other conditions or circumstances must be present as secondary causes. If these secondary causes are not present, then the primary cause does not manifest its result.

In general, karmic causes are not only associated with anger, but also very much with desire. If there is too much desire in the mind-stream of the individual, this will lead to rebirth in the Preta world as a hungry ghost. A hungry ghost continually experiences frustration of his desires, especially of great hunger and thirst which are never satisfied. This experience of suffering in the dimension of the Pretaloka is created by desire, just as suffering in the dimension of the hell worlds is created by anger. But if we have practiced many acts of generosity in our past life, then our suffering in the Pretaloka will be correspondingly less. We may have the cause for human rebirth and find ourselves reborn here on earth, but some humans are born into favorable circumstances, some are not. Some are rich and some are poor. Some may live an honest and good moral life, yet bad results come; while others live a dishonest and immoral life and good results come. They become rich and famous. This all depends on what karma the individual has accumulated in previous lives. A dishonest, ungenerous, and immoral person is accumulating bad karma in this present life, even though the results of this karma may not manifest until a future life. Their present fame and fortune are representing the results of their stock of past good karma. But this stock will be soon exhausted and they will fall and find themselves in much less fortunate circumstances. Such an individual is like a mad dog who bites many people and then dies himself. The effects of karmic causality are not limited to a single lifetime but exist within a continuum of lifetimes. So do not be deceived. The results of present actions will surely come.

There are cases where we tell lies, and do other things to help people which are normally considered bad, such as killing a bandit who is threatening to rob and harm many people. It all depends on our intention. If the intention is good, even though the action itself was bad, the results are much less than if we had the intention to do harm. And the same applies to good actions. In general, generosity is a good action, but providing guns to Iraq is something that would cause great harm to others. So it is not sufficient just to look at the act, we must always consider the intention, and it is our intention that fundamentally conditions our karma. That is why we must pay so much attention to motivation, to Bodhichitta.

One function of the Khorde Rushan exercises is to provide us with experiences, many experiences of all the six realms of rebirth and this, in turn, provides the conditions or secondary causes for many karmic causes to manifest their results. Normally these karmic causes are unconscious, we do not even know of their existence, but here, in the context of Rushan practice, we provide a space for their results to manifest. The consequences of these causes manifest as samskaras or unconscious impulses. By imitating or acting out the activities of body, speech and mind of diverse beings from the six realms, we allow the unconscious impulses deposited in the Kunzhi, which are associated with these realms, to manifest in consciousness at the present time. With complete abandon and with no inhibitions whatsoever, we allow the impulses to manifest and we yell, scream, run about frantically, weep. We do whatever the impulse directs. We act completely like a hell being, or like a Preta, or some animal such as a lion or like a bird. We may act like a Deva or an Asura, or many different kinds of people. There is no limitation. We imitate gods and goddesses such as Siva and Vishnu and Uma. Even though we become the god Siva and have the experience of Siva, we still remain in Samsara. Even though we are Siva, Uma is still constantly making trouble for Siva as her husband. So we discover that wherever we may be reborn in Samsara, we find no peace or refuge, and no permanent happiness. Even the Devas still experience suffering in Samsara.

In these Rushan exercises, we pretend and we do visualizations such as actually being a denizen in hell, or a hungry Preta in a great waterless desert, or a mighty lion in Africa. And through our activities of body, speech and mind we act out what these beings do and say and think, according to what impulses spontaneously arise. The visualizations and sounds we make provide the secondary causes for the manifesting of these samskaras ('du-byed). But all of this is done in a retreat, in isolation in the wilderness, far away from people and towns. Otherwise, if people saw and heard us, they would think that we have gone mad and send the police to take us to hospital.

Once we have acted out this karma for worldly beings and have exhausted it, we then imitate the Bodhisattvas and their efforts to help other beings. This is done through visualization and speaking out loud. Then we visualize that we are the Buddha surrounded by his retinue and we are giving teachings to them. We not only visualize that we are a Buddha, but we actually speak aloud, giving teachings to this imaginary audience. Our intention is to release them from their suffering in Samsara. But even a

Buddha does not have the capacity to save everyone because they have free will. The Buddha is like the sun which sheds its light equally and impartially everywhere, but the individual must come outdoors, out of the shadows, in order to receive and enjoy the sunlight. The individual must voluntarily come to the Buddha, hear the teachings, understand them and put them into practice before any results, that is, salvation or liberation from Samsara, can be attained. The individual cannot be coerced into salvation. But a Buddha can use skillful means to subdue difficult beings, and so we next visualize ourselves as a wrathful deity and subdue others, transforming them into disciples who listen. In this way we come to experience all good and bad conditions, everything of Samsara and Nirvana. These exercises and activities represent the outer Rushans.

The Inner Rushans

Then we visualize ourselves successively as the seven Buddhas, that is, the six Dulshen, plus Shenlha Odkar. The latter, Shenlha Odkar (gShen-lha 'od-dkar), is the Sambhogakaya aspect of the Buddha. He is a radiant white in color and is attired in all the costly jewels and silks worn by a great prince, thus signifying the richness and inexhaustible abundance of the Sambhogakaya. The six Dulshen ('dul gshen drug) are the six Nirmanakaya Buddhas projected into the six realms of rebirth in order to teach the path to liberation to the sentient beings imprisoned there. According to one system, these six Dulshen are as follows:

1. Mucho Demdrug (mu-cho ldem-drug) is blue and red in color; he appeared in the hell realms in order to transform anger and hatred by means of unconditional love and friendliness.

2. Sangwa Ngangring (gSang-ba ngang-ring) is red in color; he appeared in the Preta realms in order to transform greed and desire by means of total generosity.
3. Tisang Rangzhi (Ti-sangs rang-zhi) is blue in color; he appeared in the animal realms in order to transform ignorance and confusion by means of great wisdom and total knowledge.
4. Drajin Pungpa (Gra-byin spungs-pa) is golden in color; he appeared in the human world in order to transform envy and jealousy by means of total expansiveness.
5. Chegyal Parti (lCe-rgyal par-ti) is light blue in color; he appeared in the Asura realms in order to transform pride and arrogance by means of total peacefulness.
6. Yeshen Tsugphud (Ye-gshen gtsug-phud) is white in color; he appeared in the Deva realms in order to transform indolence and sloth by means of total diligence and vigor.

All of these figures are emanations or projections of the Nirmanakaya Buddha, Tonpa Shenrab Miwoche, who lived in Olmo Lung-ring in Tazik some 18,000 years ago. He manifested in each of these dimensions in order to purify these realms and teach the path to liberation and enlightenment.

We practice being these Buddhas successively for seven days and recite their mantras. We visualize rays of light in different colors coming out of our hearts and purifying these six realms. We send these rays of light into the hell realm, into the Preta realm, and so on, and manifest Nirmanakaya Buddhas who teach there in those realms. The beings who reside in those realms turn to the right and listen to the teachings. We also visualize Yidams appearing in different world systems. They emanate lights and recite mantras to purify all these realms and the beings inhabiting them. This method here is very much like Tantra, involving a lot of visualization and transformation, although that is not the usual

Dzogchen practice. We practice in a retreat in this way for forty-nine days and these exercises represent the Inner Rushans.

The Secret Rushans

Now we come to the Secret Rushans. All things are created by our minds. When we look back into ourselves, we see how good things, like the activities of the Buddhas and the Bodhisattvas, and how bad things, like the sufferings of Samsaric beings, are all created by the mind. Thus Samsara and Nirvana are equally created by the mind.

Now visualize a white Tibetan letter A in the space in front of us. Focus on this acutely and do this as long as possible without agitation or distraction. Then look back and see who it is who is focusing on this white letter A. We discover that the watcher and what is watched simultaneously disappear. Again focus on empty space, just the location in space where the white A had been, but without visualizing anything. Just gaze into space without thinking anything. And look to find where the mind is. When we focus on an object like the white A, we find that the mind becomes calm and one-pointed. Now we search to find the mind. Where is it located? Is it inside the body or outside? Does it have any color, shape, or form? What qualities does it have? We must do this research and thorough examination in order to discover for ourselves what the mind is and where it is. What do we find? We try to search for the Nature of Mind in this way. We must do this until we are satisfied.

We observe our thoughts: From where do they come? Where do they stay? Where do they go? Do they arise from inside the body or from outside? We just focus our gaze into empty space and remain for some time that way. We just observe; we just look at where thoughts arise, stay and go. What is their nature? What are their qualities? We must continue to do this until we are satisfied.

We should do this practice only in short sessions, and then stop. After a break, do it again. Gradually we can extend the period of time when we are not distracted or disturbed. In retreat, do four sessions during the day and four sessions at night. If in the beginning, we stay in the session too long, or try to force ourselves, we will lose our focus. But if we practice only in short sessions, things will develop much better. If we become disturbed, we take a break and go outside and face east or focus west (gazing into the sky with our back to the sun) and try again. When the mind is not much distracted, we try to keep it one-pointed. We discover that the mind never goes away; it is always present. And although we find an incessant movement of thoughts, the mind is not something material.

Recognizing the Nature of Mind

We have been continuously searching for the mind. But if we try to do or correct anything while we are focusing, agitation will disturb us and thoughts will come more and more. But check to see what is the condition of the mind, where is it and what does it do. Is it material or not? Material things have size, shape, and color. Does the mind have these qualities? Seek to find the mind. However, success in this searching for the mind will depend on the skill and capacity of the practitioner. If we are trying to follow the teachings, but we just think the mind must be like this or that, this thinking itself becomes an obstacle. Searching for the mind means just looking; it does not mean thinking or speculating philosophically. If we find something from all this looking, then we must discuss it with the Lama. But if we just read what is said in the texts or hear explanations, and then think the mind is this or that, it is not sufficient, even though we utter the correct answers. Why? Because these explanations, whether correct or not, are only thoughts created by the mind; they are not the mind itself. The teachings indeed say the mind is like this or that, and we may think of the correct answer and repeat it verbally, but this answer is only something created by mind.

Here in Dzogchen, we are not thinking or creating concepts; we are simply looking directly at our own immediate experience. When we discover this experience for ourselves, then we can compare it with what the texts say. Searching for the Nature of Mind is not just thinking thoughts about the Nature of Mind. We are searching for the real truth, what is really there. Thoughts are secondary; they are one or more steps removed from our immediate experience. They are about the past, but our immediate experience is here and now in the present moment. What is our immediate experience? Do not think about it; just look at it. What do we find?

From these Rushan exercises we come to know experientially that everything of Samsara and Nirvana is created by mind. But just to know this is not good enough. We see these thoughts, whether good or bad, arise but now we must search for the Nature of Mind which is beyond thoughts. It is not necessary to search for thoughts because thoughts are always there; they arise incessantly. Now we search for the Nature of Mind which is beyond thoughts and beyond the mind. We must realize by way of our direct immediate experience what is mind, the incessant arising of thoughts, and what is the Nature of Mind.

If we do not recognize the import and nature of Dzogchen, and only cultivate small virtues, this will bring us temporary happiness, but we will not realize the ultimate result. This is because we have not gone to the root of the matter. We will only come back and circulate again in Samsara. So the practitioner must understand the necessity of doing practice. According to the Dzogchen teachings, we must first recognize the Nature of Mind. Once we have recognized it, then it is not necessary to keep checking our Nature of Mind to see if it is correct or not. That checking is the working of the mind, and any working of the mind interferes with being in the Natural State. The very act of checking or examining immediately changes the whole situation, so it is no longer the Natural State. Therefore, any thinking or examining is done after the session and not while we are in contemplation.

When we practice, disturbances may come. We can use various methods to get rid of them and thus our meditation will become more stable. But this meditation, if we do not examine it, is ordinary meditation (according to the Sutra system), or is it Dzogchen? Is it merely a state of meditation created by the mind or is it real contemplation, a state beyond the mind? We look back at the mind and simultaneously the watcher and what is watched disappear. But is this statement correct or not? Does something remain behind? When the thought dissolves, we just leave everything as it is until the next thought arises. Is there an empty space or gap between these two thoughts? Is it really empty? Is it clear? At that moment when the thought dissolves, is that space clear and bright? If, in that gap, our presence is very clear, even though there is no thought there, then we are aware and alert. We are not sleeping. At that moment we have the possibility of realizing the Natural State. But if we think that it must be like this because it says so in the text, then this is only a thought created by the mind. It is not immediate experience. Once we know what the Natural State is, then we do not need to check in order to decide whether or not we are in the Natural State. If we do so, then we have fallen out of the Natural State.

So we should simply observe thoughts without trying to change or modify them. Just keep everything as it is and thoughts will dissolve by themselves. This is self-liberation. They self-arise and they self-liberate. But we should not think "empty" or "dissolved" because that is thinking, which is the operation of mind. The Natural State is beyond the mind, and if we start to think, we lose it. So just leave everything as it is. This state that we discover is inconceivable and inexpressible. There is nothing to create here, nothing to develop or visualize. It is totally complete and perfected just as it is. That is why we call it Dzogchen or the Great Perfection. There is nothing to be added to it or subtracted from it; nothing to be modified or corrected. It is just as it is, totally perfect. Everything is already there. So just leave it as it is. There is no problem; so do not create any problems.

Just after a thought dissolves, we may have an experience of no thought and of emptiness that is inexpressible. After the session is over, we can examine and think about this experience; we can even discuss it and check to see whether our mind is like this or not. We have a memory of the experience, so we are able to check it. But when we are in contemplation, in the Natural State, we do not do any examining or checking because that is the mind working. Each of us needs to have our individual experience of this. We look back into our mind at the thought, and then it dissolves. Does this happen or not? Do we find this gap between thoughts?

If we realize the Natural State for the moment, then there is no special description to be made of the state of calm or of the movement of thoughts. There is just this presence, whether there is calm or movement, it makes no difference. But this Natural State of Rigpa is not the same as just relaxing and having a blank mind with no thoughts present for a little while, or like deep sleep without dreaming, or like unconsciousness generally. This is because a bright clarity is present here in the Natural State. We are aware and we are alert, although we are not thinking. This is nothing special and it is quite normal, but usually we are unaware that we are aware.

It is also normal for thoughts to arise, and we should recognize this process, as well as the gaps between thoughts. And in those gaps we find an awareness or presence. That is Rigpa and this gives us the opportunity to see the Nature of Mind directly and nakedly, that is, without interference from mind and thoughts. But normally we do not recognize this, just as we do not recognize the presence of the sun in the sky when it is entirely filled with clouds. Although we do not see the face of the sun, the sun is there all the time. If it was not there, we would have no illumination at all. So we do not think about anything, but just remain in this state of presence as long as we can. This is the real meditation.

When the next thought arises, we do not try to do anything or change anything. We just let it arise and leave it as it is. But we are totally aware. It is like a mirror reflecting whatever is set before it. The mirror does not have to do anything; it is just its inherent quality to reflect and it does this effortlessly and naturally and spontaneously. And when we do not interfere by means of the mind, then the thoughts just liberate by themselves. We do not have to do anything. It is like the wind blowing the clouds from the sky; they dissolve into space without our having to do anything. We just watch the thoughts as we watch the clouds in the sky. We do not care one bit, whether they come or not. The thoughts liberate and we remain in a state of awareness. We have no expectations and no regrets. At the beginning of meditation practice, we wait for the thought to dissolve. This is by way of an introduction; later we do not need to do this. Dzogchen means that we leave everything just as it is. We do not need to focus or to expect or to wait. We do none of these things, yet we are globally aware and present. So there is nothing special here; we are simply like the bright, empty sky.

Meditation

Usually meditation means that the mind is working, and there are stages in this process. We begin with Shamatha, or the calm state of mind, and eventually this develops into Vipashyana, or higher insight. Things are explained this way in the Sutra system. The mastery of Shamatha brings with it a pleasant sensation in the body, a feeling of blissfulness. There are also experiences of clarity and of being empty without thoughts. These experiences occur naturally as the result of our meditation practice. When we practice meditation successfully for some time, we realize four successive stages as the result of meditation. These are known as the four Dhyanas and, as a consequence of realizing them, we have the possibility of rebirth in the Brahmalokas, the higher mental planes which are the dimensions of the Brahma gods.

There are sixteen levels or mental planes called Brahmalokas and they belong to the Rupadhatu, or world of mental forms. Three of these levels, or Brahmalokas, are correlated with the first Dhyana, the next three with the second Dhyana, three more with the third Dhyana, and the seven highest levels with the fourth Dhyana, that is, a total of sixteen, though some traditions count seventeen. The highest among all these levels is the Brahmaloka called Akanishtha, or Ogmin ('og-min), and here dwell the gods of pure light ('od lha). These Brahma gods are higher than the Devas and the Hindu gods who dwell on the astral planes of the Kamadhatu or Desire World. The Desire World is so-called because all of the beings who dwell within it experience sense desires, whereas the Brahmas live a purely abstract mental existence, although they inhabit subtle bodies of light. Beyond the Rupadhatu is the Arupadhatu, or formless dimensions, consisting of four Samapattis or levels of cosmic consciousness. There are also gods, higher even than the Brahmas, who dwell in these dimensions, but they have passed beyond form and are invisible.

Nevertheless, all of these levels of existence belonging to the Kamadhatu, the Rupadhatu, and the Arupadhatu are still part of Samsara because they are brought about by causes and are impermanent. The cause of the Dhyanas and the Samapattis is meditation. The first Dhyana is characterized by examination, analysis, bliss, rapture, and one-pointedness of concentration. These factors are progressively reduced as we ascend through the Dhyanas, until one-pointedness alone remains. Nevertheless, the mind is operating throughout, and the duality of subject and object persists. The four Samapattis are far more abstract because there are no concrete objects of meditation but just open, unobstructed space. With the first Samapatti, our meditation is empty and expansive like infinite space. At the second Samapatti, our consciousness becomes infinite. But in both cases there is still duality and grasping, whether at an infinite empty space like the sky, or at consciousness itself. At the next two levels there is nothing whatever specific to grasp or apprehend because only a very subtle consciousness exists. It is focused as a single point and yet, at the same time, it is infinite. But consciousness is still there because we are alive and the body is not dead. There is focusing and apprehension, so there is still duality, and this is not the same as Rigpa or the Natural State.

The Dhyanas and Samapattis are conditioned states of being brought about by causes. Therefore, they are impermanent and belong to Samsara. But the Natural State of Dzogchen is without any grasping or duality. It is a state beyond the mind and beyond meditation because it is totally unconditioned. But otherwise, in our development in meditation, we have these four stages of Dhyana or concentration, and these bring experiences of pleasurable sensation to the body and of bliss to the mind. [2]

We need to have some experience of this. We are trying to attain a recognition of the Nature of Mind, but these Dhyana states are not the Nature of Mind. It is a mistake to think so. Rigpa is not meditation. Meditation is work done by the mind. It is not simply a matter of having a blank mind or no thoughts; such a state on its own is not the Natural State. Just being empty like the sky is not the Natural State. Emptiness as such, or focusing on emptiness, or being as empty as the sky, or nothing existing, or focusing just on consciousness; none of these Samapattis is the Natural State. They are experiences created by the mind; they are conditioned and impermanent. In these Dhyanas and Samapattis, a very subtle consciousness continues to exist and we focus and apprehend, but this is not the Natural State according to Dzogchen. We have to find this Natural State which is beyond the mind for ourselves, and then remain in it as long as possible. This is what is known as Thekchod and it is not meditation, but beyond meditation. It is non-meditation.

When we practice Dzogchen, our state is clear and bright, even though we do not apprehend anything. We are simply aware. This non-meditation is the correct meditation. And in this way we discover the Nature of Mind. Now in our practice, we may allow thoughts to dissolve, but then we may find that our awareness or sense of presence is not clear. We may find that we can stay in this state of a blank mind. This simply looks like unconsciousness. This dull blank state of mind is called Lungmaten (lung ma bstan) and it is not the correct meditation. Some practitioners are able to stay in this Lungmaten condition for hours without distraction, but this state is only an experience; it is not the Natural State or Rigpa. Certainly, it is a very deep state, but it is not true samadhi, for real samadhi is without any grasping, and it is also bright and clear. Ordinary Shamatha is just a calm state of mind; it is just an experience. In this dull state of Lungmaten, we cannot even move, so it is like being asleep. It is a deep, but a dull, meditation. To confuse this with Dzogchen is a mistake.

When we practice in this way, suddenly we may experience a very strong grasping like "my!" or "myself!" This arises in a very uncalled-for way. This event represents the grasping at the inherent existence of a self as something independent. If we allow ourselves to pursue this and identify with it, we will mix it into everything and it will come to disturb us. We develop a sense of self, of self identity, and it comes to pervade all our experience. And if we continue to meditate and develop profound levels of concentration, then when we die we will find ourselves reborn among the long-lived gods in the Brahmalokas of the Rupadhatu. Nevertheless, this result is impermanent, even though it may last for an exceedingly long period of time. Rebirth in heaven does not represent liberation from Samsara.

Or, on the other hand, we may practice and have an experience of emptiness and no thought, and then we may conclude that ultimately nothing exists. All mind, all bliss, all karma, and so on, simply vanish. If we pursue this experience, it is possible that we may fall into a nihilistic view This is not correct.

Or, we may observe the arising of thoughts and then grasp at them very strongly, thinking "my country", "my family", or whatever. This will not bring us to the real practice of Dzogchen in meditation. But, at other times, we may meditate and keep ourselves in the pure Dzogchen view. Thoughts may arise, but we do not interfere with them or grasp at them with the mind, and so they dissolve again of their own accord. They self-liberate (rang grol). But even though they dissolve, our awareness or sense of presence, our sense of being there, remains very bright and clear. All of the senses are functioning at their optimum, and yet we do not move from the Natural State. That is the correct Dzogchen practice and the right view.

Sometimes we may feel that we do not want just to remain in the Natural State, but that we want to practice the visualizations of the deities and mandalas, and so on. So, it is better at that time to do some sort of Tantric practice. Indeed, some people are not satisfied at all with the Dzogchen view and want to do visualization practice. Let them do it, by all means. But if we want to be a Dzogchenpa, we must realize that there is nothing here to be created by the mind. If something is created by the mind, it is artificial and temporary; it is not the Natural State. If we have not discovered the Nature of Mind and the inseparability of clarity and emptiness, then all of this visualizing of mandalas and deities will only prove to be a disturbance, and we will not find ourselves in the Natural State.

Continuing in the View

We have described some wrong meditations where we actually do not find ourselves in the Natural State. What is it that we can do? Just remaining continuously in a bright sense of presence without grasping at anything will bring us a sense of inexpressible bliss. We will continue to see all of the mountains, lakes, trees, houses, people, and so on, that exist in the world, but we will not be distracted by anything that we see or hear. We remain in a sense of presence (rig-pa) that is bright and clear, just like a mirror that reflects all of these same things in the world, but is not affected or changed by what it reflects. We become like that mirror. It will be the same whether we are reflecting the human world, as we are doing now, or the hell realms, or the Pretaloka, or the Asuraloka, or the Devaloka, or whatever. All of them are merely reflections and they make no changes or modifications to our Natural State.

No matter what circumstances or what worlds we find ourselves in, we are without any expectations or changes. We are just what we are, the Natural State which is like a mirror. It is clear and empty, and yet it reflects everything, all possible existences and all possible lifetimes. But it never changes and it does not depend on anything else. It is just itself, and nothing special. Even if the mind finds itself dull or drowsy or agitated, the Natural State is in no way disturbed or modified by this. So there is nothing to be removed and nothing to be purified in any particular way. For example, this is like the sun shining in the sky. It occurs naturally; no special work or effort is required. It is like a lamp illuminating a dark room; it does this effortlessly. It is just the nature of the sun or the lamp to illuminate. There is nothing special to be done to remove the darkness. This is the pure view of Dzogchen.

How to Practice Meditation

Now we come to the second part of the text. In the above, we have provided a direct introduction and attempted to correct some wrong views. Now once we have discovered and recognized the real nature of Dzogchen, which is the Natural State, how are we to practice it? When we are beginners, if we attempt long sessions of practice at first, we will become restless and develop other problems such as headaches, pain in the eyes, and so on. We will grow tired and become fed up with meditation. Therefore, we should begin practicing with many short sessions, taking breaks in between, rather than attempting prolonged sessions. This will keep us in a good condition, and thus we will become familiar with the practice. Later, when we are more familiar with it, we can extend the sessions little by little. In this way, meditation will become more of a habit. But we must judge this for ourselves according to our feelings, because every practitioner is different.

What is the time to practice? It is best to begin in the spring. Also, it is best to stop at midday, otherwise we will become tired. Then it will be very difficult to make progress in meditation. Midday and midnight are not good times to practice. If we persist in meditation at those times, sleepiness will tend to overcome us. Also, after drinking wine is not a good time for the same reason, or after hard physical labor. If we try at those times, then our feelings will be like a fever. Before meditating, we should not eat too much or eat rich or heavy foods, especially onion and garlic, which will make us overly warm and feel heavy. In the early morning, in the afternoon, and in the evening, these are the best times to practice because our clarity is at a maximum. So, at these times we keep to ourselves to practice contemplation. We should make a precise timetable and keep to it habitually. But sometimes we can change the time because if we remain too rigid, this will create problems and we will not want to meditate.

What do we do between sessions? Our normal position is sitting crosslegged, with our two hands in the equipoise gesture, our necks are bent, and our gaze not too open and not too closed, looking down at nose level. Sometimes we need to move or shake our body. If we sit for too long without moving, we will become very uncomfortable. Our eyes gaze out into space. But when practicing contemplation in the Natural State, it is also possible for us to practice in other positions, for example, while lying down, or sometimes standing up and moving about slowly, or even walking. Someone who is really proficient at contemplation can even be in the Natural State while eating or when speaking to others. But the point is always that one is not distracted. Someone who is proficient can even go into a crowd of people and still do practice. Such a person can practice while engaging in the four activities of sitting, standing, lying down, and eating, and this will not disturb the Natural State. This is a sign that our meditation has become stable.

What is a suitable place for practice? The best is a solitary place which is pleasant and very quiet. A mountain should not be too high and a valley not too close. The water nearby should be clean and it will be good if there are many flowers blooming and many herbs growing. It is a place with few distractions; no people, no tourists, no robbers, no television, no cars, no airplanes. Here we set up a comfortable seat in the shade, and any necessary shelter. The food we eat is nutritious and light, not too heavy. In our hermitage, or our tent, or our cave, we can practice at any time. Once we have become familiar with the meditation, then we can change the site; we can go higher into the mountains, or into the rocks, or to the lake, or to the place where water flows. Generally we choose pleasant places which do not disturb us. But sometimes we can use a difficult and unpleasant place. Wherever we practice meditation, we should look for the signs that show we are familiar with the practice.

Disturbances to Meditation

When we are practicing meditation, there are several kinds of disturbance that can arise. For example, we may be in meditation but we lose awareness, and it seems as if we are sleeping. This is a sign of a loss of energy. We need to renew our strength and our clarity, but not to counteract drowsiness to such an extent that we are then disturbed by agitation. We need these three things: strength, clarity and calmness. If we find that we have lost awareness and things are not clear, what can we do? There are several methods to apply according to the cause of disturbance.

If you find yourself afflicted by drowsiness, go to practice in a high place where the air is fresh, or to an open space, or if you are inside, open the window and let more light into the room. If this is not sufficient, go to some place where there is a strong wind. If we find that we are still disturbed, we can wash our head and face, as well as our hands and feet. The cold water will refresh us. Also, changing the site of practice may help. Try practicing without any back support or pillow. Get up and move about and do some deep breathing and yoga exercises.

Or we may find that we are disturbed by agitation. We may try to concentrate, but the concentration is too weak and we find ourselves disturbed by thoughts arising. Or external sights and sounds may disturb us. Move to a quieter, more remote place, or try practicing in a relatively dark room. If our bodily health is not good or our diet poor, this can bring agitation. In this case, we can take some nutritious meat broth and a little chang (beer or wine) to make us feel warm, relaxed and comfortable. But these are to be used as medicine. Nevertheless, we must judge matters for ourselves.

Sometimes when we practice meditation, thoughts will come automatically. For example, thoughts of money, or personal affairs, or sex, and so on, and these can also agitate and disturb us. But we should consider that all of these thoughts, good and bad, of friends and enemies, are only experiences in a dream. They have no inherent existence, and so there is no point in grasping at them and following after them. Remember that everything is like an illusion. Do not give any support to these thoughts; just let them go.

Also, when we are practicing meditation, we may have thoughts like: "Is this the Natural State or not?" and "Is this the pure Dzogchen view or not?" and "Is this clear or not?" and "Am I really meditating, or is this just my delusion?" And other kinds of doubts may also arise in our mind. All of these represent the self-agitation which we create and encourage. This is an indication that we do not know much about the Dzogchen view, so we must do more reading and studying of the Dzogchen teachings in order to overcome the deficiency. Also, it is good to discuss one's doubts with the Lama, if possible. These doubts, at first very subtle, can grow and cause us a great deal of agitation. We must examine to see and decide whether our meditation is good or not. Continue for a time meditating and then check it. But there is no checking or examining while we are in the Natural State, otherwise, we fall out of it. Or, we may have many subtle thoughts moving subliminally. Try to recognize this when it is occurring. These thoughts are like thieves and there is no special antidote to them. Just let them liberate by themselves without clinging to them. If we can do this, disturbances will become less and less.

Sometimes our body will shake spontaneously, or we feel as if we have no head, or our psychic channels shake, or our mind feels light and spacey, or we have pains in our joints. At that time do some self-massage. Perhaps we hear loud sounds in our ears. In that case, take some heavier food and massage yourself with oil. But in any event, do not try to force yourself.

Sometimes we start the practice and we find that we are not pleased with it and become fed up. Our eyes hurt, we have headaches, we cough a lot. These are all signs that we are trying to force our concentration too much. Just relax and gaze loosely into space. Do not hold the mind too tight. And always practice in many short sessions, none of them too long.

We may have the desire to do something with our hands, to sing or to watch television; this is a sign that we are not sufficiently devoted to the Dzogchen view. Therefore, we need to study this view more and think about the unique opportunity provided by a precious human rebirth, the impermanence of life and so on. Remember that everything in the world is a delusion and we cannot depend on it. Recall the hell realms, the Preta worlds, and so on, and the suffering experienced in all of them. These thoughts will motivate us to devote ourselves to the practice of the Dharma. If we do not know these things, we need to study them.

Signs of Right Meditation

Practicing meditation correctly means that we will grasp at things much less and that our clarity will increase. There is no specific way to apprehend either clarity or emptiness. We should just continue in a relaxed state without grasping. But our awareness (rig-pa) is very present and bright, and we remain this way. Thoughts arise spontaneously and they liberate spontaneously. And the thoughts become less and less, and our awareness is stable and clear. When we are practicing, there is no special feeling to be explained. But when this immediate sense of presence is very bright, we call that Vipashyana. These are all signs that we are practicing the right meditation. Also being unable to explain it is a sign that it is the right meditation.

When we are practicing meditation and our drowsiness disappears, that is also a sign. If, when we are meditating, we suddenly think "My master is so kind; I am practicing so well and I am satisfied", that also is a good sign. If we have been practicing meditation during the day, and then at night, we dream that we are meditating, that also is a positive sign. If our appearance remains young, that is a good sign. Our thoughts remaining calm is a good sign. Not having strong thoughts when our relatives come to visit, that is a good sign. These are all signs that our meditation is going well. When others slander or praise us and we do not care, this is a good sign also. Even though we receive teachings from the Buddha himself, we do not have any expectations. We are not disappointed if there are no results. These are good signs. We can see inside our body, or see omens or practice telepathy; these powers come naturally. We can see the six realms of rebirth and see the sufferings of the beings therein. At night, it is no longer dark for us and we can see clearly. This is a sign. These are all good signs and there is nothing better than this. We meditate and, spontaneously and effortlessly, these results come. We feel comfortable and undistracted. We always remain at the same level of evenmindedness. We are disturbed by neither happiness nor sorrow.

When we continue in a feeling of comfort and happiness, it is a sign that the earth element of our body has been brought under control. If we practice meditation and we feel as if we are sinking into water, this is a sign that our meditation is now controlling the water element. Sometimes our meditation is clear and strong and we feel warm; this is a sign that our meditation now controls the fire element. Sometimes we feel light and experience a floating sensation; this is a sign that our meditation controls our air element. Sometimes our experience is very bright and the distractions of the senses do not disturb us, and we feel clearer and more empty; this is a sign that our meditation now controls the space element.

When these signs arise, we do not worry or speculate about them. There is no need to do anything about them. Just leave everything as it is. And gradually our normal illusions will lose their rigidity and disappear. [3]

CHAPTER 9

Introduction to Thekchod and Thodgal

Talk by Lopon Tenzin Namdak,
Devon, May 1991.
Compiled and edited by John Myrdhin Reynolds.

The Natural State

In Dzogchen, it is the Natural State that is emphasized, and this state we must realize for ourselves in our own experience. It is machopa (ma bcos-pa), that is, there is nothing to change or modify or create or correct in it. We let it remain just as it is. Thoughts may arise in the Natural State and yet it remains just as it is. There is no employment of an antidote as in the Sutra system and no transformation of anything as in the Tantra system. If we realize this Natural State, that is the real nature of Dzogchen. It is Thekchod (khregs-chod). [1]

We discover this Natural State through a direct introduction, and not by way of reasoning. The method is to observe how thoughts arise, how they remain, and how they go. We look back at our mind and observe it. But we do not interfere or modify anything; that is not the method. We just let things be and watch what happens. We will observe that when we do not interfere with them or try to change them, then thoughts will dissolve of themselves and leave nothing behind. What do we find? We find that there is nothing there. This Natural State is inexpressible and inconceivable. It is empty, but this emptiness is not just nothing because there is an awareness there. But this awareness or Rigpa is not the same as our ordinary consciousness (rnam-shes). That consciousness is dualistic; there is a subject that apprehends and an object that is apprehended. But here there is an awareness (rig-pa) where the seer and the seen are united and inseparable, like fire and warmth. However, when we practice the Natural State, it is not necessary to make an examination and check what is subject and what is object. In the Natural State, the practitioner does not examine anything; one is simply Rang-rig or self-aware.

The word Salwa (gsal-ba) means "clarity", but this is not a physical, visible light. Here "clear" (gsal-ba) means present and aware. Tongpa (stong-pa) means empty, and these two are Yermed (dbyer-med) or inseparable. This is like the daytime sky, where the sky is emptiness (stong) and the sun is luminosity (gsal). When we remain in a state of presence or immediate awareness (rig-pa), this state has three qualities: Essence, Nature, and Energy, which means emptiness, awareness, and their unification. They are never separate. We only separate them in order to talk about the Natural State, such as in a commentary. In actuality, they are never distinct and separate. In general, Dzogchen teaches this, but in the Longde (klong-sde) series of teachings, there is more emphasis put on the side of emptiness (stong-cha), whereas in the Semde (sems-sde), there is more emphasis put on the side of clarity (gsal-cha). But this is only a matter of emphasis and not one of real distinction or separation. In this context, long (klong, vast expanse) means tong (stong, empty), and sem (sems, mind) means sal (gsal, clear). Then Upadesha or Manngagide emphasizes their inseparability (gsal stong dbyer-med). So there are different methods to be found here in these three series of Dzogchen teachings.

The Three Series of Dzogchen Teachings

In the three series of Dzogchen teachings (rdzogs-chen sde gsum), that is, the Semde (sems-sde), the Longde (klong-sde), and the Manngagide (man-ngag gi sde) or Upadesha, the Natural State is precisely the same because it exists as the unification and inseparability (dbyer-med) of emptiness and awareness. However, the view in each of these three series of teachings is different because emphasis is placed on the one side or on the other. With such an emphasis, the process of realization takes longer because we must equalize the emptiness side (stong-cha) and the clarity side (gsal-cha). There must be Yermed, or unification, for there to be any real Dzogchen. All of this is very well explained in the *Nam-mkha' 'phrul mdzod*, which is a Dzogchen Semde text belonging to the Bonpo tradition. It is a Terma, or hidden treasure text, rediscovered in central Tibet (dbus-gter) and also an oral transmission from the master Tsewang Rigdzin (Tshe-dbang rig-'dzin). [2] This text does not speak about Thodgal, but it does speak a lot about unification (dbyer-med).

The Semde texts explain matters by way of knowledge (ye-shes), immediate awareness (rig-pa), and the Nature of Mind (sems=sems-nyid), especially the latter. Hence, this series of Dzogchen teachings is called Semde (sems-sde), or the Mind series, where sem (sems) means "mind." Here everything is influenced by mind, whereas in the Upadesha, everything is influenced by the Natural State. But this "mind" (sems) is just as it is and, therefore, the real significance of the word is not mind but the Nature of Mind (sems-nyid). However, the explanation found in the Dzogchen Semde is somewhat similar to the Chittamatra (sems-tsam) view because this sem (sems) lies more on the awareness side (rig-cha) than on the emptiness side (stong-cha). Then one proceeds to practice by means of the four contemplations (ting-nge-'dzin bzhi). [3]

Then, in the Dzogchen Longde (klong-sde) or Space series, the nine empty spaces (klong dgu) are found. Here the Natural State remains just as it is. It is empty. There is nothing substantial or tangible to be found anywhere; there is nothing moving or visible. Here the emphasis is on the side of emptiness (stong-cha) and this emptiness is very much like the Madhyamaka notion of

Shunyata. There is no inherent existence. There is nothing visible externally and nothing visible internally. But there are nine aspects on the object side with reference to emptiness. In the Madhyamaka system there are sixteen Shunyatas, but here there are nine. Thus the nine vast empty spaces (klong dgu) represent the object side of things. Then on the subject side, which is the practitioner, there are three stages in the meditation: harmonious meditation (mthun sgom), internal meditation (nang sgom), and spacious meditation (klong sgom). This is the way one proceeds with the practice.

Why are there these Dzogchen Desum (rdzogs-chen sde gsum) or three series of Dzogchen teachings? It is because there are these three qualities to the Natural State: awareness, emptiness and their unification (rig stong dbyer-med). Even though the *Nam-mkha' 'phrul mdzod* is mainly a Semde text, it explains that if we proceed only on the side of awareness or on the side of emptiness, we will fall away from true Dzogchen. There are no special texts devoted to Longde preserved in the Bonpo tradition, although quite a number of them were translated by Vairochana (eighth century C.E.) and have been preserved in the Nyingmapa tradition. The principal Bonpo Dzogchen texts are all Dzogchen Upadesha.

From the practice of the Longde alone we will not be able to realize the Rainbow Body because there is no Thodgal practice to be found here. Properly speaking, Thodgal is the cause for realizing the Rainbow Body ('ja' lus) and this is found only in Manngagide. Through the practice of Thekchod alone it is possible to realize the Body of Atoms (rdul lus) where the material body is dissolved into the atoms (rdul) of its constituent elements, and then these disappear into space, leaving nothing visible behind. However, there is still some substance (albeit atoms) remaining, although this is invisible to the eye. But this is not what is meant by the Rainbow Body. The Illusion Body (sgyu-lus) is created by quite a different cause, according to the Dzogrim (rdzogs-rim) practices of the Tantra system. Also, according to the Longde system, a method does exist for making the material body disappear, but this is not done according to the process of Thodgal so it is not the same at all. However, we Bonpos do not have the texts for this Longde method; it is strictly a Nyingmapa matter.

Thekchod and Thodgal

Most of the extant Bonpo texts dealing with Dzogchen are Upadesha. In the Upadesha or Manngagide (man-ngag gi sde), the emphasis is put on Thekchod and Thodgal. Thekchod means entering into and remaining in the Natural State. This is mainly concerned with the state of primordial purity (ka-dag), but Thodgal is the other half of Upadesha practice and refers to spontaneous self-perfected manifestation (lhun-grub). Here the practitioner uses posture, breathing and gazing. But nevertheless, as the base and foundation for this Thodgal practice we first need to establish our Thekchod firmly, which means being able to continue with stability in the Natural State.

Thekchod means that we enter into and continue in the Natural State. We begin practice by turning inward and observing the mind. But there is no visualization practice to be done here. We do not need to become engaged in the activities of Kyerim and Dzogrim as is the case with Tantra. All we have to do is to be aware without distraction and observe the arising of thoughts. We observe that they dissolve again without leaving a trace. As long as we remain in the Natural State, no visualization is needed. If we need the supports of visualization and mantra in our practice, then we are not ready for Dzogchen. When we are actually in the Natural State, we do not examine whether it is good or bad. There is no judging or thinking about something as, for example, when we watch TV. If we are examining or judging or focusing on something, this is the work of the mind, and therefore we are not in the Natural State. If we focus the attention, we lose the Natural State. Any focusing or fixating of attention is the work of the mind, and then we are no longer in the Natural State. So we do not judge in any way the thoughts that arise. If we relax our fixation on an object like the white A, then it seems as if more thoughts arise. They become like rough water in a mountain stream. But if we continue the practice, later the mind becomes like a slow-moving river and, eventually, like a calm sea.

At first we will need a quiet place to practice because many distractions come to disturb us. And also we may have problems with drowsiness, dullness and agitation. However, methods exist for overcoming these problems. Drowsiness and dullness mean that our energy is not there. For drowsiness, we need fresh air and to find a higher place. For dullness, we need to add energy in order to make things clearer. Agitation can be coarse or subtle. The first is easy to recognize, whereas the second is very difficult to detect and we do not realize that we are distracted. If agitation is very rough, we need to stop practice and do something else for a time. This is how to practice Thekchod.

Thodgal Visions

The reason why we do Thodgal practice is in order to realize that the vision of ordinary normal life is equally illusory and insubstantial. We think that our impure karmic vision, that is, the world as we see it as human beings, is solid and real and concrete. But this vision is all a projection arising from causes. Because we all have the cause for human karmic vision, we humans see the world in more or less the same way. But we must understand the illusory nature of our karmic vision. The practice of Thodgal may also serve as a preparation for the after-death experience, where visions arise in the Bardo.

As an example of such spontaneous visions, close the eyes and press with the fingers on the eyelids and the eyeballs. We will

Introduction to Thekchod and Thodgal ~ 195

see lights. These are not actual Thodgal visions, but just a kind of introduction. Thodgal visions are natural and not artificial. They are not deliberately created, as a visualization is, by the mind. In a dark room, we can also have ordinary visions that are not Thodgal. But for our vision to develop, we must employ the Dzogchen methods. We must understand that these spontaneous visions exist in, and develop in, the Natural State. However, all of these visions are illusions; there is nothing substantial there. Thodgal vision may at first appear different from our normal everyday vision, but we should realize that these two kinds of vision ultimately have the same nature. They are both projections and until we realize this, we are not ready to do Thodgal practice.

In Dzogchen, we are introduced to there being one source, rather than Two Truths. For example, we put our fingers in our ears and what happens? We hear self-originated sounds (rang sgra). In order to hear, normally we need the ear. But here we hear a sound, and not through the ear consciousness. Or again, press the fingers on the lids covering the eyeballs, then suddenly release them and open the eyes. We see self-originated lights (rang 'od) and self-originated forms and colors, technically called "rays" (rang zer). We see them when the eyes are closed and we continue to see them when the eyes have opened. When we have our eyes open, we usually see through our eye consciousness but, in this case, the lights and colors are not seen by means of the eye consciousness; they are only seen by Rigpa. This is only an example in order to introduce us to Thodgal.

In Thodgal, everything that appears is natural and spontaneous; it is not a visualization made by mind. It is not something artificial. Dzogchen just does what is natural, therefore, it represents a much shorter path to enlightenment. Besides Kadak, or primordial purity or Shunyata, the Natural State has this quality of Lhundrub or spontaneous manifestation, and this is not something recognized by Madhyamaka. The method of Madhyamaka represents a *via negativa* (negation), but it neglects the positive side of the Natural State. Dzogchen, on the other hand, emphasizes both equally, because Kadak and Lhundrub are Yermed, that is, inseparable in the Natural State.

Thodgal possesses methods using various sources of light, such as sunlight, moonlight, lamplight, crystals, and so on. Then there are methods for gazing into the clear, empty sky and for retreats in total darkness. In all of these cases, the Thodgal visions that arise are not perceived by the eye consciousness, but by our Rigpa. Although sunlight, and so on, represent secondary causes for the arising of the visions, the visions themselves do not arise from some external source; they arise from within us.

There are no limits to these visions. Certainly visions of deities may arise, but impure karmic visions may also arise, especially at first. But whatever visions arise, they arise spontaneously and naturally. According to some Dzogchen teachings, we are instructed to do the practice for seven sessions, signifying the six realms of rebirth, plus the Bardo. And so, visions of animals, ghosts, demons, and many other kinds of worldly beings may arise. According to the dark retreat found in the Zhang-zhung Nyan-gyud, there are seven sessions, but these are not according to the six realms.

Visions of thigleys (thig-le), or spheres of light, arise and inside them we may see deities, such as the famous Zhitro (zhi-khro), or Peaceful and Wrathful Deities. But this is not at all the same as the Kyerim and the Gyulu practices described in the Tantras because they are things created by the mind. Rather, the Thodgal visions arise out of the Natural State naturally and spontaneously. The Natural State, although diffused throughout the physical body, is principally located in the hollow space within the physical heart (tsitta). The Thodgal visions, even in dark retreat, appear only in front of us because the translucent Kati channel links the heart to the eyes. Inside the eyes, we find two separate channels, one is the vehicle for the normal operation of the eye consciousness, known as the optic nerve, and the other is the Kati channel which functions as the passageway for the movement of Rigpa. The Kati goes up from the hollow in the physical heart to the back of the brain and then divides into two before entering into the eyes. This Kati is not used for the normal functioning of vision. It is called the translucent crystalline channel Kati (ka-ti shel gyi rtsa). In Thodgal, the visions arise in the heart, pass along the Kati channel, emerge from the eyes, and are perceived in the space immediately in front of us. It is like having a lamp inside a hollow earthen vessel with two holes on one of its faces. The light inside is then seen in the darkness outside the vase, but its source is in the interior.

With the practice of Thodgal, our visions develop and gradually become more stable. At first we may see normal things like trees, mountains, and so on. Later we will most likely see letters, deities, and so on. At first these visions will not be stable, but will move about quite a bit. Moreover, we may only see parts of the deities, such as a face, or a torso. But with the third stage in the development of vision, we will see deities in yab-yum and entire mandalas, and all of this will be complete and perfect and bright. At the fourth stage, which is known as consummation (zad-pa), all the visions dissolve and all that remains is the Natural State. Since there are no more obscurations, there is nothing more to appear.

However, Thodgal is not like Tantra where we must do much visualization practice first in order for visions of the Yidams to appear. If the visions arise from some positive karmic causes, such as Kyerim, then we do need to practice in a special way. In that case, the resultant visions would be conditioned by our previous visualization practice. But these would not be Thodgal visions because they arise from causes created by the mind.

Furthermore, we must compare our Thodgal visions with the vision of ordinary life in order to discover that they come from the same source. The Thodgal visions are insubstantial. We can easily see that they are illusions. We see them come and we see them go. But our normal life vision appears to be very stable and seemingly solid. We think that this vision is real, but this is only our ignorance. So the practice of Thodgal provides us with an example. Thodgal vision is like a key to the realization that normal life is also a projection and an illusion. We can bring the knowledge gained from Thodgal practice to bear on the vision of normal life. We compare them and we discover that all of our so-called normal life is an illusion. If we cannot make this comparison, then perhaps it is better just to watch TV. Now while we are in the Natural State, we do not do any checking and examining because this is the work of the mind, but at other times we can examine the various qualities of the visions and compare them with the vision of ordinary life.

Through making this comparison of the Thodgal visions with normal vision, we gradually come to sense that the external world is equally unreal. Our ordinary life seems to have the same quality as the Thodgal visions, that is to say, as unreal and as insubstantial. This culminates with the third stage in the development of vision. The visions of the deities and mandalas come to overlay and even replace our ordinary impure karmic vision. At the fourth stage, all of these visions dissolve and go back to their source. They return to the Natural State and there is nothing left except the Natural State. If we die at a time when we have realized the first stage, then in the Bardo and in our next life we will meet the masters and the teachings again and again, and so continue to practice until we attain liberation. If we die at a time when we have realized the final stages, we will be reborn in a pure dimension.

The Thodgal visions come spontaneously and without anticipation. When they go, they leave no traces. Our keeping in the Natural State purifies all obscurations and the main obscuration is ignorance. The three principal methods are through sunlight, total darkness, and empty space. But in order to practice Thodgal, first we must realize the Natural State. So Thekchod, which means just remaining in the Natural State undistracted by thoughts, is something that is always necessary in Dzogchen practice. If visions arise and we become attached to them, then this is no different from Samsara. When we have visions in the practice of Thodgal, we have no grasping ('dzin-pa) at them because we are in the Natural State. In the vision of daily life, on the contrary, we are constantly grasping at one thing after another. Through the perfection of Thekchod, we may even be able to think and to do Tantric practice while still remaining in the Natural State, and then this will be like gazing at the moon reflected on the sea.

Development of Visions

Without Thekchod, we cannot practice Thodgal. Visions may come, but they will not be Thodgal visions. First we must practice Thekchod and make our remaining in the Natural State stable, then we can go on to practice Thodgal. In this way our visions will be stable. In Thodgal both pure and impure visions can come, but gradually the visions will become clearer and clearer, and then more and more integrated with our normal vision. In the end this integrated vision will dissolve into the Natural State, both Thodgal vision and normal vision.

The ultimate purpose of practicing Thodgal is to realize the Rainbow Body of Light. This occurs after all of our vision has been integrated. Our physical body is also part of our karmic vision, so when all of our vision dissolves into the Natural State, our physical body dissolves into empty space. The method for realizing the Rainbow Body ('ja' lus) may be either gradual or instantaneous. In terms of its gradual realization, we speak of the four stages in the development of vision, or Nangwa zhi (snang-ba bzhi). These are as follows:

1. The vision of the visible manifestation of Reality (bon-nyid mngon-sum). At this initial stage only small thigleys, or tiny spheres of rainbow light, appear in the sunlight.
2. The vision of the increasing of experiences. Now chains and networks of thigleys appear. Also, the faces and torsos of deities may appear inside the thigleys.
3. The vision of developing to the full measure of Awareness. This stage represents the full development of the pure visions of the deities and the mandalas, including the Peaceful and Wrathful Deities. Some of the thigleys may be as small as a mustard seed, while others are as large as a shield.
4. The vision of the final consummation (mthar-thug zad-pa). All of the visions dissolve back into the Natural State, and only that remains.

These visions are not always stable. When they dissolve spontaneously, it may be a sign that we are ready to realize the Rainbow Body. Visions have two alternative qualities: pure and impure. At the final stage, all of our visions are pure. But at the moment our normal everyday life vision is impure. There are two doors that must be opened: the pure and the impure. Inside them there are four doors apiece, making a total of eight doors. This is according to what kind of visions come.

Thodgal visions arise spontaneously from our Natural State, and how they develop depends on our individual capacity, level of purification, and so on. But if, for example, a master appears before us and gives us some teaching, this is not a Thodgal vision but a pure vision (dag snang). It is conditioned and brought about by some cause or karmic link. Examples of this are the visions some Tertons have had of Guru Padmasambhava. These pure visions come about because of a cause or seed planted in the Terton's stream of consciousness in a previous life when he was a disciple in personal contact with Guru Rinpoche. A Thodgal vision, on the other hand, has no external cause; it arises solely from within, from out of one's Natural State residing in the heart. It is natural and spontaneous, without any antecedent cause. It represents the free spontaneous creativity (rtsal) inherent in the Natural State which is our innate Buddha-nature.

The Four Lamps

In the practice of Thodgal, we speak of four lights or Four Lamps (sgron-ma bzhi), or sometimes of Six Lamps (sgron-ma drug). These Four Lamps are as follows:

1. The lamp of the self-originated wisdom (shes-rab rang-byung gi sgron-ma)
2. The lamp of the completely pure dimension of space (dbyings rnam-dag gi sgron-ma)
3. The lamp of the (globe-like eye of) water that lassos everything at a distance (rgyang zhags chu'i sgron-ma), and
4. The lamp of the empty spheres of light (thig-le stong-pa'i sgron-ma).

The First Lamp or light (sgron-ma) is Thekchod. We first need this lamp if we are to see anything. Thekchod is the fundamental practice and the principal practice. It means continuing in the Natural State with stability. This is intrinsic immediate awareness (rig-pa). Here Self-originated Wisdom (shes-rab rang-byung) means not the discriminating wisdom (shes-rab) of the Sutra system; in this context, it means Rigpa, the clarity aspect, in union with Kunzhi, the emptiness aspect. It is explained as being like the empty, open sky illuminated by sunlight. Certainly we must understand that the Natural State is empty, but also that it has three qualities and these are inseparable. First, this emptiness is immaterial and insubstantial, and so it is like the sky or Namkha (nam-mkha', sky, space). That is its quality. Whatever we do or take from it, this emptiness is always there as the Base.

Even if we fill everything up and make clutter everywhere, this emptiness of space is still there as the container of everything. Whatever we do, Shunyata is always empty; it is not any bigger or any smaller by virtue of what it contains. Whatever we put into it or take out of it, it remains the same and undiminished as the Base. This aspect is called Ying (dbyings) or dimension. It is the dimension in which everything originates and happens. And this emptiness never changes whatever we do; it is never increased or diminished. That aspect is called Long (klong) or vast expanse. These are the three qualities to emptiness: space (nam-mkha'), dimension (dbyings), and vast expanse (klong).

As for the Second Lamp: it is somewhat like watching a film show in the cinema hall. The Thodgal visions appear to manifest in the space before us, just as the cinema show does. When we do Thodgal practice, we gaze into the clear open sky and focus our gaze in this space without blinking. Then, at the horizon, or the tops of the trees, or on the side of the window frame, wherever we are gazing, we find that the space at this border becomes whiter and, at the center of our vision, it grows darker. If we are gazing out through a window, for example, we find that the sky will be lighter and whiter next to the window frame and darker at the center. As we continue to gaze, this light part around the border or at the edge becomes larger. However, the visions will only appear in the darker center. This is the dimension in which the Thodgal visions manifest. And they will be like the cinema pictures projected onto the screen in front of us.

The Third Lamp refers to the physical eye as a doorway. The Kati channel connects the physical heart to the physical eye organs. In dark retreat, the visions are clearer and brighter than in daylight, but the principle is the same. In Thodgal practice, the eye organ is given this rather unusual name (rgyang zhags chu'i sgron-ma), where *rgyang* means "distance" or "at a distance", *zhags* means "lasso" or a rope with a noose at the end, and *chu* means "water." The eyeball is filled with water, so *chu* refers to the eyeball. When we gaze into space, our visions appear at some distance from us and our sight goes out to them and grasps them like lassoing a wild horse. We watch our visions develop with full awareness. That is the meaning of *rgyang zhags*. The eye organ is connected with the kidney which is ruled by the water element, therefore "water." According to ancient Bonpo medical science, the outer organs are controlled by the inner organs. This information, such as the correspondences eye-kidney-water element, nose-lung-air element, tongue-spleen-earth element, and so on, is given in the account of embryology found in the Zhang-zhung Nyan-gyud and elsewhere.

As for the Fourth Lamp, it is like small white or black spots seen in the sky, or like the rainbow thigleys seen in sunlight. At first they are very tiny, but then they develop because we remain in the Natural State. Their nature is empty (stong-pa). They are called thigley because *thig* means "essence" as well as "a line drawn on a paper" to demarcate a mandala, and signifies being related to the essence or Natural State, and *le* means "very clearly," that it is very bright and clear. Therefore the meaning of thigle is that it is clear and connected with the Natural State.

The Rainbow Body

To become a real Jalupa ('ja'-lus-pa) means that we have practiced Thodgal. These visions are not specifically created by the mind, but appear spontaneously in the presence of secondary causes like sunlight, the open, empty sky, and so on. They arise naturally and spontaneously from the Natural State, and no Kyerim or Dzogrim practice must be done first as a preparation. We only need to stabilize our Thekchod practice. Then the visions come automatically. Gradually all of the Peaceful and Wrathful deities appear to us and these visions develop until completion. Then they dissolve again into the Natural State.

This final stage in the development of vision is called the Exhaustion of Reality (bon-nyid zad-pa). Nevertheless these visions have the same quality and the same source as our normal vision in everyday life. Because our material body is part of our karmic vision and has the same source as the Thodgal visions, at the time when all of our visions dissolve, our material body will also dissolve. This occurs at the point of actual death when the impure elements of our material body will revert back (ru-log) into the subtle pure forms of the elements, which are clear, coloured lights. These lights manifest as rainbows, which then dissolve into the space of the sky. All that remains behind at the end of the process are the practitioner's clothes, hair and nails, because these things have not been suffused with consciousness. The material body had been part of one's impure karmic vision but now, for the practitioner, the pure visions become the actual Jalupa or Rainbow Body, which is the real Sambhogakaya and Nirmanakaya, and one becomes perfectly purified.

In terms of Dzogchen, the Dharmakaya is realized through the practice of Thekchod, whereas the Form Body, that is, the Sambhogkaya and Nirmanakaya, is realized through the practice of Thodgal. The attaining of the Rainbow Body by a master is a sign or indication that this has occurred. But this is not the end, even though liberation and enlightenment have been attained. The Jalupa can subsequently reappear, even appearing as substantially material, to sentient beings in order to teach them the Dharma. However the Sambhogakaya can only be seen by the Aryas, that is, the Great Bodhisattvas who have ascended the first through the ninth stage of the path. They can see the Sambhogakaya and hear the teachings. But ordinary sentient beings, their minds still obscured with defilements, cannot see or hear the Sambhogakaya. Therefore the Nirmanakaya manifests to them and reveals itself in time and history, generally in human form.

Lopon Tenzin Namdak

Khenpo Tenpa Yungdrung

Khenpo Tenpa Yungdrung explaining points of the teaching.

*Khenpo Tenpa Yungdrung with the translator at
Triten Norbutge Monastery, Kathmandu.*

Monks debating.

Monk challenging one another in debate.

APPENDIX
The Biography of Lopon Tenzin Namdak

The Venerable Yongdzin Lopon Tenzin Namdak Rinpoche [1] is an accomplished scholar and practitioner of the Bon tradition, in particular of Dzogchen and the Ma Gyud or Mother Tantra, and the foremost and most learned expert on Bon outside Tibet. Since the 1960s he has also been in the forefront of reviving Bonpo religious culture among the Tibetans living in exile from their homeland in India and Nepal, where he has established Bonpo communities and monastic educational institutions.

Lopon Rinpoche was born in 1926 in Khyungpo Karru (khyung-po dkar-ru) in Khyungpo district of Kham province in eastern Tibet. His father was a farmer with land in the Chamdo district, where he possessed many yaks, sheep, horses, goats, dogs and other animals. At the age of seven, in 1933, [2] he entered Tengchen Monastery (steng-chen dgon-pa), which was the local monastic establishment in the same district. [3] His uncle, Kalzang Tsultrim (bsKal-bzang tshul-khrims), was the Umdze (om-mdzad), or chant leader, among the monks at the monastery. Tengchen Monastery belonged to the tradition of Old Bon (bon rnying-ma), otherwise known as Yungdrung Bon (g.yung-drung bon) in contrast to New Bon (bon gsar-ma) [4] and had close affiliations with Menri Monastery and Yungdrung Ling Monastery in central Tibet. This monastery had the only school in the district at the time and here young Lopon Rinpoche was taught to read and write, thus beginning his extensive education. It was here also that he took his novice monk vows at the age of fourteen.

In 1941 when he was fifteen years old, Lopon Rinpoche traveled with his uncle to Yungdrung Ling (g.yung-drung gling), one of the two leading Bonpo monasteries in central Tibet. [5] Coming from a family famous for its many artists, from 1941 to 1943 he was largely engaged in helping to execute a series of wall paintings or frescos in the new temple at this monastery. The Lopon had been trained as an artist and painter since the age of eleven, and this training in drawing and painting has served him throughout his entire life. [6]

In 1944 at the age of eighteen, he went on pilgrimage to Nepal with two other monks, first visiting Solu-Khumbu and then Kathmandu, where he meditated at the holy hill of Swayambhunath at the western end of the valley, a location which had once been graced and blessed by the presence of the Buddha Tonpa Shenrab himself. [7] Lopon Rinpoche returned to Tibet by way of Pokhara and Mustang, the latter also being an area of Bonpo settlement in Nepal. From there he went on pilgrimage to the Mt. Kailas region of west Tibet, which lies at the heart of the old Zhang-zhung kingdom.

In 1945, Lopon Rinpoche returned to Yungdrung Ling to begin his studies in philosophy (mtshan-nyid). From 1945 to 1950, he lived more or less a hermit's existence with his tutor and master Gang-ru Tsultrim Gyaltsan Rinpoche (sGang-ru Tshul-khrims rgyal-mtshan). This master was an exceedingly learned Lama in the Bonpo tradition and for some eighteen years he had been the Lopon at Yungdrung Ling Monastery. After retirement from this monastery, Gang-ru Rinpoche lived in a meditation cave at Namtso (gnam-mtsho) Lake in northern Tibet. The young Lopon Rinpoche lived in the cave with this master for four years. With the master, he studied the same subjects as those taught at Yungdrung Ling, namely, grammar (sgra), poetics (snyan-ngag), monastic discipline ('dul-ba), cosmology (mdzod-phug), and the stages of the path to enlightenment (sa-lam).

Following his master's advice, in 1950 he went to Menri Monastery [8] in Tsang province, near Sakya Monastery in central Tibet, in order to complete his studies in preparation for the Geshe (dge-bshes) degree examination, the Tibetan equivalent of a Doctor of Philosophy. Here he underwent a full course of scholastic studies. At this time, his principal teacher was Lopon Sangye Tenzin (slob-dpon Sangs-rgyas bstan-'dzin). At Menri, he studied Tibetan and Sanskrit grammar, poetics, astrology and medicine, as well as chanting and ritual practices. His advanced studies included Prajnaparamita, Madhyamaka philosophy, Abhidharma, Vinaya, Tantra and Dzogchen. In 1953, at the relatively young age of twenty-seven, he passed his oral examinations and was awarded the Geshe degree from Menri Monastery. In the same year, due to his outstanding learning and scholarship, he was elected to serve in the position of Lopon or head teacher for the academic course of studies at the college of the monastery, succeeding his own master Lopon Sangye Tenzin. From 1953 until 1957, he remained in this position only to retire in that year as the conflict between the native Tibetans and the encroaching Chinese Communists increased in central Tibet.

Until 1960, he remained at Se-zhig Monastery on the Dang-ra lake in northern Tibet. March 10, 1959, saw the Lhasa uprising against the Chinese Communist tyrannical rule over Tibet. Many of the most famous living Lamas of Tibet, including H.H. the Dalai Lama and H.H. the Gyalwa Karmapa, were forced to flee from their homeland and a flood of Tibetan refugees entered India and Nepal. In 1960, after his long retreat, Lopon Rinpoche also sought to flee, seeking refuge in India. But on the way south he was shot by Chinese soldiers and incarcerated in a Chinese military prison for nearly ten months, where he endured great hardships. Finally, he was able to make an escape, leading a small party of monks. They traveled by night and hid during the day for some twenty-two days until they reached safety in Nepal by way of the small principality of Lo Mustang.

Coming finally to Kathmandu, Lopon Rinpoche stayed for some months at Najyin (gna'-sbyin) Monastery. In 1961, while residing in Kathmandu, Lopon Rinpoche met and was befriended by the celebrated English Tibetologist, Dr. David Snellgrove, of London University who invited him to London, along with Lopon Sangye Tenzin and Geshe Samten Karmay. Thus, receiving a Rockefeller Foundation Grant in the Visiting Scholar Program, the Lopon came first to the University of London and then he resided for a time at Cambridge University. Towards the end of his stay in England, he made a retreat at a Benedictine monastery on the Isle of Wight.

During this time, in 1967, his collaboration with Professor Snellgrove resulted in the publication, by Oxford University Press, of *The Nine Ways of Bon* which contains translated extracts from the famous *gZi-brjid*, the most extensive hagiography of the Buddha Tonpa Shenrab. This was the first scholarly study of the Bonpo tradition from original sources to be made in a Western language. [9] Lopon Rinpoche remained in England for three years, from 1961 to 1964.

In 1964, the Lopon returned to India from England and was subsequently employed as a Tibetan expert by the American Library of Congress in New Delhi where, under the PL 480 Program, the American Government purchased diverse books published in India in around fourteen different languages, including Tibetan. The project of purchasing Tibetan texts was under the supervision of the celebrated Tibetologist, E. Eugene Smith, from the University of Washington, a famous center for Tibetan studies in the United States. It was Mr. Smith who was initially responsible for encouraging Tibetan Lamas, including the Lopon, to republish Tibetan texts by way of photo offset in India. This program ensured that these precious texts would not be lost to Tibet or to the world.

While in New Delhi, the Lopon was also befriended by Dr. Lokesh Chandra of the International Academy of Indian Culture and their collaboration led to the publication, by way of photo offset, of a text made from a block-print at Menri. It was an anthology or collection of texts from the Zhang-zhung snyan-rgyud. [10] Published in New Delhi in 1968, the book was entitled *History and Doctrine of Bon-po Nispanna-Yoga*. [11]

Among the nearly one hundred thousand Tibetan refugees who had fled the Chinese Communist occupation of Tibet, a small number belonged to the Bonpo tradition. [12] After escaping from Tsang province, monks from Menri Monastery, which had been totally destroyed by the Red Guards during the Cultural Revolution inspired by Chairman Mao Tse Tung, found themselves in the Kulu-Manali district of Himachal Pradesh state in north-west India. Impoverished, they were forced to secure a livelihood as road workers. Among their number was Sherab Lodro (Shes-rab blo-gros), the thirty-second Abbot of Menri Monastery (1935-1963). Finding the road work exhausting in an alien climate, many of the monks died or suffered from serious illness, as did the Abbot himself.

Thus, when Lopon Tenzin Namdak returned to India in 1964, he undertook the task of raising funds and finding land in order to establish a Bonpo settlement in northern India. From 1964 to 1967, the Lopon worked desperately to keep the Bonpo people and their culture alive in exile. In 1967, with the financial help of the Catholic Relief Service, he purchased a piece of undeveloped forest land at Dolanji, near Solan in Himachal Pradesh, and began to establish a settlement there. The first Bonpo families who settled there initially lived in tents on the cleared land. Later the new monastery developed nearby.

In 1967 the settlement was formally registered with the Indian Government under the name of the Tibetan Bonpo Foundation. About seventy families transferred there from Manali and each received a house and a small piece of land, the size depending on the number of people in the family in question. The Tibetan Bonpo Foundation possessed its own constitution and administration, with the Abbot of Menri acting as president. The new settlement at Dolanji was given the name Thobgyal Sarpa (thob-rgyal gsar-pa) after the village of Thobgyal in Tsang province, located near the original site of Menri Monastery. However, most of the Tibetans in the new settlement came from the Mt. Kailas region and Upper Tsang in the west as well as Hor, Kongpo, Derge, Amdo and Gyarong in the east.

After the death of Sherab Lodro, the thirty-second Abbot of Menri in 1963, the Abbot of Yungdrung Ling, the second most important monastery for Bonpos in central Tibet, became the spiritual head of the Bonpo community in exile in India. He came to Dolanji in 1967, together with a group of monks, and founded a new monastic community, overseeing the erection of small houses and a small prayer chapel for religious services. In 1969, the Abbot of Yungdrung Ling arranged the ceremony to find a successor to the deceased Abbot of Menri to be chosen by lot. The names were put into a vase and while prayers to the Bonpo deities were being chanted, the vase was churned until a name fell out. The selection of the office fell to Jongdong Sangye Tendzin (lJong-ldong Sangs-rgyas bstan-'dzin), who thus became the thirty-third Abbot of Tashi Menri Monastery. At that time, Sangye Tenzin was working at the University of Oslo, Norway, in collaboration with the celebrated Tibetologist, Dr. Per Kvaerne. For the rest of the year, he and the Abbot of Yungdrung Ling worked together on the monastery project. Following the death of the Abbot, Jongdong Sangye Tendzin assumed the spiritual leadership of the Bonpos in exile. More houses were erected, as well as a library, and an abbot's residence (bla-brang) was constructed. Monastic life was organized around the ordinances of the Vinaya ('dul-ba). The foundation for a main temple was laid in 1969 and completed in 1978. This temple was given the name Pal Shenten Menri Ling (dpal gshen bstan sman-ri gling). The whole complex was designated as the Bonpo Monastic Centre and it formed part of the Tibetan Bonpo Foundation. At the time, this was the only Bonpo monastery in India. [13]

The Lopon made a second visit to Europe in 1969 where, at the invitation of Professor Helmut Hoffmann of the University of Munich, he was a visiting scholar at the University of Munich, contributing to the monumental Tibetan-German-English dictionary being compiled there, and yet to be published. The Lopon stayed in Munich for seven months

From 1967, when the first monks came to Dolanji, the teaching was largely given by Lopon Sangye Tenzin, the former teaching master at Menri in Tibet, assisted by his successor, Lopon Tenzin Namdak, the founder of the settlement at Dolanji. From 1970 to 1979 Lopon Rinpoche continued to teach and write while residing at the Bonpo Monastic Centre and, in addition, he was much engaged in the publishing in New Delhi of a large number of important Bonpo texts. Due to various difficulties, especially a lack of basic canonical books, the teaching was only partial and consisted mainly of training the young monks in the practices of the Dzogchen tradition, especially the *Zhang-zhung-snyan-rgyud*, which was considered by both Lopons to be of prime importance. In 1977, when Lopon Sangye Tenzin died after a protracted illness, Lopon Tenzin Namdak was assigned full responsibility for the education of the younger generation of monks. In the next year, he conducted funerary and post-mortem rites for his teacher Lopon Sangye Tenzin.

By 1978, a sufficient number of important Bonpo texts had been published, many having been borrowed from the collection housed at Samling Monastery in Dolpo, Nepal, and reprinted in New Delhi, so that classes could be organized around them as a curriculum. Moreover, premises for use as classrooms were now available. Thus, a Dialectics School, or Shedra (bshad-grwa), was established in 1978, organized under the guidance of Lopon Rinpoche, who served as one of the two professors at the college.

The official name of this institution was Yungdrung Bon Shedrub Lobnyer Dude (g.yung-drung bon bshad-sgrub slob gnyer 'dus-sde). In that year the full training in Bonpo academic studies began and in 1986 the first class of monks graduated. [14]

In 1978, Lopon Rinpoche, together with the new Abbot, Jongdong Sangye Tenzin, visited H.H. the Dalai Lama, head of the Tibetan Government in exile at Dharamsala in order to inform him of the purpose of establishing the Bonpo settlement at Dolanji and the Lama College or Dialectics School, with its nine-year program of Geshe studies. Moreover, they requested official recognition, by the Tibetan Government in Exile in Dharamsala, of Menri Trizin Rinpoche, the Abbot of Menri Monastery, as the head of the Bonpo school in general among Tibetans. Thus, Jongdong Sangye Tenzin became the present throne-holder, or thirty-third Abbot of Menri, under the name H.H. Lungtog Tenpai Nyima (sKyabs-rje lung-rtogs bstan-pa'i nyi-ma dpal bzang-po). Normally, His Holiness resides at Dolanji, but he has now visited the West on a number of occasions. Moreover, H.H. the Dalai Lama and his Government officially recognized the Bonpos as the fifth Tibetan school and granted them representation on the Council of Religious Affairs at Dharamsala.

In 1978, Namkhai Norbu Rinpoche, together with a group of his Italian students, came to visit Dolanji and, because of his wide non-sectarian interest in Dzogchen, he requested from the Lopon the initiation for Zhang-zhung Meri, the Yidam or meditation deity practice closely associated with the *Zhang-zhung snyan-rgyud*. This had been the personal Tantric practice of Gyerpungpa himself. It is traditional to receive this empowerment before entering into the practice of Dzogchen according to the Zhang-zhung tradition. [15] Years later, when the Lopon visited Merigar, the retreat center of Norbu Rinpoche in the hills of Tuscany north of Rome, he gave the complete Lung, or scriptural authorization, to Norbu Rinpoche and the latter's students in the Dzogchen Community.

From 1976 to 1986, Lopon Rinpoche educated the young monks at Dolanji and wrote several texts himself, including some that are used in the Dialectics School. In 1986 Geshe degrees were awarded to the first six young monks to complete the nine-year training at Dolanji. For three years Lopon Sangye Tenzin taught the Dzogchen teachings of the Zhang-zhung snyan-rgyud to a group of about fifteen monks and when he had completed this first cycle of teaching, he was requested to teach it again to the same group. But in the middle of this second cycle he became seriously ill and Lopon Tenzin Namdak took over the burden of teaching. Lopon Sangye Tenzin died in 1977. He had requested that the money left over from his estate after his death be spent on the dialectics school. With his departure this left as teachers Lopon Tenzin Namdak and Geshe Yungdrung Langyal. Lopon Rinpoche continued to teach Dzogchen. Geshe Yungdrung Langyal, who was a Geshe Lharampa in both the Bonpo and the Gelugpa traditions, having studied at Drepung, was the principal teacher for around twelve students in philosophical studies focusing on Madhyamaka and logic required for the Geshe degree.

The purpose of this new Dialectics School at Dolanji was to preserve the tradition of education in philosophy (mtshan-nyid) first established and developed at Yeru Wensakha, where philosophical analysis and logic were applied to the understanding of the *mDo sngags sems gsum*, that is to say, the teachings of Sutra, Tantra and Dzogchen. At Tashi Menri in Tibet, the monks studied the five scriptural systems (mdo gzhung lnga) in the philosophy college, but all of the instruction in Tantra and Dzogchen was done in a more private context with individual masters. The five scriptures, actually five collections of texts, are:

1. tshad-ma – pramana or logic and epistemology;
2. phar-phyin – Prajnaparamita or the Perfection of Wisdom Sutras;
3. dbu-ma – Madhyamaka philosophy;

4. mdzod-phug – Abhidharma or cosmology, and
5. 'dul-ba – Vinaya or monastic discipline.

However, at the revived Menri Monastery at Dolanji, students also study Tantra and Dzogchen in the college, as well as the five above-mentioned scriptural systems that pertain to the Sutra level of teaching. Also included in the course of studies are the secular sciences (rig-gnas), such as grammar, poetics, astrology, medicine and so on. [16] The school has a nine-year program of studies that prepare the student for the Geshe degree examination.

In 1986, Lopon Rinpoche made a return visit to Tibet to visit the site of Menri Monastery and other important Bonpo monasteries, seeking to inspire the few remaining monks who were living under Chinese occupation. He also traveled to eastern Tibet, including his native district of Khyungpo. Here he enthroned Sherab Gelek (Shes-rab dge-legs) as the new Abbot of Tengchen Monastery and offered donations for the restoration of the monastery, which was at that time in a sorry state of disrepair. These repairs and restorations continue today under the direction of the Abbot. Subsequently, he was reunited with his mother for the first time after forty-five years. He then returned to Lhasa and flew to Chengdu in China in order to visit temples and the holy mountain of Langchen Gyingri. By way of Lhasa again, he returned by air to Kathmandu.

Once in Nepal, he donated all the remaining money he had collected in Tibet and elsewhere to acquiring a small piece of land at the foot of Nagarjuna hill to the west of the famous hill of Swayambhu at the far end of the Kathmandu Valley, in order to build the future monastery of Triten Norbutse (khri-brten nor-bu-rtse). The monastery was formally founded in 1987 and one of his former students from Dolanji, Geshe Nyima Wangyal, was put in charge of the project. Later the Geshe became the first Khenpo or Abbot of the new monastery. In 1988 Lopon Rinpoche contracted jaundice, but continued his regular teaching schedule after first moving into a small building erected on the land. [17]

Unique to the Bonpo monastic tradition and the education developed by Lopon Rinpoche provided to the monks, is debating of the view of Dzogchen in relation to Madhyamaka and other Buddhist philosophies. Unlike the Nyingmapa tradition, which generally transmitted Dzogchen in the context of secret meditation instructions conferred in private between master and disciple, the Bonpos developed a system of logic and debate specifially related to the Dzogchen teachings and thereby, in a certain sense, brought Dzogchen out of the closet into the philosophical market place of discussion of ideas. This has elicited some criticism from Lamas belonging to other Tibetan schools. However, in 1988 H.H. the Dalai Lama, who is himself also well versed in Dzogchen and a practitioner of it, visited the Dialectics School at Dolanji and was quite pleased with the fact that the Bonpo monks use debate and logic as a method of studying Dzogchen, especially in relation to other philosophical systems. With much delight and enthusiasm, His Holiness observed the monks debating various philosophical points of the Dzogchen view. [18]

In 1989, Lopon Tenzin Namdak Rinpoche, made his third visit to the West, this time to England, America and Italy, at the invitation of the Dzogchen Communities of Namkhai Norbu Rinpoche in those countries. During the course of several months, Lopon Rinpoche presented to interested Western students Dzogchen teachings according to the Bonpo tradition of the *A-khrid* and the *Zhang-zhung snyan-rgyud*. In Los Angeles, the Healing Light Center generously paid the hospital costs for a badly needed operation to extract six gall-stones. Thereafter Lopon Rinpoche recovered completely and was subsequently able to visit Italy, both Rome and Merigar, the retreat center of Namkhai Norbu Rinpoche in Tuscany, before returning to Nepal.

Again the Lopon was invited to the West in March and April by students of the Dzogchen Community, first to Bischofshofen in Austria and then to Rome and Merigar in Italy and to south Devon in England. Thereafter the Lopon taught for the first time in Amsterdam in the Netherlands. At this time, he was accompanied by Geshe Nyima Wangyal, the first Khenpo or Abbot of Triten Norbutse in Nepal. After his return to Nepal in August, a small group of English students met with the Lopon at Triten Norbutse where, every morning for two hours, he presented an exegetical commentary on a Dzogchen text composed by the famous Shardza Rinpoche (1859-1933) [19] known as the *Kunbzang snying-thig*. The edited transcripts of this teaching resulted in the publication in 1993 of *Heart Drops of Dharmakaya*. [20]

In October he came to New York City at the invitation of H.H. the Dalai Lama to attend the Kalachakra initiation and to give a lecture on the Nature of Mind as the representative of the Bonpo tradition of Tibet. For this lecture, the Lopon had previously composed a paper while teaching in Devon entitled: "The Condensed Meaning of an Explanation of the Teachings of Yungdrung Bon," which was published in time for the presentation, before the actual Kalachakra initiation. [21] He taught briefly in New York City and Amherst, Massachusetts. After a tour of the American Southwest and various American Indian reservations, he taught on Dzogchen at Coos Bay, Oregon, in November. The transcripts of these teachings were published later in 1992 and privately circulated by the Bonpo Translation Project as *Bonpo Dzogchen Teachings*. [22]

In 1992, he returned from Nepal to Dolanji to attend the Geshe examinations and give the initiation for the Ma Gyud, or Bonpo Mother Tantra, the most extensive of all Bonpo Tantric initiations, requiring seven days to complete the cycle. At this time, the Lopon also enthroned Geshe Nyima Wangyal as the first Abbot of Triten Norbutse in the presence of H.H. Menri Trizin, the current Abbot of Menri at Dolanji.

That summer, Lopon Rinpoche again visited Tibet, first going on a pilgrimage of the Lhasa area, and then proceeding to the

Nag-chu region of Kham or eastern Tibet where he gave many teachings and initiations. He made a return visit to Tengchen Monastery in his native district of Khyungpo, which had been rebuilt since his previous visit in 1986. He remained at the monastery for a time, giving the Mawe Senge initiation and teaching the Vinaya to the monks. He visited adjacent regions and then his mother once again. Thereafter he returned to Lhasa, where he purchased a small piece of land in order to build a reception house for the Bonpos living in the city, that is, a place where they could meet and assemble for religious practices.

In 1994, Lopon Rinpoche traveled again to Lhasa and Nag-chu, but conditions had changed in China and he was not able to give any teachings or initiations. When he returned to Triten Norbutse Monastery in Kathmandu, he performed the consecration (rab-gnas) of the new Lhakhang, or temple and assembly hall, at the monastery. The event was also attended by H.H. Menri Trizin from Dolanji and the latter officially inaugurated the Dialectics School (bsad-grwa) and Meditation School (sgrub-grwa) at the monastery.

At the Dialectics School, every week one monk is subjected to an exhaustive and thorough examination by Lopon Rinpoche and all the other monks enrolled in the Geshe degree program. Each monk in turn poses questions to the examinee, with even the youngest monks taking their turns at asking questions. It is not unusual for such an oral examination to last five to six hours. In the course of one year every monk in the program is tested two or three times in this manner. Upon successful completion of the thirteen-year Geshe program, during the course of the graduation ceremony, the monks are awarded the distinguished Geshe degree by the representative of H.H. the Dalai Lama.

In addition to the Geshe Degree Program, Lopon Rinpoche provided personal guidance and daily meditation instruction to a small group of advanced practitioners who focus their study and practice on Dzogchen. Lopon Rinpoche also oversaw the monastic education of a small group of orphaned boys who received pre-Geshe training and instruction that also include training in debating.

In early 1994, there were only twenty monks in residence at Triten Norbutse, but after the inception of the Dialectics School, the monastic population increased dramatically in a matter of months. Currently there are over one hundred monks in residence and new monks arrive at Triten Norbutse, at times on a daily basis. Most come directly from Tibet, but some also from Dolanji in India and some from the border regions of Nepal, including Dolpo and Mustang. Also in recent years, a number of Bonpo nuns have fled Tibet and come to the monastery in the hope of receiving teachings from the Lopon and other senior monks.

Since the Cultural Revolution in China and Tibet in the 1960s, the availability of Bonpo teachings in Tibet has become quite limited. Currently, monks can only receive teachings at the Sutra level because in general there are no qualified teachers available to give the higher level teachings of Tantra and Dzogchen. The Bonpo education currently available in Tibet focuses upon the preliminary practices, zhine meditation, and the one-hundred-day Tummo (or psychic heat) retreat. As a result, in order to receive a complete education in the Bonpo tradition, monks and nuns must leave Tibet to obtain these teachings from Lopon Rinpoche. The primary purpose behind the Lopon establishing the Dialectics School is to train Bonpo monks in exile so that they can eventually take the Bonpo teachings back to Tibet. [23]

Since 1995, Lopon Rinpoche has visited Europe regularly in order to give Dzogchen teachings from the Bonpo tradition, in particular the *Zhang-zhung snyan-rgyud* and the *A-khrid*. From time to time, he has also visted the United States at the invitation of his former student from Dolanji, Geshe Tenzin Wangyal, and others. Since this time, Lopon Rinpoche has regularly taught retreats every spring or summer in France, where the Association Yungdrung Bon was set up by his Western students to facilitate his work in the West and in particular Europe. In 2001 this process led to plans to establish a permanent Bonpo teaching, research and retreat center in France, and this project was realized in the summer of 2005 with the purchase of a chateau in France. This institute and retreat facility is now known as Shenten Dargye Ling (gshen bstan dar-rgyas gling), meaning "the place for the spreading of the teachings of the Buddha Tonpa Shenrab."

For further information regarding the monastery, its programs and future plans, as well as Shenten Dargye Ling in France, contact:

Khenpo Tenpa Yungdrung
Triten Norbutse Bonpo Monastery
Ichangu, G.B.S. Ward No. 6,
G.P.O. Box 4640, Kathmandu, Nepal
E-mail: triten @wlink.com.np.

The Curriculum of Studies at Triten Norbutse Monastery

The program of philosophical studies (mtshan-nyid, Skt. Lakshana, definitive characteristic) held at the Dialectics School (bshad-grwa) at Triten Norbutse Monastery in Kathmandu, Nepal, since 1994 has been extended by Lopon Rinpoche to thirteen years, and even to fourteen or fifteen years because the Geshe examinations are not held every year. [24] This provides an opportunity to study more texts than in the usual curriculum. When acting as head teacher or Lopon at Menri Monastery in Tibet, Lopon Rinpoche had already begun to revise the traditional curriculum of studies. Then at the re-established Menri Monastery at Dolanji in India, he included the study of Tantra and Dzogchen as studies in the Geshe program.

The course of Geshe studies commences with the study of Pramana (tshad-ma) or Logic, that is, with the methods of correct logical thinking and arriving at valid cognitions. At Triten Norbutse, these preliminary studies in methodology and logic extending over the first three years are known as the first successive year course in logic studies (tshad-ma lo rim dang-po), the second successive year course in logic studies, (tshad-ma lo rim gnyis-pa), and the third successive year course in logic studies (tshad-ma lo rim gsum-pa). [25] In a formal sense, Bonpo logic is similar to the Buddhist logic developed in India by Dignaga and Dharmakirti. However, in the Bonpo tradition, the origin of logic is attributed to the Primordial Buddha himself, Kuntu Zangpo, [26] rather than to historical figures like Dignaga and Dharmakirti.

Pramana, in the narrower sense, means valid cognition. And in terms of debate and philosophical discussions with Outsiders (phyi-pa), that is to say, non-Buddhists and non-Bonpos, there are two sources of valid cognition:

1. direct perception (mngon-sum tshad-ma, pratyaksha-pramana) and
2. inference (rjes-dpag tshad-ma, anumana-pramana).

When engaged in discussions with Insiders (nang-pa), that is, other Bonpos, then scriptural authority represents a third source of valid cognition. This is because an enlightened being like the Buddha is a reliable witness and would not lie or be mistaken in any way.

The thirteen-year course of studies at the Dialectics School is as follows:

Sutra System Studies:
I. *Tshad-ma* (initial three years).
   Studies in logic, terminology, and methodology, representing a three-year course in basic knowledge and correct thinking.
   A. *bsDus-grwa* (first year).
      Studies in terminology and methodology.
      Thun-mong bsdus-grwa'i rnam-bshad by Khenchen Nyima Tenzin.
      Bon-can zur-bkod gsal-byed by Khenchen Nyima Tenzin.
   B. *rTags-rigs* (second year).
      Studies in epistemology. [27]
      bsTan-bcos chen-po tshad-ma rnam-'byed by Ponlob Yontan Gyatso.
   C. *Tshad-m*a (third year).
      Studies in formal logic. The practice of debate (rtsod-pa) begins with the first year and continues throughout the entire course of studies. [28]
      Tshad-ma rnam-'byed 'phrul gyi sgron-me by Nyammed Sherab Gyaltsan. (Root text in 14 folia).
      Students are required to memorize these root texts (rtsa-ba) and the others that follow below.

rNam'byed 'phrul gyi sgron-me'i 'grel-pa, auto-commentary to the above root text.

II. *Theg-rim* (fourth year).
Studies of the successive vehicles to enlightenment, Sutra system section only.
Theg-pa'i rim-pa mngon du bshad-pa'i mdo rgyud, root text and commentary attributed to Tonpa Shenrab. (Root text in 6 folia to be memorized).
Theg-'grel (three different commentaries).

III. *Sa-lam* (fifth year).
Study of the five paths and the ten stages.
Sa-lam 'phrul gyi sgron-me by Nyammed Sherab Gyaltsan (Root text in 26 folia).
Rang-'grel, his auto-commentary, plus another commentary.

IV. *Phar-phyin* (two years).
   A. *Phar-phyin* (sixth year).
      Studies in the *Khams brgyad* or Prajnaparamita Sutra.
      Phar-phyin skabs dang-po by Nyammed Sherab Gyaltsan. (Root text and commentaries for Chapters 1-2).
   B. *Phar-phyin* (seventh year).
      Studies in the *Khams brgyad* or Prajnaparamita.
      Phar-phyin skabs gnyis-pa by Nyammed Sherab Gyaltsen. (Root text and commentaries for Chapters 3-8).

V. *dBu-ma* (eighth year).
Studies in Madhyamaka philosophy.
dBu-ma bden gnyis kyi gzhung by Meton Sherab Odzer (Root text in 6 folia).
Two commentaries by Nyammed Sherab Gyaltsan and Lopon Tenzin Namdak.

VI. *mDzod* (ninth year).
   Studies in the Abhidharma or cosmology.
   Srid-pa'i mdzog-phug, attributed to Tonpa Shenrab. (Root text in 16 folia).
   Srid-pa'i mdzog-phug rtsa 'grel, attributed to Dranpa Namkha.
   Lung mtshan-nyid srid-pa'i mdzog-phug klad don, by Azha Lodro Gyaltsan.
   sNang-srid mdzod-phug gi gzhung 'grel-pa, by Nyammed Sherab Gyaltsan.

VII. *'Dul-ba* (tenth year).
   Studies in the Vinaya or monastic rules and ordinances.
   'Dul-ba rtsa sdom rgyal btsan gsal-ba'i rgyan (Root text in 11 folia).
   Two commentaries by Nyammed Sherab Gyaltsan:
   'Dul-ba mdor bsdus kyi 'grel-pa
   'Dul-ba kun las btus-pa sa-gcod

Tantra System Studies:
VIII. *sNgags* (eleventh year).
   Studies in the system of the Father Tantras (pha rgyud).
   Theg-rim (Tantra section only).
   bKa' 'grel by Lopon Tenzin Namdak.
   gSang-ba bsen thub kyi 'grel-pa by Azha Lodro Gyaltsan.

IX. *Ma rGyud* (twelfth year).
   Studies in the system of the Mother Tantra.
   Ma rgyud sangs-rgyas rgyud gsum 'grel-pa, attributed to Milu Samlek.
   Ye-shes thig-le mchan 'grel by Lopon Tenzin Namdak.

Dzogchen Studies:
X. *rDzogs-chen* (thirteenth and fourteenth years).

Theg-'grel (Dzogchen section only).
Nam-mkha' 'phrul-mdzod, attributed to Dranpa Namkha (Root text with 7 folia).
Nam-mkha' 'phrul-mdzod 'grel-pa, attributed to Dranpa Namkha` (commentary).
gTan-tshigs gal mdo rig-pa'i tshad-ma, attributed to Lishu Tag-ring.
Gab 'grel, attributed to Dranpa Namkha.
Zhang-zhung snayan-rgyud bka' rgyud skor bzhi, attributed to Tapihritsa.
(This is the *bKa'-rgyud* only, not the *Nyams rgyud*. The *Zhang-zhung snayan-rgyud* and the *A-khrid* are both mostly practice oriented, and so are not studied in the Dialectics School. A portion of the *Ye-khri mtha'-sel* is also studied, if time permits.

Parallel to this course of academic studies, taught in morning classes, there are the study and practice of the secular sciences and arts (rig-gnas). These classes are usually in the afternoon. The traditional list of these sciences in the Buddhist context is as follows:

1. Sanskrit linguistics (sgra rig-pa)
2. healing and medicine (gso-ba rig-pa)
3. arts and crafts (bzo rig-pa)
4. external sciences, such as astrology, etc. (phyi rig-pa)
5. internal sciences, which are religious and spiritual (nang rig-pa)

At Triten Norbutse, eleven such sciences are taught to the students as follows:

1. Tibetan spelling (dag-yig ming-gzhi)
2. Tibetan grammar (brda-sprod)

3. poetics (snyan-ngag)
4. Sanskrit linguistics (sgra rig-pa)
5. composition and stylistics (sdebs-sbyor)
6. calendrics, similar to Chinese astrology (nag-rtsis)
7. Indian astrology and horoscopes (dkar-rtsis)
8. consecrations for stupas, statues. etc. (gzungs-rdzong)
9. proportions for stupas, mandalas, etc. (thig-tshad)
10. medicine and healing (gso-ba rig-pa), and
11. arts and crafts (bzo rig-pa)

When the sciences of linguistics and composition are combined, that makes ten secular sciences

Usually there are six to eight graduates examined at any one time, but this depends on the circumstances. The examinations consist of testing the student's memorization of the root texts, his skills in debating, a written examination, the making of an astrological chart for an individual, calculating a one-month calendar according to Indian astrology, designing a stupa and a mandala, a written poem, a written prose composition, and constructing a poem grid diagram (sgra 'khor). Upon completion of all the examinations, the graduate is presented by the Abbot or Khenpo with a certificate of graduation (lag-khyer) and a white silk scarf (kha-btags)

The Meditation School (sgrub-grwa) is independent of the Dialectics School and a student may enter it separately without first enrolling in the Geshe Studies program. This represents a four-year program of the study and practice of Dzogchen in a semi-retreat situation, one year each being spent on a different system of Dzogchen, as follows:

First year   : *A-khrid*, attributed to Meuton Dongdzod Ritrod Chenpo.
Second year : *rDzogs-chen*, attributed to Dranpa Namkha.

Third year : *Zhang-zhung snyan-rgyud*, attributed to Tapihritsa, and
Fourth year : *Ye-khri mtha'-sel*, attributed to Dranpa Namkha.

For the graduate completing four years, there is a similar graduation ceremony and certificate.

Notes

Notes to the Preface of the First Edition
1. Originally published as an appendix in John Myrdhin Reynolds (Vajranatha), *Yungdrung Bon: The Eternal Tradition* (1991).
2. See Reynolds, *The Oral Tradition from Zhang-zhung* (2005).
3. See Namkhai Norbu, *Drung, Dreu, and Bon* (1995) and *The Necklace of gZi* (1981).
4. On the two authentic traditions of Dzogchen in Tibet, see Reynolds, *The Golden Letters* (1996) and Reynolds, *The Oral Tradition from Zhang-zhung* (2005), especially Chapter One.

Notes to the Introduction to Bon
1. In the Bonpo tradition, Maitreya, the future Buddha, is known as Tonpa Thangma Medron (sTon-pa thang-ma me-sgron).
2. On the Bonpo understanding of the Trikaya, or Three Bodies of the Buddha, see Chapters One and Two in Reynolds, *The Oral Tradition from Zhang-zhung* (2005).
3. However, this similarity of the Bonpo texts to many Indian Buddhist texts and teachings was explained as simple plagiarism in medieval Tibetan histories written by Buddhist monk scholars. Shenchen Luga was considered the main perpetrator here. Until recently, before the actual Bonpo texts became known, most Western scholars accepted this accusation at face value. However, most of the Tertons (gter-ston), or discoverers of hidden treasure texts, were simple illiterates and not learned scholars. They could have hardly composed these texts. On Bonpo Terma discoveries, see Karmay, *Treasury* (1972).
4. There are three principal biographies or hagiographies of Tonpa Shenrab in the Bon tradition:

(1) *mDo 'dus* or *Dus gsum sangs-rgyas byung-khungs kyi mdo*,
(2) *gZer-myig* or *'Dus-pa rin-po-che'i rgyud gzer-myig*, and
(3) *gZi-brjid* or *'Dus-pa rin-po-che dri-ma med-pa gzi-brjid rab tu 'bar-ba'i mdo*.

A summary of the hagiography of Tonpa Shenrab, drawn from the *gZer-myig*, will be found in Helmut Hoffmann, *The Religions of Tibet* (1961), pp. 84-98. A brief version of the hagiography may be found in Sangye Tandar, *The Twelve Deeds: A Brief Life Story of Tonpa Shenrab, the Founder of the Bon Religion* (1995). Although the monastic career of Tonpa Shenrab in his later life bears many resemblances to the account of Shakyamuni Buddha's Great Renunciation and subsequent teaching activities, as found, for example, in the *Lalitavistara*, his life story is otherwise of an origin quite independent of anything remotely Indian Buddhist. Indeed, the noted Russian scholar Kuznetsov sees Tonpa Shenrab as being of Central Asian or Iranian origin. See B.I. Kuznetsov, "Who was the Founder of the Bon Religion," in *Tibet Journal* (1975). Certain contemporary Tibetan scholars see Tonpa Shenrab as a native-born Tibetan, rather than a prince or priest of Central Asian origin. See Namkhai Norbu, *The Necklace of gZi* (1981). Karmay also appears to suggest this. See Samten G. Karmay, "A General Introduction to the History and Doctrines of Bon," in *The Memoirs of the Research Department of the Toyo Bunko* (1975), pp. 171-218. Lopon Tenzin Namdak, following Bonpo tradition, is adamant in asserting that Tonpa Shenrab was not a Tibetan, but originated in *'Ol-mo lung-ring*, which he identifies with Shambhala. In that case, *'Ol-mo lung-ring* was a mystical domain and not a precise geographical location. On the significance of *'Ol-mo lung-ring* and Shambhala, see Edwin Birnbaum, *The Way to Shambhala* (1980), pp. 12-13, 44, 79-81, 102; and especially see Daniel Martin, *Mandala Cosmology* (1994). On the signicance of mystical geography in general, see Mircea Eliade, *The Sacred and the Profane: The Nature of Religion* (1957), and also Henry Corbin, *Spiritual Body and Celestial Earth* (1977).

5. On Shambhala and Olmo Lung-ring, see Burnbaum, *The Way to Shambhala* (1980).
6. See Sangye Tandar, *The Twelve Deeds* (1995).

7. On the origin of the word *bon*, see Geza Uray, "The Old Tibetan Verb Bon," in *Acta Orientalia Academiae Scientarium Hungaricae* (1964).
8. According to Lopon Tenzin Namdak, the translations of these technical terms *chab dkar* as "white water" and *chab nag* as "black water" are problematic. Indeed, *chab* does mean "water" in Tibetan, but the word may originally have been a Zhang-zhung term and held a different and now forgotten meaning. In the old Bonpo usage, the terms "white" (dkar) and "black" (nag) did not have the moral connotations that they have in English, such as "white magic" done for good purposes and "black magic" done for evil purposes. In this context, "white" refers to invoking the aid of the gods and spirits, drawing positive energy to oneself, while "black" refers to the exorcizing and expelling of negative energies, perceived as a process of purification. The exorcised negative energies are felt to appear black in color, but the intention here is positive, namely, that of purification.
9. According to Karmay, the name *'Phan-yul* designates the district of *'Phan-yul* to the north of Lhasa. This may have been the location where the Bonpo translation of the Prajnaparamita was made in the early period, to be later concealed in a different region before rediscovery by *gShen-chen klu-dga'* in the eleventh century. However, the Lopon disputes this theory and holds that *'phan-yul* was probably a Zhang-zhung word whose meaning has been forgotten. The Tibetan term *'bum*, literally meaning "one hundred thousand," is the usual designation in the Buddhist tradition for the entire collection of the Prajnaparamita Sutras, the largest of which consists of one hundred-thousand verses. See Karmay, *Treasury* (1972).
10. See Snellgrove, *The Nine Ways of Bon* (1967).
11. On *'Chi-med gtsug-phud* and the lineages for the Bonpo Dzogchen teachings, see Chapter Three with the translations of the *Yig-chung* and the *rNam-thar* in Reynolds, *The Oral Tradition from Zhang-zhung* (2005).
12. On the Zhang-zhung language, see Erik Haarh, "The Zhang-zhung Language: A Grammar and Dictionary of the Unexplored Language of the Tibetan Bonpos," in *Acta Jutlandica* (1968). On the relationship of Kinnauri to the Zhang-zhung language, see D.D. Sharma, *A Descriptive Grammar of Kinnauri* Delhi (1988).

13. See Karmay, *Treasury* (1972).
14. On the *sMar-yig* script of Zhang-zhung, see Tshering Thar, "The Ancient Zhang Zhung Civilization," in *Tibet Studies* (1989). Also see Namkhai Norbu, *The Necklace of gZi* (1981).
15. On the Bonpo Terma tradition, see Karmay, *Treasury* (1972). All of the early Terma discoveries of the Bonpos were *sa-gter*, that is, the actual physical texts written in previous times and concealed in various places of Tibet and Bhutan. Most of the actual discoverers of these collections of Terma texts were not learned Lamas, but simple farmers and hunters, who could not have possibly forged or otherwise plagiarized these texts. Among the most famous of these early "Tertons" were three Nepalese thieves known as the three Atsaras, who in the year 961 CE stole a heavy locked chest from the *Cha-ti dmar-po* temple at Samye Monastery. Escaping into the mountains with their loot and thinking that it contained gold, they broke into the chest. But when they opened it, they found only some old texts. Greatly disappointed, they sold these old books to some local village Bonpo Lamas for gold and a horse.
16. According to Lopon Tenzin Namdak, *sTang-chen dMu-tsha gyermed* was a disciple of Dranpa Namkha, the prince of Zhang-zhung and not the later Tibetan Dranpa Namkha who lived in the eighth century as claimed by Karmay, *Treasury* (1972), pp.xxxvii, xxxviii. This sage appeared to Lodan Nyingpo in a series of visions, dictating a number of texts which the latter wrote down. At this time, it is said, Lodan Nyingpo was 23 to 24 years old and these visions came to him spontaneously without his conscious control. Even though this process would be designated a Mind Treasure (dgongs-gter) or a pure vision (dag-snang) by the Nyingmapas, the Bonpos classify such vision revelations as *snyan-brgyud* or oral transmissions, even though they do not represent a continuous oral transmission from the earliest time. In all, Lodan Nyingpo received four cycles of oral transmissions in visions from the Vidyadharas and the Dakinis. See Karmay, *Treasury* (1972), pp. 183, 340.
17. On the Nyingmapa Terma tradition, see Eva Dargyay, *The Rise of Esoteric Buddhism in Tibet* (1977). Also see Tulku Thondup, *Hidden Teachings of Tibet* (1986), and Tulku Thondup, *The Tantric Tradition of the Nyingmapas* (1984).

18. The Three Cycles of Precepts that are Outer, Inner and Secret (bka' phyi nang gsang skor gsum) are as follows:
    (1) The Outer Cycle (phyi skor) contains the Sutra system of teachings (mdo-lugs) relating to the Path of Renunciation (spong lam).
    (2) The Inner Cycle (nang skor) contains the Tantra system of teachings (rgyud-lugs) relating to the Path of Transformation (sgyur lam), otherwise known as the Secret Mantras (gsang sngags).
    (3) The Secret Cycle (gsang skor) contains the Upadesha teachings (man-ngag) relating to the Path of Self-Liberation (grol lam), otherwise known as Dzogchen, the Great Perfection.
19. On the Central Treasures, see John Myrdhin Reynolds, *Yungdrung Bon: The Eternal Tradition* (1994). And also Lopon Tenzin Namdak and John Reynolds (tr), *The Condensed Meaning of an Explanation of the Teachings of Yungdrung Bon* (n.d.). Also see Tenzin Wangyal, *Wonders of the Natural Mind* (1993), pp. 35-37, 203-208.
20. Oral communication.
21. Shenchen Luga (gShen-chen klu-dga', 996-1035) discovered the largest single cache of old Bonpo texts. See Karmay, *Treasury*, p. 126-135.
22. On the *A-khrid* system and *rMe'u-ston dGongs-mdzod ri-khrod chen-po*, see Per Kvaerne, "Bonpo Studies: The A-khrid System of Meditation," Part One: "The Transmission of the A-khrid System," in *Kailash* (1973), pp. 19-50. Bru-chen rGyal-ba g.yung-drung (1242-1290) composed the practice manual entitled the *A-khrid thun mtshams bco-lnga-pa*, "The Fifteen Sessions of Practice for A-khrid." For the translation of most of this text, see Per Kvaerne and Thubten Rikey, *The Stages of A-khrid Meditation: Dzogchen Practice of the Bon Tradition* (1996). And on the *A-khrid* system generally, see Per Kvaerne, "Bonpo Studies" in *Kailash* v. I, n. 1 and n. 4 in *Kailash* (1973).
23. On the *rDzogs-chen sems-sde*, see Reynolds, *The Golden Letters*, ibid. and also Namkhai Norbu, *The Crystal and the Way of Light: Sutra, Tantra, and Dzogchen*, Arkana Penguin Books, London (1993).

24. *sNya-chen Li-shu stag-rings* was said to be a contemporary of the Tibetan king Trisong Detsan and was actively involved in the concealing of Terma texts. He is said to be the source for the *rDzogs-chen yang-rtse'i klong-chen*. See Karmay, *Treasury* (1972).
25. Usually it is said that the Rainbow Body ('ja'-lus) is accomplished at the point of death. However, the Rainbow Body of the Great Transfer ('ja'-lus 'pho-ba chen-po) is accomplished while the master is still alive. He simply dissolves into space and then reappears in a Body of Light ('od-lus). Among those who are believed to have attained the Great Transfer were Padmasambhava, Vimalamitra, and Tapihritsa.
26. On Tapihritsa and Gyerpung Nangzher Lodpo (Gyer-spungs snang-bzher lod-po), see Chapters Five, Six, and Seven in Reynolds, *The Oral Tradition from Zhang-zhung* (2005).

Notes to Chapter One: Introduction to the Practice of Dzogchen

1. *gCig brgyud*, transmission to a single disciple only. On the Twenty-four Masters, all of whom become Jalupas ('ja'-lus-pa) who realized the Rainbow Body ('ja'-lus), see Chapter Four in Reynolds, *The Oral Transmission from Zhang-zhung* (2005). Unlike the other traditions of Bonpo Dzogchen, the *Zhang-zhung snyan-rgyud* was never a Terma (gter-ma), or hidden treasure text, concealed during the eighth century persecution of Bon and rediscovered centuries later. For the traditional account of why this was not the case, see Chapter Seven in Reynolds, *The Oral Tradition from Zhang-zhung* (2005). On the Bonpo Termas in general, see Karmay, *Treasury* (1972).
2. The Guardians (bon-srung, bon-skyong) are the guardian spirits of the teachings of Bon. Some of them are emanations of enlightened beings, others represent nature spirits and pagan gods subdued and converted to Bon or Dharma by Tonpa Shenrab and other great masters in the past, such as Gyerpung Nangzher Lodpo. Among the Bonpos, the chief guardian of the Dzogchen teachings is the goddess Sidpa Gyalmo (srid-pa'i rgal-mo), who is a direct emanation of the Primordial Wisdom, Sherab Jyamma (shes-rab 'byams-ma). The former corresponds to Ekajati in the Nyingmapa system and to Paldan Lhamo (dpal-ldan lha-mo) in Tibetan Buddhism in general.

It was Sidpa gGalmo who, in a vision, urged Lopon Sangye Tenzin, formerly the Lopon or chief teacher at Menri Monastery in Tibet and later Lopon at the refounded monastery at Dolanji in India, to make the Dzogchen teachings more available, lest they be lost to humanity in these difficult times. On the goddess Sidpa Gyalmo, see Reynolds, *The Healing Practice for Sidpa Gyalmo* (1996) and on the Bonpo guardian Nyipangse, see Appendix Three in Reynolds, *The Oral Tradition from Zhang-zhung* (2005).

3. First translated from the Zhang-zhung language into the Tibetan language by Ponchen Tsanpo in the ninth century, see Chapter Eight in Reynolds, *The Oral Tradition from Zhang-zhung* (2005).

4. According to an article by Prof. Uray, the word bon may come from an old Tibetan verb *'bond-pa*, meaning "to invoke the gods." This would correspond to the Zhang-zhung word *gyer*, which was taken into Tibetan as a noun and as a verb *gyer-ba*, "to chant." Beckwith gives an alternative possibility, namely, that bon comes from the Sogdian *bwn* (pronounced bun) meaning Dharma. See Uray (1964) and Beckwith (1986).

5. The Tantra system speaks of yuganaddha, or unification (zung-'jug), where two separate things are brought together and then blended or merged into one, like pouring water into milk. In Dzogchen, the idea is not unification, but inseparability (dbyer-med), that is to say, they have never been separated. Although one may speak of two aspects for the sake of human understanding, in actual fact, they have never been separate, like water and wetness.

6. On the practice of Refuge and Bodhichitta in Bon, and on the Ngondro (sngon-'gro), or the preliminary practices in the Bonpo tradition, see Appendices One and Two in Reynolds, *The Oral Tradition from Zhang-zhung* (2005).

7. Whereas the individual enters into the practice of the Sutra system by way of taking vows and into the Tantra system by way of taking initiations, one enters into Dzogchen by way of receiving a direct introduction (ngo-sprod). After engaging in some preliminary practices, such as semdzin (sems-'dzin), or fixating the mind on a single object of meditation such as the white Tibetan letter A, and other Rushan exercises (see below), in order to impart some immediate experience of what is meant by mind (sems), the Lama points out to the practitioner what is the Nature of Mind (sems-nyid) and its in-

trinsic awareness (rig-pa). But to be directly introduced in this way alone is not enough. One must practice Rigpa, or contemplation, again and again in order to become familiar with it and remove all doubts with regards to its nature. Only then can one have confidence in it. This process corresponds to the Three Statements of Garab Dorje. On this and direct introduction, see Reynolds, *The Golden Letters* (1996).
8. The method of meditation proper to Dzogchen is that of self-liberation (rang-grol). See Reynolds, *The Golden Letters* (1996).
9. On Guru Yoga combined with Dzogchen or contemplation practice, see Appendix One in Reynolds, *The Oral Tradition from Zhang-zhung* (2005).
10. This practice of looking back at thoughts and searching for their source, or for the mind, is not unique to Dzogchen. Nevertheless, it represents a practice done at the beginning and later it is not necessary for the advanced practitioner, according to Lopon Tenzin Namdak.

Notes to Chapter Two: The Attaining of Buddhahood according to Sutra, Tantra and Dzogchen

1. According to Lopon Tenzin Namdak, the more immediate aim of the practice of the Higher Tantras is creation, by way of the practices of the generation process (bskyed-rim) and the perfection process (rdzogs-rim), of a Gyulu, or illusory body (sgyu-lus) comprised of mind (sems) and prana or subtle psychic energy (rlung). Such a subtle psychic body has the form of one's Yidam (yi-dam lha), or personal meditation deity, whether this form be peaceful or wrathful, male or female. This Yidam image represents a purified vision of oneself, a self-deification, that is in contrast to the normal impure karmic vision one has of oneself in everyday waking-state consciousness. By meditation upon oneself in this purified archetypal form the practitioner, during the course of sadhana practice, accesses those virtuous qualities, capacities, and wisdoms associated with that particular deity. Then, at the time of death, when the material body and the conscious mind separate, as a practitioner one transfers one's consciousness (rnam-shes) into this subtle body of the Yidam, which has been previously prepared by way of medita-

tion practice in one's lifetime. Although this in itself does not represent enlightenment and one needs to do further practices in order to purify subtle obscurations, one is no longer the passive victim of the various visions created by one's past karma in the Bardo, or after-death experience.

2. The two obscurations (sgrib-pa gnyis) are the emotional defilements, or kleshas, and the intellectual defilements, or distorted, wrong ideas about the nature of reality.

3. This example was added later by the Lopon by way of further explanation. On this question of the one and the many, see also the Appendix in Reynolds, *Self-Liberation* (1998).

4. The practices with sunlight, with total darkness, and with the empty sky are not the cause of the Thodgal visions but, rather, they serve as the supports (rten) for the manifestation of these visions, much as does the screen for a cinema show.

5. The generation process, or stages of generation (bskyed-rim), refers to the process of visualizing oneself in the form of the Yidam meditation deity in the sacred space of the mandala. When totally identifying oneself with this divine form or pure vision during the course of the sadhana or Tantric transformation process, the practitioner develops a divine pride (lha yi nga-rgyal). But none of this has any inherent existence. Before generating oneself as the deity, one dissolves all impure karmic vision, the way one sees things now in samsaric existence, into the state of Shunyata, emptiness or pure potentiality, which is like the clear, empty sky. The practitioner may succeed in totally identifying in concentration with the Yidam deity during the course of the sadhana or meditation session but, at the conclusion, the visualization is dissolved again into the pristine state of Shunyata, and one enters into formless contemplation (mnyam-bzhag) for a time. Even though there is no image or discursive thought in this state of even contemplation for focusing and anchoring consciousness, one is not unconscious. Rather, one is totally present and aware like the clear, open sky devoid of clouds but filled with sunlight. The dissolving of the visualization of oneself as the meditation deity before returning to the mundane waking state consciousness of reality (rjes thob), ensures that one does not confuse levels of reality and suffer ego inflation, that is to say, the false

identification of the empirical ego (impure karmic vision) with the pure archetype.
6. This clarification was added later by the Lopon.
7. That is to say, the Paths of Vision (mthong lam), Meditation (sgom lam), and Culmination (mthar thug lam), the latter also being known as the Path Beyond Training (mi slob lam).

Notes to Chapter Three: Four Essential Points for Understanding Dzogchen

1. The *Nam-mkha' 'phrul mdzod*, "The Magical Treasury of the Sky," attributed to Dranpa Namkha (eighth century), a contemporary of Guru Padmasambhava, belongs to one of the four principal cycles of Dzogchen teachings in Bon, the *Ye-khri mtha'-sel*, rediscovered by Lungton Lhanyen (Lung-stong lha-gnyan) in the eleventh century.
2. The Two Truths (bden-pa gnyis), the Relative Truth (kun rdzob) and the Absolute Truth (don-dam), refer to the understanding of reality according to the Sutra system and, in this context particularly, the Madhyamaka philosophy. The Two Truths are also applied in the Tantra system but Dzogchen has a different, non-dual, understanding.
3. On the understanding of the Primordial Buddha in Dzogchen, see Chapter Two in Reynolds, *The Oral Tradition from Zhang-zhung* (2005).
4. Thigley Nyagchik (thig-le nyag-gcig) has been translated as unique essence, single point, unique sphere, and so on, with reference to the non-dual totality of being. But this does not mean that Dzogchen is positing the existence of a single substance out of which all forms are fabricated, like a series of pots all made of clay. Nor is it postulating a single ocean of being into which all individual selves, like so many raindrops, fall and dissolve upon their liberation from the cycle of rebirth. Nor is it postulating a great "One Mind" in which all partial minds participate. As the Lopon pointed out, if there existed only One Mind, then when the historical Buddha attained enlightenment, all sentient beings would have become enlightened. Or again, if Kuntu Zangpo is primordially enlightened as the One Mind, then diversity would have never come into ap-

pearance. Nevertheless, this reflects the perennial problem of the one and the many, and how the latter can be derived from the former. The Thigley Nyagchik transcends this dichotomy in the view of Dzogchen. On this problem in relation to universality and individuality in terms of Buddha enlightenment, see the Appendix in Reynolds, *Self-Liberation* (1998).

5. This Buddhist teaching that a self does not exist as an eternal unchanging entity, Anatmavada, contrasts with the Hindu Vedantic view that the self (atman) is all that exists. For the Buddhist view, the self is unreal and insubstantial, lacking any essence or inherent existence. By means of practicing meditation and observing the mind, one discovers not some unchanging abiding entity or substance that can be designated "the self" but, rather, a constantly changing stream of consciousness. The Buddhist view, however, also contrasts with the dualistic view of Samkhya and similar movements in Ancient India that postulated two distinct orders of reality, originally existing independently, that is to say, Nature (prakriti), which is constantly in flux and undergoing evolution, as against a plurality of spirits or selves (purusha), who are the passive witnesses to the activities of Nature. Nature is active, but blind and unconscious, whereas Spirit is conscious, but passive and inactive, like an audience watching a dancing girl. Whereas the Buddha rejected Samkhya's radical dualism, the dialogue between the Buddhist and the Vedantist points of view is much more subtle.

6. Here, in one's meditation practice, there is a two-fold investigation into the meaning of Atman or self (bdag). First, there is the conventional notion of a self in persons and the grasping at this supposed self as real (gang-zag gi bdag 'dzin), as a permanent entity or substance having an essence or inherent existence. Second, there is the conventional notion of a substance in or behind phenomena, a stuff that they are made of, and the grasping at the reality of that stuff (bon gyi bdag 'dzin). The first kind of no-self in persons (gang-zag gi bdag-med) is realized in Hinayana, whereas, in addition, the second kind of no-self in phenomena, their insubstantiality, is realized in Mahayana. Note that whenever a Tibetan Buddhist text has the term *chos*, a Bonpo text will have the word *bon*. In both cases, these words translate the Sanskrit 'dharma' or 'phenomenon'.

Notes to Chapter Four: The View of Shunyata found in Madhyamaka, Chittamatra and Dzogchen

1. This transcript has been compiled from the notes I made at retreats held with Lopon Tenzin Namdak in Bischofshofen and Vienna, Austria, in Devon, England, and in Amsterdam, the Netherlands. Thus this transcript represents a compilation of the Lopon's teachings on Shunyata over the course of four retreats, and I have taken the liberty, with his permission, of adding any additional clarifications required here and any sentences needed to link the various paragraphs or topics. Also I have added subheadings for the purpose of clarification.

2. Here the Lopon is speaking on the side of the doctrinal system as formulated logically and scholastically, and not on the side of the individual practitioner who can, of course, change his or her mind or change course mid-stream. If philosophical systems postulate different bases, then logically their paths of practice will be different and consequently their results will be different. For example, if one sows barley seeds in a field, one cannot expect wheat as the harvest.

3. Note that in Dzogchen, one also requires secondary causes to bring about the visible manifestation of the Trikaya. The Trikaya is latent in the Natural State, but invisible. It is not like a statue sitting in a temple with an open door. The Lopon suggests that this may be compared with the Jonangpa view.

4. Longchenpa (Kun-mkhyen klong-chen rab-'byams-pa (fourteenth century) in his magnum opus the *mDzod bdun*, or Seven Treasuries, came to place Dzogchen in the context of Indian Buddhist teaching and clearly demonstrated it is the real teaching of the Buddha, in fact, the culmination of the Prajnaparamita, and not some heresy or import from outside.

5. These questions are discussed in another series of texts known as the *Gal-mdo*, in particular the *gTan-tshigs gal-mdo rig-pa'i tshad-ma*.

Notes to Chapter Five: The Views of Tantra, Mahamudra and Dzogchen

1. This is more or less true of all the Sarmapa schools. But nowadays, and even for some preceding centuries, the Geshes, or Lama scholars, belonging to the Menri tradition of Bon, studied and were familiar with the expositions of the Dharma by the great Tsongkhapa and certain other Gelugpa scholars, whereas they were not so likely to be familiar with Nyingmapa, Sakyapa, and Kagyudpa treatises. For example, only later while in India during exile from his homeland in Tibet, did the Lopon come to read the *mDzod bdun* of Longchen Rabjyampa and found this superb exposition of Dzogchen to be in full agreement with the Bonpo understanding. In the earlier period, Yeru Wensakha (g.yas ru dben-sa-kha), the monastery preceding Tashi Menri Monastery, lacking its own philosophy college, sent its candidate Geshes to the nearby Sakyapa monastery of Druyul Kyedtsal (Brus-yul skyed-tshal) to pursue their Sutra system studies. In later centuries, after the establishment of the Gelugpa hegemony in central Tibet in the time of the Fifth Dalai Lama, Tashi Menri Monastery, re-established in 1405 by Nyammed Sherab Gyaltsan, sent its candidate Geshes to Drepung Monastery for Sutra studies. Consequently, Bonpo Lama scholars of the Menri tradition are quite familiar with the works of Je Tsongkhapa and with Gelugpa exegesis in general.

2. In the era of the New Translations, the Prasangika Madhyamaka system was introduced into Tibet by Patsab Lotsawa (sPa-tshab lotswa-ba Nyi-ma grags). He translated the seminal texts of Prasangika into Tibetan, including the *Prasannapada* of Chandrakirti. Patsab Lotsawa lived in the twelfth century. He was a native of 'Phanyul and went to Kashmir as a boy in 1137; for twenty-three years he studied with many Buddhist scholars in India, including the two sons of Sanjana, Hasumati and Kanakavarman. When he returned to Tibet, he taught the six treatises of Nagarjuna, translated the *Prasannapada*, the *Madhyamakavatara* and its auto-commentary, and Chandrakirti's commentary to the *Yuktishashtika*. He revised the translation of Chandrakirti's *Shunyatasaptati* and translated the Sutrasamuccaya with the collaboration of Khudo Debar (Khu-mdo sde-'bar) and the Kashmiri scholar Jayananda. He gathered about him many disciples. See George Roerich, *The Blue Annals* (1974),

pp. 230, 236, 272, 341-2, 344, 350. As the result of his efforts, Prasangika Madhyamaka became the intellectual fashion in Tibet and replaced the earlier eclectic Svatantrika-Yogachara-Madhyamaka system of Shantirakshita. Generally, Prasangika Madhyamaka is now the official philosophy and party line in all Tibetan schools, including the Nyingmapa and the Bonpo, at least in terms of Sutra system studies.

3. The *Lam-rim chen-mo* represents Tsongkhapa's great exposition of the Sutra path, following in the tradition of the *Bodhipathapradipa* of Atisha (eleventh century). His *sNgags-rim chen-mo* represents his equally famous exposition of the Mantra path or Tantra system.

4. The Hwashang Mahayana was the representative of the viewpoint of Ch'an Buddhism in Tibet. According to the Tibetan histories of the Middle Ages, he was defeated in face-to-face debate by Kamalashila, the chief Indian disciple of the Abbot Shantirakshita and the leading proponent of the gradual path of Indian Madhyamaka. As the result of this encounter, Kamalashila wrote his famous treatise, the *Bhavanakrama* (sgom-rim). It is said that the Hwashang was forced to flee Tibet in disgrace, leaving behind only his shoes. But according to ancient texts (tenth century) discovered at the Tun Huang library in Central Asia, the Hwashang never actually entered Tibet, but only communicated with the Tibetan king Trisong Detsan by way of correspondence. These documents preserved in Tibetan and Chinese represent his side of the controversy, expressing the sudden enlightenment point of view.

5. The Bonpo tradition has four classes of Tantras. The Outer or Lower Tantras (phyi rgyud) are:
   (1) Kriya Tantra (bya-ba'i rgyud), the Tantra of Ritual Activity, and
   (2) Charya Tantra (spyod-pa'i rgyud), the Tantra of Conduct (that is both external and internal). These designations are also employed for the Lower Tantras in the Buddhist schools. In the Lower Tantras, the Yidam, or meditation deity, is visualized in the sky or the space in front of oneself (mdun bskyed) and the practitioner prays to receive the blessings and capacities of the Yidam, thereby actualizing them within oneself. However, there is still a separation between oneself and the Yidam; its

presence is invoked out of space and at the end of the sadhana practice, it again dissolves back into space.

The Inner or Higher Tantras (nang-rgyud) are:
(3) Yeshen Tantra (ye-gshen gyi rgyud), the Tantra of Primordial Practice, and
(4) Yeshen Chenpo Tantra (ye-gshen chen-po'i rgyud), the Tantra of Total Primordial Practice.

This third class of Tantra is divided into Father Tantra (pha rgyud) and Mother Tantra (ma rgyud). In the sadhana practice here, not only does one visualize the deity and the mandala in the space in front, but also one transforms oneself in visualization (bdag bskyed) into the form and experience of the deity. The Father Tantra emphasizes this visualization or generation process (bskyed-rim). Chief among the Father Tantras are the General Collection, or Chyipung cycle (spyi-spungs skor), featuring the three Yidams: Walse, Lhagod and Tsochok, representing the Body, Speech and Mind aspects of the Buddha. The peaceful form of Lhagod is Mawe Senge (smra-ba'i seng-ge), the Bonpo form of Manjushri, who is the patron of scholarly learning and dialectic studies (mtshan-nyid). Tsochok is accompanied by a large retinue of Peaceful and Wrathful Deities (zhi khro lha tsgogs), such as those described in the Tibetan Book of the Dead. This group is further expanded into five Yidams, or meditation deities, representing the enlightened Body, Speech, Mind Quality, and Activity aspects of the Buddha. These are known as the Five Divine Citadels (gsas-mkhar mchog lnga), namely,
(1) Walse (dBal-gsas rngam-pa)
(2) Lhagod (Lha-rgod thog-pa),
(3) Tsochok (Khro-bo gtso-mchog mkha'-'gying),
(4) Gekhod (dBal-chen ge-khod), and
(5) Phurpa (dBal-phur nag-po).

Also in Bon, we find the Mother Tantra, or *Ma rgyud thugs-rje nyi-ma*, where the Yidam is known as Sangchok Gyalpo (gSang-mchog rgyal-po). Here the goal is explained very much in terms of Dzogchen and the emphasis is on the perfection process (rdzogs-rim), where the practitioner comes to experience internally what the Yidam experiences. These six yogas for Method (thabs-lam), Sleep (gnyid), Dream (rmi-la), Bardo (bar-do), Chod (gcod), and Consciousness Transference ('pho-ba) are similar to the Six Yogas of Naropa. However, in the Mother Tantra, the male aspect (yab) represents Shunyata or space (dbyings) and the female aspect (yum) represents wisdom or awareness (ye-shes). The final class, Yeshen Chenpo, consists mainly of Guru Sadhana practices and is even more closely connected with Dzogchen.

6. This was my own experience in Darjeeling years ago with Kangyur Rinpoche and Kalu Rinpoche who definitely asserted that Mahamudra and Dzogchen were the same. But this was the Mahamudra of Gampopa. As pointed out by Namkhai Norbu Rinpoche also, both possess four yogas or contemplations (rnal-'byor bzhi, ting-'dzin bzhi) described in almost identical terms, for Mahamudra: *tshe-gcig, spros-bral, ro-gcig, bsgom-med*, and for Dzogchen: *gnas-pa, mi g.yo-ba, mnyam-med, lhun-grub*. See Namkhai Norbu, *The Crystal and the Way of Light: Sutra, Tantra, and Dzogchen* (1993).

7. Here the Lopon is not speaking specifically of the Mahamudra of Gampopa, which has been propagated widely by the Kagyudpa school of Tibetan Buddhism. Gampopa received this transmission from his own master Milarepa, who had been influenced previously by the Dzogchen Semde (sems-sde) teachings of his Nyingmapa Lamas. Rather, we are concerned here with Mahamudra as defined in various commentaries on the practice of Anuttara Tantra where Mahamudra represents the culmination of the Tantric practice of transformation.

8. The Path of Vision is the third among the five successive paths in both the Sutra and the Tantra system, namely, the Path of Accumulation (tshogs lam), the Path of Unification (sbyor lam), the Path of Vision (mthong lam), the Path of Meditation (sgom lam), and the Path Beyond Training (mi slob lam), also known as the Ultimate Path (mthar thug lam). These five paths are combined with the ten stages, or bhumis (sa bcu), pertaining to the career of the Bodhisattva. The first bhumi belongs to the Path of Vision, the remaining ones to the Path of Meditation.

9. This is in accordance with strict logic, that is, speaking from the side of the system. From the side of the individual practitioner, it is a different matter, because one can always change course. One counter-argument runs: If we want to go to New York City, we can take a jet plane, or a train, or a bus, or a car, or a bicycle, or even walk — but in every case we come to New York City. So different methods can lead to the same goal. But here the Base is the same:

the human being who decides to go to New York; only the means of transportation differ.

10. Among the three methods or approaches to the spiritual path, the Path of Renunciation (spong lam) of the Sutra system employs antidotes to the negative emotions, the Path of Transformation (sgyur lam) of the Tantra system employs visualizations in meditation and transforms these negative emotions, and the Path of Self-Liberation (grol lam) of Dzogchen simply allows the energies of these negative emotions to dissolve of themselves, or self-liberate (rang grol).

11. According to Tibetan scholasticism, any spiritual path or philosophical system can be analyzed in terms of the base or foundation (gzhi), the path or practice (lam), and the fruit or result ('bras-bu). The base of any system will logically and inevitably define and condition both the practice and the final result. Therefore, if the bases are different, the results will inevitably be different, according to this logic.

12. The method of practicing the fruit as a cause on the path means visualizing oneself as the meditation deity in the mandala and thereby accessing within one's mind-stream its powers, capacities and wisdoms. This method is in agreement in aspect with the result or the fruit, that is to say, the Rupakaya.

13. The Jonangpas were a school, in some ways affiliated with the Sakyapas, which produced some great Lama scholars like Dolpopa and Taranatha. Moreover, they were famous for their exegesis of the *Kalachakra Tantra* and for their interpretation of Madhyamaka that differed from that of Chandrakirti. They were suppressed in the time of the Fifth Dalai Lama, largely for political reasons, and disappeared from the scene in central Tibet. However, they have continued to flourish as an independent school in eastern Tibet until the present day. The Jonangpas also asserted an interpretation of the Tathagatagarbha, or inherent Buddha Nature in all sentient beings, in some ways similar to Dzogchen, but they did not know the practice of Thodgal that provides the secondary causes for the visible manifestation of Buddha enlightenment, the Rupakaya.

14. Thigleys (thig-le, Skt. Bindu) are energy droplets occurring in the system of subtle psychic channels of the body of the yogi. These energy droplets are activated through the practice of Tummo (gtum-mo), or inner psychic heat, known in Hindu yoga as Kundalini.

Notes to Chapter Six: The View of Dzogchen

1. On the Dharmakaya and the masters in the lineage for the Zhang-zhung Nyan-gyud, see Reynolds, *The Oral Tradition from Zhang-zhung* (2005), Chapters Two through Nine.
2. Geshe (dge-bshes, Skt. kalyanamitra), literally "good spiritual friend," is the term used not only in Bon but also in the Sakyapa and Gelugpa schools, for an individual who has completed the course of Sutra studies
3. The two principal systems of Bonpo Termas, or hidden treasure texts discovered from the tenth century onwards are (1) the system of the Southern Treasures (lho gter lugs), chiefly the discoveries of Shenchen Luga (gShen-chen klu-dga') in 1017 in southern Tibet, and (2) the system of the Central Treasures (dbus gter lugs), so-called from their discovery at Samye Monastery and other locations in central Tibet. In both cases, these discoveries consisted of actual physical texts from an earlier era. They are said to have been concealed by Dranpa Namkha, Lishu Tagring, and other Bonpo masters during the persecution of Bon in the eighth century. The description of the Nine Successive Ways of Bon (bon theg-pa rim dgu) differs in these two systems. A translation of the description of these Nine Ways found in the *gZi-brjid* will be found in Snellgrove, *The Nine Ways of Bon* (1967). The Nine Ways in the system of the Central Treasures is more similar to the Nyingmapa system of Nine Ways.
4. On Tapihritsa and Gyerpungpa, see Reynolds, *The Oral Tradition from Zhang-zhung* (2005), Chapters Five through Seven.
5. The designations of these three classes of Dzogchen teachings properly belong to the Nyingmapa system. See Reynolds, *The Golden Letters* (1996). The principal Bonpo traditions of Dzogchen, including the Zhang-zhung Nyan-gyud, represent Dzogchen Upadesha (man-ngag gi sde). However, according to the Lopon, some of the texts among the Central Treasures, such as the *Nam-mkha' 'phrul mdzod* of Dranpa Namkha, could be classified as Dzogchen Semde (sems-sde). The class Dzogchen Longde (klong-sde) is not extant in Bon.
6. The Lopon later explained that this matter was discussed much more elaborately in the text known as the *Gal mdo*.

Notes to Chapter Seven: The Practice of Dzogchen

1. Tazik (stag-gzig) was the name in Tibetan for Ancient Central Asia, the region now known as Tajikistan, Uzbekistan, and northern Afghanistan. Uddiyana (o-rgyan) may also be identified with eastern Afghanistan. It was not simply the tiny Swat valley in modern day Pakistan. See Upasak, *History of Buddhism in Afghanistan* (1990).
2. Lung-ston (var. Lung-bon) Lha-gnyan, b. 1088, is said to have met in person the sage Tsewang Rigdzin (Tshe-dbang reg-'dzin), who was disguised as a Hindu sadhu. Tsewang Rigdzin was the son of Dranpa Namkha (eighth century) and he was said to have realized the power of long life (tshe dbang) through his yoga practice and so he was still alive in the eleventh century. The cycle of Dzogchen teachings he transmitted to Lung-ton Lha-nyen is known as the *Ye-khri mtha' sel*, the removing of extreme (views) with regard to the Primordial State.
3. For the Ngondro (sngon-'gro) and the *'Bum-dgu* associated with the Zhang-zhung Nyan-gyud found in the practice manual entitled the *rGyal-ba phyag-khrid*, composed by Druchen Gyalwa Yungdrung (Bru-chen rgyal-ba g.yung-drung, 1242-1290), see Appendix Two in Reynolds, *The Oral Tradition from Zhang-zhung* (2005).
4. On the relationship of this method, the system of the ascetics (ku-su-li-pa'i lugs), to the three statements of Garab Dorje, see Reynolds, *The Golden Letters* (1996).
5. The scholastic approach to Dzogchen is known as the system of the learned scholars (mkhas-pa pandita'i lugs). The Bonpo educational program developed by Lopon Tenzin Namdak for the Dialectics School at Menri Monastery differs from that of the Nyingmapa and Sarmapa schools in that the academic study of the views of Tantra and Dzogchen are included together with Sutra system studies. In this way, the Bonpos bring Dzogchen out into the philosophical marketplace, so to speak, entering into a dialogue with Madhyamaka, Chittamatra, and other systems regarding philosophical views, rather than keeping Dzogchen strictly as a system of private meditation instruction.
6. Dzogchen may use various terms taken from the Sutra system, such as shamatha (zhi-gnas) and vipashyana (lhag-mthong), but the meanings in each case are not necessarily the same.

7. Semdzin (sems-'dzin) exercises are employed for fixating ('dzin) the mind (sems) on a single object of meditation, such as the white Tibetan letter A.
8. On Guru Yoga practice combined with Dzogchen, see Appendix One in Reynolds, *The Oral Tradition from Zhang-zhung* (2005).
9. See Reynolds, *Selections from the Bonpo Book of the Dead* (1997). Also see Reynolds, *The Path of the Clear Light*, forthcoming.
10. The higher attainments known as the dhyanas (bsam-gtan) are achieved through concentrated meditation upon forms (dmigs-bcas, mtshan-bcas) and the samapattis (snyoms-'jug) are achieved through concentrated meditation without forms (dmigs-med, mtshan-med), that is, simply fixation on a location in empty space.
11. On the distinction between Ch'an and Zen on the one hand and Dzogchen on the other, see the Appendix in Reynolds, *The Golden Letters* (1996). Also, for a Tibetan understanding of the issue, see Namkhai Norbu, *Zen and Dzogchen* (1984).
12. This represents the explanation of the cause for the realization of the Dharmakaya and of the Rupakaya according to Dzogchen. This differs from the Sutra system where the cause for realizing the Dharmakaya is the accumulation of wisdom (ye-shes kyi tshogs) and the cause for realizing the Rupakaya is the accumulation of merit (bsod-nams kyi tshogs) by virtue of the practice of the Paramitas. According to the Higher Tantras, the Rupakaya is realized by means of the meditation practices of Kyerim and Dzogrim, the generation and perfection processes, where the practitioner constructs a Gyulu (sgyu-lus), or illusion body, composed of prana or psychic energy and subtle mind.
13. The process of dissolving the gross material elements of the physical human body back into the subtle elements in their pure form of radiant light in their respective colours is known as *ru-log*, or reversal. This reversal occurs on the occasion of realization of the Rainbow Body ('ja'-lus) at the time of death. Only the clothing, hair and nails are left behind because they are not suffused with the consciousness of the individual.
14. As the Lopon has said elsewhere, all of our life is but a preparation for death and what comes afterwards. Regarding the Bardo practices and Phowa, the transference of consciousness, as preparations for death and the Bardo experience in the context of the Bonpo tradition, see Reynolds, *Selections from the Bonpo Book of the*

Dead (1997). Also see Reynolds, *The Path of the Clear Light*, forthcoming.

Notes to Chapter Eight: Rushans: The Preliminary Practices of Dzogchen

1. For the Ngondro and preliminary practices in relation to the Zhang-zhung Nyan-gyud, see Appendix Two in Reynolds, *The Oral Tradition from Zhang-zhung* (2005).
2. All of these different states of higher consciousness, the dhyanas and the samapattis, are elaborately described in the Abhidharma literature (mdzod). Among Tibetan Buddhists, the principal text for cosmological studies is the *Abhidharmakosha* of Vasubandhu (fourth century), whereas for Bonpos, it is the *Srid-pa'i mdzod-phug*, the root text being attributed to Tonpa Shenrab and the commentary to Dranpa Namkha (eighth century).
3. When one practices meditation for some time and becomes deeply relaxed, this is said to release the energies of the material elements of one's body and one has certain visions and experiences.

Notes to Chapter Nine: Introduction to Thekchod and Thodgal

1. All of the individual's tensions, rigidities and obscurations are compared to a bundle of sticks (khregs-pa) tied together with a cord or rope. When one cuts (chod) this cord, all of the sticks immediately fall to the ground. Therefore, the term Thekchod means the releasing of all one's tensions and rigidities in a totally relaxed state (lhod-pa chen-po). The latter term is also a synonym for Dzogchen.
2. Tsewang Rigdzin revealed these Dzogchen teachings, which he had received from his father Dranpa Namkha, to Lung-ton Lha-nyen in the eleventh century.
3. These four yogas or contemplations are also found in the Mahamudra of Gampopa, which he learned from his master Milarepa, who was a colleague and friend of Lung-ton Lha-nyen.

Notes to the Appendix

1. The personal name Tenzin Namdak means in Tibetan the completely pure (rnam-dag) holder of the teachings (bstan 'dzin). In general, the title Lopon (slob-dpon, Skt. acharya) designates the head teacher or professor in a monastic institution. A Lopon is principally in charge of educating the new monks both in terms of the Dharma and the Vinaya, whereas the Abbot or Khenpo (mkhan-po, Skt. upadhyaya) is, in general, the chief religious administrator of the monastery and the senior monk who administers the monastic vows to the novices and other monks. The honorific title Yongdzin (yongs 'dzin) usually designates the tutor and philosophy instructor superintending the education of high incarnate Lamas. Rinpoche (rin-po-che) does not necessarily mean a Tulku (sprul-sku) or recognized reincarnate Lama; it is the honorific term meaning "the most precious one" extended to religious personages worthy of great respect for their extensive learning and/or accomplishments in meditation practice. The Lopon belongs to the tradition of Menri Monastery, the Abbots of which, known as Menri Trizin (sman-ri khri-'dzin) or the throne-holders of Menri, are selected by lot, rather than by reincarnation. Thus, the institution of Tulkus is not very prevalent in the tradition of Old Bon, although there are some Bonpo Tulkus or recognized reincarnations in this school.

2. According to Tibetan convention, an individual is one year old at birth and so in the view of the Lopon and his family, he was eight years old when he entered Tengchen Monastery, the legal age for doing so as a novice.

3. Bonpo monasteries and practitioners predominate in the Khyungpo district of eastern Tibet or Kham. The area of Tengchen (steng-chen) consists of the valleys of the southward flowing Gachu and Ruchu tributaries of the great Selween river and those of the northwest flowing feeder rivers known as Dakchu and Kyilkhorchu. In Tibetan the word *chu* means "river" as well as "water" in general. The capital of the district is called Tengchen, also known as Gyamotang. Tengchen town is situated in a wide cultivated valley hemmed in by sandstone hills. The old Tibetan village of Tengchen-kha and the modern district town of Tengchen (altitude 3,750m) face each other across the Dakchu river. When visiting the village of Tengchen-kha, Gyurme Dorje found the people to be extremely

hospitable and tolerant. Bonpos, Nyingmapas and Gelugpas all participated together in the Tsechu or tenth-day festival for Guru Padmasambhava. Most of the monasteries in the region are Bonpo rather than Buddhist. The two most important monasteries are on the northern ridge that overlooks the river and is across from Tengchen-kha. They are Tengchen (steng-chen) Monastery and Ritro Lhakang (ri-khrod lha-khang). Tengchen Monastery is also called Namdak Pema Long-yang (rnam-dag padma klong-yangs). It was founded in 1110 by Sherab Gyaltsan and Monlam Gyaltsan. The third lineage holder after these two greatly expanded the community of yogis around Tengchen and established Ritro Lhakang hermitage above the temple in 1180. The two monasteries have close connections with the Bonpo monasteries of Menri and Yungdrung Ling in central Tibet, as well as with the Ngawa region and Nangzhik Monastery in particular. Repairs to Tengchen Monastery were made possible by donations from Lopon Tenzin Namdak on his visit to Tengchen in 1986. These renovations continue under the direction of Lama Sherab Gelek, who was enthroned as the abbot of the monastery by the Lopon. Particularly notable at Tengchen is Nampar Gyalwa Lhakhang (rnam-par rgyal-ba lha-khang) with many wall-paintings of deities and mandalas. Ritro Lhakang also has an abbot's residence (bla-brang) and many notable wall-paintings, including a chamber containing the reliquary of Monlam Gyaltsan and also other early lineage holders, namely, Nyima Gyaltsan, Kunga Gyaltsan, Jimpa Gyaltsan, Tsultrim Gyaltsan, Yungdrung Gyaltsan, and Tsultrim Nyima. Formerly both monasteries had about three hundred monks each, but nowadays (1999) Tengchen has eighty-five and Ritro Lhakang has only twenty-three. See Gyurme Dorje, *Footprint Tibet Handbook* (1999), p. 388-389.

4. As for the distinction between Old and New Bon, New Bon (bon gsar-ma) arose from the fourteenth century onwards, relying upon the discoveries of a different Terma system from that of Old Bon. As a whole, this system is quite similar to the Nyingmapa one and here Padmasambhava is also regarded as an important figure. Indeed, some Tertons, such as Dorje Lingpa, discovered both Nyingmapa and Bonpo Termas. In a text such as the *Bon-khrid*, rediscovered by Tsewang Gyalpo, it is asserted that Padmasambhava went to Uddiyana and received the Dzogchen teachings directly from the

Sambhogakaya Shenlha Odkar (gShen-lha 'od-dkar) himself. Later he transmitted these teachings in Tibet, concealing many of them as Termas meant for the use of future generations of Bonpos. According to Shardza Rinpoche also, the New Bon Movement began in the fourteenth century and continues until today. The Termas revealed to such masters as Lodan Nyingpo, Mizhik Dorje (otherwise known as Dorje Lingpa), Kundrol Dragpa, Dechen Lingpa, Sang-ngag Lingpa, Khandro Dechen Wangmo, and so on, are all considered Tersar (gter-gsar) or recent treasure text discoveries. The New Bon has flourished mainly in eastern Tibet. The Termas revealed to *bLo-ldan snying-po* (b. 1360), *Mi-zhig rDo-rje*, otherwise known as *rDo-rje gling-pa* (1346-1405), *Kun-grol grags-pa* (b. 1700), *bDe-chen gling-pa* (b.1833), *gSang-sngags gling-pa* (b. 1864), *mKha'-'gro bDe-chen dbang-mo* (b.1868), etc., are considered recent treasure text discoveries (gter gsar). Among those listed here, Dorje Lingpa is also well-known as a Nyingmapa Terton. On Dorje Lingpa, see Eva Dargyay, *The Rise of Esoteric Buddhism in Tibet* (1977), pp. 139-143. On the New Bon Termas in general, see Karmay, *Treasury* (1972), pp.182-190.

5. The three river valleys of Oyuk, Thobgyal, and Shang in Tsang province are now known as Namling (rnam-gling) district. Through these valleys flow the Nam-gung-chu, the Thobpu-chu, and the Shang-chu, respectively. Their tributaries all rise amid the southern slopes of the Nyenchen Thanglha mountain range to the north and flow southward to converge with the Tsangpo or Brahmaputra river. This is an important region in Bonpo history. Menri Monastery lies in the Thobgyal valley and Yungdrung Ling, founded in 1834 by Dawa Gyaltsan (Zla-ba rgyal-mthsan), a colleague and friend of the Abbot of Menri, Nyima Tenzin, lies in the lower Oyuk valley to the east of Thobgyal. See Gyurme Dorje, *Footprint Tibet Handbook* (1999), p. 249.

6. For example, the Lopon did all the line drawings in the study of Bon published by the Tibetologist David Snellgrove. See David Snellgrove, *The Nine Ways of Bon* (1967).

7. According to the Nepali Buddhist text, the *Svayambhu Purana*, seven Buddhas in succession have visited this hill and graced it with their presence, namely, Vipashyin, Shikhin, Vishvabhu, Krakucchanda, Kanakamuni, Kashyapa, and the historical Buddha Shakya-

muni. According to local legend, the great stupa of Baudhanath at the eastern end of the valley contains the relics of the Buddha Kashyapa. Again, an inscription of the Buddhist emperor Ashoka found on a pillar in the Tarai asserts that he once restored a stupa in this location that was said to have contained the relics of the Buddha Kanakamuni. It is said that at the time of the visit of the Buddha Vipashyin, the Kathmandu Valley was still a large Naga lake, and on a lotus growing from a small island, he saw a self-originated light (svayamabhu-jyoti). Later, according to legend, the great Bodhisattva Manjushri came to this lake from China, and intrigued by this same self-originated light, he cut a cleft in the southern hills bounding the lake at the Chobar Gorge and drained the lake. Thus, the hill of Swayambhu became visible. It is said in the Bonpo tradition that in the same way as these other six prehistoric Buddhas visited the sacred hill, Tonpa Shenrab did so as well.

8. When one follows the Thobpu-chu river northward upstream from its confluence with the Tsangpo or Brahmaputra river, one finds that the valley splits in two and the village of Thobgyal (thob-rgyal) is located near this dividing of the valley. Then when one continues following the eastern branch upstream, now known as the Zhung-chu river, by way of Gangpa one comes to the sites of the Bonpo monasteries of Yeru Wensakha (g.yas-ru dben-sa-kha), Menri (sman-ri) and Kharna (mkhar-sna). Yeru Wensakha was founded in 1072 by Druje Yungdrung Lama (Bru-rje g.yung-drung bla-ma), a follower of the famous Bonpo Terton Shenchen Luga (gShen-chen klu-dga', 996-1035), who discovered the great collection of Bonpo texts known as the Southern Treasures (lho gter lugs). This master especially entrusted his disciple Druchen Namkha Yungdrung with the preservation of *mtshan-nyid* or the philosophical texts he had recovered. For centuries thereafter this monastery was closely connected with the Dru clan (bru rigs) and many of its Geshes were sent for their academic studies to the Sakyapa monastery of Bruyul Kyedtsal (brus-yul skyed-tshal), for at this time Sakya represented the greatest monastic university in Tibet. Yeru Wensakha Monastery was destroyed in a disastrous flood in 1386, leaving little remaining. However, the ruins of this foundation are still visible. According to local legend, at that time a Sadhu came from India and felt that he was not treated respectfully at the monastery. Therefore, he performed some black magic and sent down a flood that

destroyed the monastery entirely. However, the monks were able to save the library and this was preserved at the later Menri Monastery. The villagers from nearby Thobgyal were also able to save some other things from the monastery. Rebuilt higher up the slopes of the Zhungchu valley, Tashi Menri Monastery (bkra-shis smanri), "the auspicious medicine mountain," was founded in 1405 by Nyammed Sherab Gyaltsan (mNyam-med Shes-rab rgyal-mtshan), the greatest scholar in the Bonpo tradition, ranking with Longchen Rabjampa among the Nyingmapas, Sakya Pandita among the Sakyapas, and Je Tsongkhapa among the Gelugpas. It is said that this event had been predicted by the Buddha Tonpa Shenrab himself. For centuries Menri Monastery was the most important Bonpo teaching center for Old Bon in all of Tibet. Menri would attract monk students, such as the Lopon himself, from Tengchen, Ngawa, and Gyarong districts in eastern Tibet. Prior to its destruction in the 1960s in the Cultural Revolution, it housed more than three hundred monks. Now there are only about fifty monks living among the extensive ruins. Some rebuilding has been carried out. In former times, there were four colleges, including a dialectics school or Shedra (bshad-grwa) and a large assembly hall. The oldest extant building is known as Red Hermitage (grub-khang dmar-po). Further upstream are the Kharna caves where Bonpo hermits and yogis practiced for centuries. A new monastery was founded there in 1838 by Sherab Yungdrung. See Gyurme Dorgye, *Footprint Tibet Handbook* (1999), p. 249-250.

9. See David Snellgrove, *The Nine Ways of Bon* (1967)
10. When the Lopon escaped from Tibet, he was able to bring two valuable texts with him. The first was an anthology of texts from the *Zhang-zhung snyan-rgyud* cycle, printed from blocks carved at Menri Monastery in Tibet, probably in the 1950s. This block-print edition was later republished in New Delhi. For the contents of this collection, see Chapter Ten above. The second was an *dbu-med* (headless script) hand-written copy of the *Ma rgyud thugs-rje nyima*, including the three root texts or Tantras and their commentaries from the cycle of the Bonpo Mother Tantra. These texts were also later reprinted by photo offset in India.
11. Lokesh Chandra and Lopon Tenzin Namdak, *History and Doctrine of Bon-po Nispanna-Yoga* (1968).

12. The number of Bonpo refugees was small in proportion to the total flood of Tibetan refugees, according to the official Chinese Government census of Tibet and China; the Tibetan followers of the Gelugpa school form the largest single group in the ethnic Tibetan population. However, as the second largest group among the ethnic Tibetans, the Nyingmapas and the Bonpos are tied. The various Kagyudpa groups are smaller and the Sakyapas constitute the smallest group in the Tibetan population. (Oral communication from Lopon Tenzin Namdak).
13. See Tadeusz Skorupski, "Tibetan gYung-Drung Bon Monastery in India" (1981), (1983).
14. Tadeusz Skorupski, "Tibetan gYung-Drung Bon Monastery in India" (1983). At the time when Skorupski visited the monastery, the monastic community was comprised of three groups of monks. The first group consisted of twenty older monks who had come from Tibet. Their main activities were to perform puja ceremonies at the houses of lay people, private religious practices, and participate in all the rituals in the temple at the monastery. The second group consisted of thirty-five young monks who had taken their monastic vows at the new monastery. They were being educated by the Lopons in traditional Bonpo studies and trained to live according to the Vinaya. The monastery provided these students with a mid-day meal of rice and dal, afternoon tea, and soup (thug-pa) in the evening. As for their clothing and their morning tea and bread, they had to provide these items for themselves. Their syllabus consisted of philosophy (mtshan-nyid), epistemology and logic (tshad-ma), Prajnaparamita (phar-phyin), the paths and stages (sa-lam), Madhyamaka (du-ma), cosmology (mdzod-phug), monastic discipline ('dul-ba), Tantra (rgyud), Dzogchen (rdzogs-chen), religious history (bon-'byung), poetry (sdeb-sbyor), astrology (rtsis) and grammar (sgra). The third group consisted of boys between seven and fourteen years of age. They received a primary education in the Central Government School in the village near the monastery. The normal school syllabus included Hindi and English, and in addition they were taught Tibetan grammar and history. These boys had a separate kitchen and took responsibility for collecting firewood and preparing their own meals. All boys, whether orphans or not, were maintained by the monastery. Parents were not obliged to pay for their sons' upkeep, but contributions were welcome. When a boy

joins the monastic community, he has his head shaved (symbolic of renouncing the world) and receives a new name in a short ceremony called *tshe-ring*, "long life." Thereafter he wears monastic robes when he attends puja ceremonies and ordinary clothes when he attends the government school. They do not take monk's vows until the age of eighteen, although they can take them earlier if they wish. At this age, if they fail to take the full monastic vows, they must leave the monastery and enter worldly life.

15. On the Mahasiddha and Tantric adept Gyerpungpa, see Chapter Five above and on the empowerment or initiation (dbang bskur) for Zhang-zhung Meri, see the translation of the Ngondro text in Appendix 2, Section 2, above. On the meditation deity of Meri in general, see Kvaerne, *The Bon Religion of Tibet* (1995), and Reynolds, *The Cult and Practice of Zhang-zhung Meri* (1996).

16. For the curriculum in more detail, see Krystyna Cech, "History, Teaching, and Practice of Dialectics according to the Bon Tradition" (1986), pp. 3-28.

17. The original Triten Norbutse (khri-brten nor-bu'i rtse) was founded in the fourteenth century by the great Bonpo master Shen Nyima Gyaltsan (gShen Nyi-ma rgyal-mtshan, b.1360), who belonged to the Shen (gshen) clan which claims descent from Tonpa Shenrab himself, the founder of the Bon religion. Triten Norbutse became one of the four principal monastic institutions providing Bonpo education from the fourteenth century until the Chinese Communist occupation in the later 1950s. Known for its rich cultural and academic heritage, the monastery was destroyed in the Cultural Revolution in the 1960s.

It was re-established by Lopon Rinpoche in Kathmandu in 1987, with the able assistance of Geshe Nyima Wangyal, who became its first abbot or Khenpo. The monastery is at present headed by Khenpo Tenpa Yungdrung. At present there are about one hundred and fifteen monks, both Tibetan refugees and others from the Bonpo areas of Nepal such as Dolpo and Mustang, residing and receiving their education at the monastery. The monastery was founded for the purpose of providing a complete education in Bonpo tradition and practice. This is embodied in the nine-year program of academic studies for the Geshe degree and the four-year program of meditation practice in Dzogchen. The monastery is, therefore, essentially an educational institution, and not a residential one for monks.

The education at the monastery falls into two principal sections, as was the case at Menri itself in Tibet:

(1) The first system of education is known as the system of the learned scholar (mkhas-pa pandita yi lugs). This represents the nine-year program in academic studies, culminating in the Geshe (dge-bshes) degree, and including Sutra, Tantra and Dzogchen. It entails a curriculum of Bonpo philosophy (here the emphasis is on Madhyamaka) and the principal canonical texts, as well as the secular sciences of astrology, medicine, poetics, grammar, and so on. There is also the learning of ritual practices, chanting of various liturgies and the accompanying music, religious art and architecture, and so on. But the emphasis is on scholarly academic studies by way of study and debating, rather than on meditation practice. Later this knowledge can be applied in practice, including meditation retreats, as well as in ordinary life outside the monastery. Ordinarily, unless engaged in retreat or further studies, the monk must leave the monastery after successfully completing the Geshe degree.

(2) The second system of education is known as the system of the ascetic yogis (ku-sa-li-pa'i lugs), where a four-year program focuses on Dzogchen practice in order to realize the Nature of Mind. The four major traditions of Bonpo Dzogchen texts are studied and practiced in order to develop experiential understanding in terms of meditation practice. In this system, one goes to a qualified Lama, receives instructions in the preliminary practices and does them from around three to six months. Then one returns to the Lama, receives instruction on fixating the mind (sems 'dzin) and thereafter a direct introduction to the Natural State (rig-pa'i ngo-sprod). This understanding is then developed with further retreat practices. The Sanskrit term Pandita means a scholar well-versed in book learning and intellectual knowledge, whereas a Kushali (v. ku-sa-li, ku-su-li) indicates a practitioner who has attained high spiritual realization by way of meditation practice.

In the year 2001, six students completed their academic studies and passed the oral examination and were awarded Geshe degrees. Today they teach other monks and take part in various monastic and community activites for the benefit of the Bonpo people of Nepal. This has included setting up schools in remote regions like Dolpo, and in 2001 a Tibetan medical school was also started in western Nepal under the guidance of the monastery. Three students from this school have been awarded medical diplomas.

In central Tibet itself, all wood-blocks and the books printed from them were destroyed in the Cultural Revolution. The library at the monastery, built with financial aid from Germany, possesses a complete collection of Bonpo canonical texts, both the Kangyur (bka'-'gyur) and the Katen (bka'-brten), recently reprinted in Chengdu, China. At present, there is a program to catalogue and index all these Bonpo texts as well as to put them on computer diskettes.

18. On the view of Dzogchen, especially with regard to the philosophical views of Madhyamaka, Chittamatra, and Mahamudra, see Chapter Four above.

19. Shardza Tashi Gyaltsan (Shar-rdza bkra-shes rgyal-mtshan), was born in 1859 in the village of Da (brda) in the region of Dagang (zla-gang) or Dzakhog (rdza-khog) between the two rivers of Ngulchu and Dzachu. His father belonged to the Hor clan. When he was still a boy of nine, at the urging of Lama Tenzin Wangyal (rDza-sprul bsTan-'dzin dbang-rgyal), with great reluctance his parents allowed him to become a monk. The Lama ordained him and gave him the name Tashi Gyaltsan (bKra-shis rgyal-mtshan). With this Lama, he studied Sutra, Tantra and Dzogchen, receiving his education at Dza Tengchen (rdza steng-chen) Monastery. He took all the Vinaya and Bodhisattva vows as well as Tantric vows from his Root Lama, Dzatrul Tenzin Wangyal. In terms of Tantra, there are five root vows and twenty-five branch vows for the visualization process (bskyed-rim), five root vows and one hundred branch vows for the perfection process (rdzogs-rim) and thirty vows for Dzogchen. He kept all of these vows carefully. He began his Tantra studies with the empowerment for the meditation deity Walse Ngampa (dBal-gsas rngam-pa), and he was introduced to the Nature of Mind. In total, he had twenty-four masters, among them Tenzin Wangyal, Dechen Lingpa, Duddul Lingpa, Samten Yeshe, Shengyal Tenzin, and so on.

At the age of thirty-four, he became disgusted with the world, and having decided to spend the rest of his life in retreat, he went to the remote site of Yungdrung Lhunpo on the border of his native district of Shardza or Eastern Dza. Here he built a small hut, planning to be in permanent retreat and live in solitude. In his district, the people practiced mainly New Bon, but he saw also the value of Old Bon as preserved by the five clans of Dru (bru), Zhu, Pa (spa), Meu (rme'u) and Shen (gshen). Personally he mainly followed the system of Dru (bru-lugs) because this was the lineage of Menri Monastery. He practiced both Yeshen Tantra and Yeshen Chenpo Tantra, as well as Dzogchen. He composed commentaries on all the Nine Ways of Bon, as well as many rituals and prayers.

Among his disciples was Sang-ngak Lingpa (gSang-sngas gling-pa) and his successor was his nephew Lodro Gyatso bLo-gros rgya-mtsho). Below his master's meditation hut, Sang-ngak Lingpa built a meditation center called Gethang (dge-thang) which had a small temple. Soon this became a major teaching center for Bon in Kham. Here also wood-blocks were carved for some three hundred and thirty volumes, including Shardza Rinpoche's own works in thirteen volumes. Many Bonpo Lamas and also some Buddhist ones such as Changchub Dorje, the Dzogchen master of Namkhai Norbu Rinpoche, went there to receive his teachings. When he grew old, he turned over the running of the center to his nephew. When he was seventy-six, he warned his disciples that his time had come, and he went to a solitary place called Rabzhiteng (rab zhi steng) and put up a small tent where he practiced Thodgal. In the fourth Tibetan month in 1933, he had himself sewn up in the tent. His successor Lodro Gyatso and his younger brother Tsultrin saw that his property was distributed to both Bonpo and Buddhist monasteries as he had requested. His students, who had assembled outside, saw rainbows around the tent and observed other signs such as earthquakes. Fearing that their master would disappear completely, they opened the tent and found that his physical body, wrapped in rainbow lights, had shrunk to the size of one cubit and was suspended in the air. Many hundreds of people saw this phenomenon. His disciples made a large stupa of gilded copper and what remained of his body was placed inside. See Lopon Tenzin Namdak, *Heart Drops of Dharmakaya* (1993), pp. 17-29.

20. Lopon Tenzin Namdak, *Heart Drops of Dharmakaya* (1993). As useful as this book may be, it is not actually a literal translation of the Tibetan text, but a paraphrase and explanation by the Lopon given orally, which was recorded and then transcribed and edited.

The text, *'Od-gsal rdzogs-pa chen-po'i lam gyi rim-pa khrid-yig kun tu bzang-po'i snying-tig shes bya-ba bzhugs*, which belongs to a cycle of teaching and practice by Shardza Rinpoche known as the *Kun-bzang snying-tig*, was given the title of "Heart Drops of Dharmakaya" by the editor but that is not the actual meaning in Tibetan. The translation "heart drops" makes no sense in this context. The word *thig-pa* means "drop," but *snying-thig* is an abbreviation for *snying-po'i thig-le* meaning "the Essence of the Mind," in this case, of Kuntu Zangpo, who is indeed the Dharmakaya (bon-sku) in the Bonpo system as in the Nyingmapa. The word *thig-le* (Skt. bindu) in Tantra means a tiny sphere of luminous energy resembling a ball of liquid mercury. It is spherical in shape, not like a raindrop. Guru Tapihritsa, for example, is visualized sitting within a rainbow *thig-le* or sphere of rainbow light. In the context of Dzogchen, however, the term very often means "essence", as it does here. In its ordinary usage, *snying-po* means the physical heart, and by extension the core or essence of something. But here in the Dzogchen context, *snying-po* means "Mind", not the thought process but the Nature of Mind (sems-nyid). In any event, Kuntu Zangpo does not have a "mind" in the ordinary sense of discursive thoughts (rnam-rtog) since he is primordially enlightened but, rather, non-dual primal cognitions of reality or *ye-shes*. See the discussion of the Primordial Buddha in Chapter Two above. Therefore, the above title should be translated "Here is contained the Essence of the Mind of Kuntu Zangpo, being the explanatory text for the stages of the path of the Clear Light Great Perfection."

21. The short article "The Condensed Meaning of an Explanation of the Teachings of Yungdrung Bon" was published as an appendix in John Myrdhin Reynolds, *Yungdrung Bon — The Eternal Tradition* (1992). The article was subsequently reprinted with other material as a booklet with the same title by the Bonpo Foundation, Kathmandu (1993).

22. Newly edited and published as this volume.

23. This information comes from Lopon Tenpa Yungdrung in the brochure "Triten Norbutse Bonpo Monastery Monk Sponsorship Project," n.d.

24. Oral communication, Khenpo Tenpa Yungdrung.

25. Cech calls this section "basic knowledge." See Krystyna Cech, "History, Teaching, and Practice of Dialectics according to the Bon Tradition," (1986), p.15, 25. Her description of the curriculum of studies concerned that given at Dolanji in 1983 when she did her fieldwork there.
26. This attribution of the invention of logic to Kuntu Zangpo is found in the Chapter of the Mother Tantra, entitled *Ye-shes thig-le*
27. This term *rtags-rigs* means epistemology according to the Khenpo, literally *rigs, rigs-pa* means "reasoning," and also occurs in the phrase *lung rigs*, scriptural authority and reasoning. It should not be confused with the Dzogchen term, *rig-pa*, "intrinsic awareness," which is beyond mind and thought. *rTags* means "sign, indication."
28. The term *blo-rigs*, cited by Cech (1986) is not used in the syllabus at Triten Norbutse according to the Khenpo. On logic and debate practiced among the Tibetans, especially in the Gelugpa tradition see Daniel Perdue, *Debate in Tibetan Buddhist Education*, LTWA, Dharamsala 1976.

Selected Bibliography

Beckwith, Christopher, *The Tibetan Empire in Central Asia*, Princeton University Press, Princeton NJ 1987.
Bellezza, John Vincent, "High Country Culture: A Civilization flourished in the Himalayas before Buddhism reached Tibet," in *Discovering Archaeology*, v. 1, n. 3, May-June, 1999, pp.78-83.
Bellezza, John Vincent, "A Preliminary Archaeological Survey of gNammtsho and Dang-ra g.yu-mtsho," in *The Tibet Journal*, v. 21, Dharamsala 1996, pp.58-84.
Burnbaum, Edwin, *The Way to Shambhala: A Search for the Mythical Kingdom beyond the Himalayas*, Anchor Press/Doubleday, New York 1980.
Cech, Krystyna, "History, Teaching, and Practice of Dialectics according to the Bon Tradition," in The Tibet Journal, v. XI, n. 2, 1986, pp. 3-28.
Corbin, Henry, *Spiritual Body and Celestial Earth*, Princeton University Press, Princeton 1977.
Dargyay, Eva, *The Rise of Esoteric Buddhism in Tibet*, Motilal Banarsidass, Delhi 1977.
Eliade, Mircea, *The Sacred and the Profane: The Nature of Religion*, Harcourt Brice & World, New York 1957.
Gyurme Dorje, *Footprint Tibet Handbook*, Footprint Handbooks, Bath 1999.
Haarh, Erik, "The Zhang-zhung Language: A Grammar and Dictionary of the Unexplored Language of the Tibetan Bonpos," in *Acta Jutlandica* XL: 1, Copenhagen 1968, pp. 7-43.
Hoffmann, Helmut, *The Religions of Tibet*, George Allen and Unwin, London 1961, pp. 84-98.
Karmay, Samten G., "A General Introduction to the History and Doctrines of the Bon," in *The Memoirs of the Research Department of the Toyo Bunko*, n. 33, Tokyo 1975, pp. 171-218.

Karmay, Samten G., *The Little Luminous Boy: The Oral Tradition from the Land of Zhangzhung depicted in Two Tibetan Paintings*, Orchid Press, Bangkok 1998.

Karmay, Samten G., *The Treasury of Good Sayings: A Tibetan History of Bon*, Oxford University Press, London 1972.

Kuznetsov, B.I., "Who was the Founder of the Bon Religion," in *The Tibet Journal*, Vol. I, No. 1, Dharamsala 1975.

Kvaerne, "Bonpo Studies: The A-khrid System of Meditation," Part One: "The Transmission of the A-khrid System," in *Kailash* v. I, n. 1, pp. 19-50, Part Two: "The Essential Teachings of the A-khrid System, in *Kailash* v. I, n. 4, pp. 248-332, Kathmandu 1973.

Kvaerne, Per, "Chronological Table of the Bonpo: The bsTan rcis of Nyi-ma bstan-'jin," in *Acta Orientalia*, n. 33, Copenhagen 1971, pp. 205-282.

Kvaerne, Per, *The Bon Religion of Tibet: The Iconography of a Living Tradition*, Serindia Publications, London 1995.

Kvaerne, Per, "The Monastery of sNang-zhig of the Bon Religion in the rNga-ba District of Amdo", in *Studi in Onore di Luciano Petech*, P. Daffina (ed), *Studi Orientali*, vol. 9, Rome 1990, pp.207-222.

Kvaerne, Per, and Thubten Rikey, *The Stages of A-khrid Meditation: Dzogchen Practice of the Bon Tradition*, Library of Tibetan Works and Archives, Dharamsala 1996.

Kvaerne, Per, "The Succession of Lamas at the Monastery of sNang-zhig in the rNga-ba District of Amdo," in *Les Habitants du Toit du Monde: Tibet et Himalaya*, Samten Karmay and Philippe Sagant (eds), *Recherches sur la Haute Asie* 12, Societe d'ethnologie, Nanaterre 1997, pp. 155-157.

Lokesh Chandra and Lopon Tenzin Namdak, *History and Doctrine of Bon-po Nispanna-Yoga*, International Academy of Indian Culture, New Delhi 1968.

Martin, Dan, *Mandala Cosmology: Human Body Good Thought and the Revelation of the Secret Mother Tantras of Bon*, Asiatische Forschungen Band 124, Harrassowitz Verlag, Wiesbaden 1994.

Namdak, Lopon Tenzin, *Heart Drops of Dharmakaya: Dzogchen Practice of the Bon Tradition*, Snow Lion Publications, Ithaca 1993.

Namkhai Norbu, *The Crystal and the Way of Light: Sutra, Tantra, and Dzogchen*, Arkana Penguin Books, London 1993.

Namkhai Norbu, *Drung, Dreu, and Bon, Narrations, Symbolic Languages, and the Bon Tradition of Ancient Tibet*, TLWA, Dharamsala 1995.

Namkhai Norbu, *The Necklace of gZi: A Cultural History of Tibet*, LTWA, Dharamsala 1981.

Namkhai Norbu, *Zen and Dzogchen*, Zhang Zhung Editions, Oakland CA 1984.

Perdue, Daniel, *Debate in Tibetan Buddhist Education*, LTWA, Dharamsala 1976.

Reynolds, John Myrdhin, *Bonpo Dzogchen Teachings*, Bonpo Translation Project (privately printed), Freehold and Amsterdam 1992.

Reynolds, John Myrdhin, *The Cult and Practice of Zhang-zhung Meri: The Meditation Deity for the Zhang-zhung Nyan-gyud Tradition of Bonpo Dzogchen Teachings*, Bonpo Translation Project (privately printed), San Diego 1996.

Reynolds, John Myrdhin, *The Golden Letters*, Snow Lion Publications, Ithaca NY 1996.

Reynolds, John Myrdhin, *The Healing Practice for Sidpa Gyalmo*, Bonpo Translation Project (privately printed), San Diego 1996.

Reynolds, John Myrdhin, *The Oral Tradition from Zhang-zhung*, Vajra Publications, Kathmandu 2005.

Reynolds, John Myrdhin, *Selections from the Bonpo Book of the Dead*, Bonpo Translation Project (privately printed), San Diego and Copenhagen 1997.

Reynolds, John Myrdhin, *Self-Liberation through Seeing Everything with Naked Awareness*, Snow Lion Publications, Ithaca NY 1998.

Reynolds, John Myrdhin, *Yungdrung Bon: The Eternal Tradition*, Bonpo Translation Project (privately printed), New York 1991.

Roerich, George, *The Blue Annals*, Calcutta 1974; reprint Motilal Banarsidass, New Delhi 1976.

Rossi, Donatella, "The Monastic Lineage of sNang zhig dgon pa in Amdo rNga ba," in *The Tibet Journal*, vol. 23, no. 4, Dharamsala 1998, pp. 58-71.

Sharma, D.D., *A Descriptive Grammar of Kinnauri*, Studies in Tibeto-Himalayan Languages 1, Mittal Publications, Delhi 1988.

Skorupski, Tadeusz, "Tibetan gYung-Drung Bon Monastery in India", *Kailash*, vol. VIII, nos. 1-2, Kathmandu 1981; reprinted separately by gYung-Drung Bon Monastic Centre, Solan, India 1983.

Snellgrove, David, and Hugh Richardson, *A Cultural History of Tibet*, Geo Weidenfeld & Nicolson, London 1968.

Snellgrove, David, *The Nine Ways of Bon*, Oxford University Press, London 1967.

Sangye Tandar and Richard Guard, *The Twelve Deeds: A Brief Life Story of Tonpa Shenrab, the Founder of the Bon Religion*, LTWA, New Delhi 1995.

Thar, Tsering, "The Ancient Zhang Zhung Civilization," in *Tibet Studies: Journal of the Tibetan Academy of Social Sciences*, Lhasa 1989, pp.90-104.

Tenzin Namdak, Lopon, and John Reynolds (tr), *The Condensed Meaning of an Explanation of the Teachings of Yungdrung Bon*, Bonpo Foundation, Kathmandu n.d.

Tulku Thondup, *Hidden Teachings of Tibet: An Explanation of the Terma Tradition of the Nyingmapa School of Buddhism*, Wisdom Publications, London 1986.

Tulku Thondup, *The Tantric Tradition of the Nyingmapas*, Buddhayana, Marion MA 1984.

Upasak, C.S., *History of Buddhism in Afghanistan*, Central Institute of Higher Tibetan Studies, Sarnath Varanasi 1990.

Uray, Geza, "The Old Tibetan Verb Bon," in *Acta Orientalia Academiae Scientarium Hungaricae*, v. 17, n. 3, Budapest 1964, pp.323-334.

Wangyal, Tenzin, *Wonders of the Natural Mind*, Station Hill Press, Barrytown NY 1993, pp. 35-37, 203-208.